Olive Mason

Norfolk Within Living Memory

GW00372397

Compiled by the Norfolk Federation
of Women's Institutes from notes sent by
Institutes in the County

Published jointly by
Countryside Books, Newbury
and
NFWI, Norwich

COUNTRYSIDE BOOKS
3 Catherine Road
Newbury, Berkshire

ISBN 1 85306 339 8

The cover photograph shows the siding at St Germans.

Designed by Mon Mohan
Produced through MRM Associates Ltd, Reading
Printed by Woolnough Bookbinding Ltd., Irthlingborough

Contents

NORFOLK FEDERATION OF WOMEN'S INSTITUTES

Wells

Hunstanton

Fakenham

Sandringham

CO U

King's Lynn

East Dereham

Swaffham

O F

Downham Market

NORF

Thetford

MILES

6 12 18

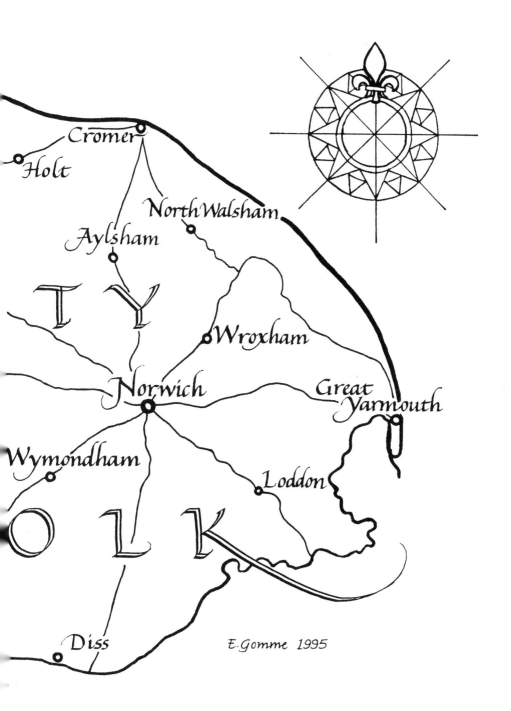

Cromer

Holt

North Walsham

Aylsham

T Y

Wroxham

Norwich

Great Yarmouth

Wymondham

Loddon

O L K

Diss

E. Gomme 1995

Foreword

What changes many of our members will have seen since our Federation was formed over 75 years ago. From a virtual farming community with few facilities, other industry has developed and towns and villages have grown to house the people moving from other parts of the country to the peace and quiet of Norfolk. Although roads have recently improved, Norfolk is mainly still unspoilt.

This is the second *Within Living Memory* to be written by members and I am sure it will be equally as interesting and enjoyable as the previous one.

I would like to thank everyone who has contributed to the book and especially our co-ordinator Mrs Eileen Gomme who has given so much time to make it possible.

Brenda Preston
County Chairman

Acknowledgements

Norfolk Federation of Women's Institutes would like to thank all WI members who supplied material, whether written or photographic, for this project.

Unfortunately we were unable to include extracts from all the articles that were submitted; to do so would have meant some duplication of content, and naturally we had to take into account the total amount of space available in the book.

Nevertheless all the contributions were of value in deciding the shape and content of the book. We were very grateful to receive them all.

We are indebted to all those members who supplied photographs and our thanks are also due to Julia Newson who provided the charming line illustrations for the book.

Linda Hacon
County Secretary

TOWN & COUNTRY LIFE

NORWICH PAST

Norwich before the bombs of the Second World War, and before modern industrial and road development – that is the city so many of us remember. The market on a Saturday night, the blacksmith at work, the fairs at Christmas and Easter, the 'chocolate box' men, the 'dear old Hippodrome' – memories of Norwich past.

MEMORIES FROM THE EARLY 1900s

'Most people lived in terraced houses, streets of them, a great number of which were destroyed in the air raids in the war. The roads and streets were lit by gas lamps; these had two hanging chains "on and off" which were operated by lamplighters on cycles at dusk and dawn each day. Houses mostly had gas for lighting and cooking but many people used oil lamps.

The early electricity works were by the river in Duke Street. Coal for the purpose was brought from Yarmouth by wherries, pushed along if there was not enough wind for sailing by quant (punting pole) until engines were introduced. Some coal came by rail. I cannot say when the first power station was built but I remember the present one at Thorpe being built close to the river.

In my early years the streets were continually swept by corporation employees, very necessary as all vehicles were horse-drawn. In dry weather sprinkler carts would patrol the roads to lay the dust.

The bread van came daily, also milk on a horse-drawn float in large cans from which the man filled a smaller one and brought it to the door with pint and half-pint measures, to go straight into customers' jugs. Never mind the dust if the roadmen were busy! Greengrocery and fish arrived on hand barrows, and if one put in a fair-sized grocery order that would be delivered too. Some butchers employed delivery boys on cycles.

Outside the city boundary, sanitation was very primitive. Some people had a wooden hut in the garden, others were of brick, with buckets under wooden seats and a low door at the back from which the bucket was removed and emptied on Fridays, after dark. The council workers on this job had a large horse-drawn covered van, which locals called "the chocolate box". It was most unpleasant to be outside even several hours after the task was done. On Saturday mornings householders would rinse out the buckets with Jeyes' Fluid and plenty of Jeyes' powder, trying to be as hygienic as possible. After the Second World War pressure was very keen on the council, and flush toilets were installed and, where houses had room, bathrooms were added.

On Good Friday mornings from 6 am, bakers' men and boys would bring trays, carried on their heads, of hot cross buns, calling out "Hot cross buns, one a penny, two a penny" – large ones a penny each, two a penny for small ones. People would rush out to buy and then eat them in bed while still nicely hot.

Bakers did not bake bread on Saturday nights, but they would use the remaining heat in their ovens to bake joints of meat for some of their poorer customers who would take the meat in their own tins, and it would cook beautifully overnight. For a few pence the baker would add a few yeast dumplings. On Sunday mornings men and boys would come, calling out, selling freshly-cooked cockles, mussels, winkles and shrimps, a treat for Sunday tea.'

THE CITY I LOVED

' "I remember, I remember, the house where I was born" . . . I suppose we all learned that poem at school. I remember where I was born so well, it was in one of the unlovely yards that sprawled off Oak Street, with names such as Dog, Talbot, Fellmonger Yards, and Jenkins Alley (called locally "Chafe Lug" because it was so narrow). Then there was Ragged School Yard, so called because it once housed a school for which the pupils paid approximately one penny a week, Flower-in-Hand and Baldwin's Yards, and many more. Here there were shops where one penny bought a bar of chocolate, Devon Dairy Cream toffees or an aerated drink, Vantas. These could all be bought in the cottages in the Gildencroft Lane. These houses are still there, having been preserved, thank goodness.

Barn Road was once a row of small houses, each with its own small well kept garden. At the St Benedict's end was a smithy, and I often watched the smith and his assistant fit a glowing red-hot iron tyre on to a wooden cartwheel – a thing of the long distant past now. At the other end of Barn Road, by St Martin's bridge stood the City station. Here the railway supplied the more rural areas and it was here that cattle were unloaded and driven to the cattle market – it was all destroyed by enemy bombs, including Heigham Street school, the Wincarnis factory, and a house which was brought from Whitlingham and rebuilt in the corporation supplies yard. It is all now an industrial area.

One of the highlights of our week in those days was to visit the market on a Saturday night. The whole place and the atmosphere was a source of free entertainment. There were the stalls for secondhand clothes and just about everything else. "Alf the Purse

King" would be proclaiming in his cockney/Jewish accent. He would take a purse or handbag and turn it inside out, and then challenge one and all to find a fault with it. I can never recall anyone actually doing so! He was a master "speiler" and he would enthral the crowd with his stories. Then there was the "Phostrogene" seller, stripped to the waist, and with chest expanders and weights he would demonstrate the wonders of his wares. Alongside him would be a maker of cough humbugs, who would pull and stretch at his magic mixture until it was to his liking, then it would be cut into small or large pieces, as the customer wished. Further along were the "China men". No, not from Peking but from London, pure cockneys. All manner of items made of china were sold, and because the market had to be cleared by half past nine, the best time to be there was about half an hour before the deadline. One of the dealers would have the tea/dinner set up for sale, he could hold the six dinner plates and six tea plates in his hand like an enormous fan. He would then offer the two sets for "Six parnds – no, what about five parnds ten, four-ten." At this time, if there were no takers he would say, "Right, if you don't want it neither do I, and I ain't taking it home wiv me," and with a flick of his wrist he would throw the lot into the bin, where it smashed to smithereens . . . Oh! the market was a joy in those days!

The market place was cleared completely each Saturday night so that it was ready for the religious groups on Sunday mornings, when the Church Army, Salvation Army and various other sects would fill the square. The afternoon was completely different, this being given over to the politicians. Labour, Communists etc would shout and try to convert the listeners. This was the norm, but I remember one afternoon when the Brown Shirts (complete with band playing, and with Sir Oswald Mosley in command and flags flying) marched onto the square. Their appearance was extremely smart and well trained. However, when their leader started to speak a fight broke out among the other parties and for a while it was complete mayhem, but the police arrived to separate the fighting factions before things got completely out of hand. An order was given and the Fascists formed into three ranks and marched off.

During my youthful years of the 1930s life was hard, with low pay, long hours and a great deal of unemployment, but etched in my memory is the entertainment we had in Norwich. The dear old Hippodrome for variety shows, circus acts, comedy and revues, or the Theatre Royal for opera, ballet, dance bands, notable singers and the "classier" type of entertainment. There were six or seven cinemas, ranging from the Haymarket down to the Empire – the Haymarket was my favourite, you entered a different world, one of soft carpet underfoot, subdued amber lighting, perfumed air and soft seats, which were sheer bliss to sink into. I remember staying there one afternoon from two o'clock until my distraught mother came to find me at ten o'clock that night (sorry, Mum!). I had been watching *All quiet on the Western Front* – I must have watched it twice right through.

For the more energetic there were dance halls galore, from the majestic Thatched Ballroom to simple church and parish halls which abounded in Norwich in those days. The Lido was my favourite and that of my friends as well, we could afford to go there and have a couple of drinks. Dancing was also a great feature of the summer in the Chapelfield Gardens, around the bandstand. All sorts of people enjoyed this, young and old alike, and no "louts" of any description spoiled it for us. St Luke's on Aylsham Road was a very good hall until the new vicar refused to allow the dances – he thought it was sinful to dance.

I served in the Third Norwich Scouts, the Boys' Brigade, and when older, the Priory Gym. I learnt from various friends of the weekend camping at Hemsby, so from May until September a group of us were to be found there from Saturday lunchtime until Sunday evening; we had a tent, and it was enormous fun. Sunday evening would mean leaving the campsite around six o'clock, a quick ride home (we were all cyclists), and a wash and change to get to the "Chicken Run" (Prince of Wales Road) before all the girls had gone home. The situation was the girls would parade on one side of the road, and the boys on the other, and gradually "the twain would mix".

The other enjoyment we all looked forward to were the fairs. The main fair appeared twice a year, at Christmas and Easter. These fairs were preceded by a small contingent which took up residence in the Agricultural Hall, usually various stalls and a large dodgems or Noah's Ark for a couple of weeks before the main event. When this opened, all of the old cattle market, now the Castle Mall, was a jostling mass of shouting, laughing, happy people, all with one idea in their minds, to have a good time, and this they certainly did. The raucous music, the sounds of the steam engines which supplied the motive power, be it belt-driven or the new-fangled electric generator, all added to the din. The girls on the "Shamrock" screaming, sailors on the "chara-planes" shouting to pals, singing, talking, added to the cries of the "barkers" calling out the wonders of the world hidden inside (such as the Spider Girl, the calf with two heads, bearded lady, strong man, boxers willing to fight one and all for £1 a round), such was the working class's quest for simple pleasures and happiness. All went home broke – but happy!

The younger, more adventurous could always go to the cattle market on a Saturday to help move the cattle from pen to truck

11

for transport to the new owners' farms, or go to the City station at the bottom of Barn Road (Halfords occupies the spot now) and help drive the sheep or cows to the market. Locals called this "bullock whoppin". Alternatively one could go and watch the horses being put through their paces on the ground opposite the Castle Hotel (now gone the way of many of Norwich's old buildings). Nearby was Orford Place where the trams used to turn around the island – the Germans moved that!

As with other towns, Norwich had "juvenile troupes" of youngsters who sang and danced. One such group was "Madame Ozine's" and whenever I could scrounge a penny or two I would go to the local hall and watch. I loved the little girl who sang *Won't you buy my pretty flowers* and *Mistakes* – all the performers were good, I thought.

During the summer months the boatyards along the river, the *Eagle* and the *Dolphin*, all did a roaring trade, for here one could hire a two- or four-oared skiff and row to the mills at Hellesdon, stopping on the bank for a smoke or a drink (or a cuddle if your girlfriend was with you, of course). There were times when through horse-play an oar or rudder was lost, but a quick "whip round" when back at the yard would satisfy the boatman. He knew that the lost item would be returned to him by someone finding it, or it would be brought home again by the river flowing past his yard. Real vandalism was not much in evidence then.

The form during the winter months was to go into the Castle museum. At the turnstile was a gentleman in uniform with a red waistcoat, and wearing a top hat. Each time we entered we had to endure his lecture on behaviour, solemnly warning that "we would be turned out if we didn't behave". We used to wander around hoping to find something new, but all the artefacts, animals etc always seemed to be the same. After doing the rounds we would wander outside, meeting school mates, or if we were lucky, girls! Then a slow walk home, the day was over, with the rest of the family now all listening to the radio – sorry, wireless, as it was known then.

I finally joined the RAF in 1938, and was away from Norwich on and off for about 34 years – and the Norwich I had known and loved was gone, but the memories of those seemingly halcyon days remain. Perhaps, in some ways they were not truly "the good old days", there was dreadful poverty and hardship, but there was a camaraderie which no longer seems to exist in this modern world. I am glad that I was born and lived through the years that I now hold close to my heart.'

SOME OTHER TOWNS AND VILLAGES REMEMBERED

From Old Hunstanton to the hamlet of Roudham, Cromer to Saham Toney, life in our villages has changed almost beyond recognition since the Second World War. Here are just a few memories of life as it used to be in Norfolk – and a reminder of that dreadful night in 1953 when the floods burst into our homes.

CROMER

'I came to Cromer in 1925, aged six, to live with my widowed mother in a three-bedroomed terraced house in Mill Road, Suffield Park (a suburb of Cromer). We had an outside flush toilet but no bathroom. However, we were fortunate in having a full-sized bath installed in the kitchen, covered with a white-wood table top when not in use. Water was heated in the gas copper, also used for laundering sheets. My grandparents lived next door and many friends and relations came to stay in the summer and to enjoy the sea shore from our beach hut on the East Beach. The hut had been included with the sale of the house and we practically lived down there in the summer.

Suffield Park was the home of many railway workers – engine drivers, porters, restaurant car staff, booking clerks – for the station looking down on us from the hill was the terminus for the London and North Eastern Railway for through trains to and from Liverpool Street. It was known as the "Top Station". Some railway workers also lived at the other end of Cromer near the Beach Station. Its name used to be picked out in whitened stones on the bank on the way to the station but now these are overgrown. This was a station for the Midland and Great Northern line, known as the "Muddle and Goes Nowhere". Journeys to anywhere over about ten miles in length were extremely long and involved many changes. Now it is our only station. We could also travel by bus but mainly along the coast, and good road services did not really come into use until after the war. There were private coaches (or charabancs as they were known) which made enjoyable trips in the summer and often drove private outings and Sunday school treats. Taxis were available at the stations and there was even a horse-drawn vehicle available there until the early 1930s.

There were several private schools in Cromer in pre-war years including one known as St Rhadegund's and one at the convent in Cliff Avenue (now flats). The main school in Mount Street announces over the three entrances that one is for boys, one for girls and the other for infants. Many Cromer people will have memories of the "happiest days of their lives" in this building which has nearly attained its century. The high school (at first the secondary modern school) moved in the late 1940s and the infants school to Mill Road, Suffield Park in the late 1960s. There are records of small dame schools in private houses, and the Goldsmith's School, an old foundation for boys in Overstrand Road, later a doctor's surgery and now a holiday home, is now remembered in the Goldsmith's Charity to help Cromer boys and, of latter years, girls with a grant to help with their education.

Cromer never was an industrial town but of course there was and always has been a fishing industry. It is still a lovely sight to see the boats going out to sea and come home again with their catch. The fishermen still risk their lives and many of them also are devoted members of the famous Cromer Lifeboat crew. The present coxswain is a great-nephew of the renowned Coxswain Henry Blogg. However, the greatest industry used to be the holiday trade, in hotels, boarding houses and in small homes where the resident family had to sleep in outhouses or one-room dormitories to make space for the visitors. The housewife hoped to make enough from her summer visitors to pay the rates on the house and many of her lodgers would come year after year. There was, and still is, much unemployment especially in winter.'

'An aunt and uncle of mine lived during the 1930s in a cottage in Tower Lane, Sidestrand, a few miles from Cromer. The previous tenant of the cottage who had recently died was a Miss Louise Jermy. She had been the daughter of the local miller, and had gained notoriety during the Edwardian era for giving hospitality to many of the literary figures of the age who stayed at the Mill House. The poet Swinburne resided there for many months, and wrote about the area, calling it "Poppyland" and Louise Jermy the "Maid of the Mill". In her old age Louise Jermy moved to the cottage in Tower Lane and must have become rather eccentric with magpie instincts. My aunt and uncle had to remove a great mass of old scrap metal which had been attached to the beams and walls of the cottage; this consisted of old keys, nails, gin-traps, lanterns etc which Louise Jermy had collected during her sojourn there. A veritable paradise for a scrap metal dealer! Alas, Tower Lane and its row of cottages is no more, having succumbed to cliff erosion many years ago.'

'My brother in law was a coastguard at Cromer, and after the First

14

World War I used to go and stay with him and my sister at Cromer. The lifeboat at that time was a rowing boat, and when the alarm sounded everyone from the town who could used to run to the beach to help the launch. The boat was kept in a hut on the beach. I vividly remember how we were given a rope to pull, how often we fell down struggling to haul the boat, and the relief when the boat was finally in the sea and rowing away.'

'I remember as a young child of eight walking back to school, after lunch, on a very cold and stormy afternoon in December. Crowds of people were lining the cliffs, looking seaward. On joining them my friends and I watched the plight of an old sailing barge which was stranded about 200 yards from the shoreline, and the abortive attempts being made to launch the No 2 lifeboat from the beach.

We children made our way down to the promenade but had to return to the cliff top because of the hard, stinging sand swept off the beach by the gale force winds and cutting at our legs and faces. I remember the excitement that filled the air when a slowly enlarging speck was observed approaching from the distance. The shout went up that it was Coxswain Blogg and the *H. F. Bailey* returning from another rescue and making for Cromer.

For the next hour or so we watched, enthralled, the most courageous act of seamanship I have ever seen. Finding it impossible to stay alongside the barge because of the rough seas Blogg allowed the crest of a huge wave to surf him on to the deck of the barge so that the two men and a boy could be grabbed from the rigging and pulled into the lifeboat. He then waited for another such wave to lift him off the barge's deck. Having damaged his boat in the process he steered straight for the shore and beached it.

I remember the people cheering and the church bells ringing, and later in life I realised that in watching this rescue of the crew of the barge *Sepoy* we eight year olds had witnessed one of the most gallant feats in the history of the Cromer lifeboat. It was well worth the reprimands received from school and home for non-attendance at school that afternoon.'

BROOME

'The churches of Broome and Thwaite went together when I was at school in the 1920s and came under the Loddon Deanery, the rector living at Broome vicarage. The Rev Wingfield was an army colonel and on Armistice Sunday, wearing uniform, he paraded the ex-servicemen from Broome school to the church.

There was a dairy farm where the dried flower farm now stands and the milk was delivered in Ditchingham and Broome by bicycle

15

Fisherman on Sheringham beach in the 1920s.

to the door, measured in one pint and half pint measures from cans. There was a private laundry in Sun Road where three women used to wash and iron, now a private house. Sun Road was an unmade road, with just two cottages. There was a shoemaker in the village and his sister sewed gloves for Nurseys; they worked in a lean-to shed next to a house nearly opposite the post office.

There was no village hall until 1926, when my father and Mr Easthaugh went to Salisbury Plain and selected two army huts (one for Ditchingham). The sections came by train to Ditchingham station and the hall was erected by them both, being carpenters. Mr and Mrs Mortimer, who lived at Broome Place for 20 years, gave a full sized billiard table for the villagers to use. There was a football pitch on the heath and the teams changed in the hut. The pitch was later dug up to provide gravel and now there are lakes there. After the First World War there were trenches on the heath where we used to play house – we had no worries in those days, we only came home when we were hungry.

My mother, who was born in 1889, went to Broome school and in her day there were two headmasters, Mr Wilson and Mr Sibring (who had the first car in the village). Over 100 children attended the school in my day, the infants being taught in a room by themselves and the big room divided by a curtain between the two teachers. The dentist came once a year, when a surgery (of its day) was brought to the playground. If you were frightened of the dentist, it didn't help seeing it there all the weekend. A nurse used to come once a month to look in our hair for nits.

We belonged to the chapel Sunday school and went to Gorleston for our outing. We went in Mr Lambert's charabanc. The seats went straight across with a door each end, and if it rained the hood was brought over the entire coach. When we got to Haddiscoe Bridge many of us had to get out as it was too heavy for the wooden bridge, and join it the other side. A man stood at the top with a red flag to stop any other traffic coming through.'

NORTH WOOTTON

'The biggest area of the village belonged to the Castle Rising estate with the Howard family being the lords of the manor. It was an agricultural village in the 1930s when there were two large farmers and five or six smallholders who between them supplied most of the work for the villagers.

Mr Henry Thompson was the marsh farmer who had nine tied cottages at the top of Marsh Farm and the same down the "bottom farm" as they used to call it. These were very remote places where the people had to drink water from cisterns that caught the rainwater from the house roofs. They had to cycle or walk three miles to catch the train to go to Lynn to do the shopping as the buses did not go down there until 1937. There were roundsmen who delivered goods such as bread and meat. Milk was mostly supplied by the foremen as they were allowed to keep a cow. It was a hard life down there in the winter months as there were very few windbreaks for shelter. Most of the land work was done by horses but Mr Thompson did keep two steam ploughing engines for deep winter ploughing and cultivating. He employed gangs of men and women from King's Lynn during the setting and harvesting of potatoes which was one of his main crops. He even built a "paddy house" for groups of Irishmen to live in during the potato picking in the autumn.

The Failes brothers were the biggest farmers in the village, they were tenant farmers at Home Farm where they kept a herd of about 100 cows. This provided work for six cowmen, milking and preparing food like grinding mangolds and turnips, mixing it with chaff and filling the racks with hay. The cows used to sleep in the cow sheds during the winter months then. The milk was cooled and put into churns to be transported to King's Lynn for distribution. Most of the smallholders kept a few cows; some delivered milk around the village and the remainder sent it to King's Lynn.

The smallholders mostly relied on the allotments to grow their mangolds and turnips, and common rights so the cattle could graze during the summer and leave their meadows to grow the hay for winter feed. Most of the Castle Rising estate houses had common rights so those that did not have cows or horses used to rent them to the smallholders.

The houses that were not tied to the farms paid rent to the Castle Rising estate office at Michaelmas Day, which was 11th October. Some of the smallholders paid half yearly so it was October and 6th April, Lady Day. The cows walking through the village during the winter from the cow sheds to the fields made the village roads a sea of mud which gave the roadman a continuous job scraping the roads clean.

Times were very hard for the farm labourers in those days as wages were poor and most of them had large families to keep. It was mostly a case of the children handing clothes down from the eldest to the youngest, clothes having to be repaired over and over again. Some children never wore socks and this was cold and not very comfortable in hobnail boots. Most houses had a boot-last or boot-boy as they were known and it was the father's job to put new nails in the boots after examination at the weekends. The boys mostly wore jerseys and short trousers and the girls below-the-knee dresses. The women of the village wore long dresses or skirts and blouses over which they always wore an apron; a hessian one for the rough work such as scrubbing and a white linen one for light work.

The men wore breeches and buskins for warmth during the winter. Some buskins were of leather clipped at the bottom and with strap and buckles at the top, others had corduroy leggings buttoned up at the front. Most wore corduroy trousers with a strap below the knee, called yorks. They all wore good jackets with a large inside pocket, with mostly a flat cap or trilby. Men used to use hessian sacks as aprons and wrap them around their legs for warmth and protection against mud. They even wore them over their shoulders when it rained.'

SAHAM TONEY

'In the 1920s there were mainly two classes of homes, the very rich landowners and the workers, with few middle class people. The workers lived in tied cottages, many in very lonely places.

Water was supplied by a well which probably served several properties. In very hot summers these would dry up and this would mean travelling quite a distance to one that still had a supply – it was not until the 1950s that a main supply came to the village. The parish council maintained a well to provide water for residents in part of the village and during very dry times this was kept locked and water rationed during certain times of the day. Every drop of

The quay at Wells in about 1912. Harbours were busy working areas, full of interest.

water was precious and every cottage had a water butt to collect rainwater from the roof.

The main work in the village was farming or gardening for the large houses or domestic work, very few were able to obtain work as shop assistants in the nearby market town. Harvest was a very hard time for the farm worker and a bargain would be made that the worker would be paid a fixed sum for a month to get the harvest in. This would involve very late set hours, and if it rained so harvest work was impossible the worker still had to work the same amount of hours, usually clearing the manure from the cattle yards in preparation for the winter. Many women took in washing from the better off, and it was traditional that washday would be on a Monday. The copper was situated in the outside shed and this would be lit very early and a linen line would be stretched the full length of the garden. Sometimes the fire would not burn, having been fuelled by all kinds of rubbish causing it to get clogged with soot, and this would be cleared by placing a small amount of gunpowder in the fire to cause an explosion.

The village was mostly self supporting. This was a very long, straggly village and we had two post offices which were also general stores, two coal merchants and two millers, a fish and chip shop and five public houses. At one time there were eight. The village bobby was one of the most important people in the village and our policeman was also responsible for the next parish. Many a time you would hear of his tussles with a poacher or a drunkard. He dealt with the situation on the spot, often with a good hiding.

The folk in the large houses were well respected – they were the main source of employment, and to fall out with them meant it was very difficult to obtain work in the area. The squire would take his place in the front pew of the church and take a leading part in the running of it. The schoolmaster would also play a prominent role; discipline was very strict and any child caught misbehaving outside school hours would be dealt with next day. Practically every need was brought to the village; baker, butcher, fishmonger (one fishmonger who used to come with his horse and cart would shout his wares and you could hear him a long time before he entered the village), the draper would also call and goods could be paid for at so much a week. The chimney sweep was a resident and a regular caller.

Sport in the village was a must, with a cricket and football team. There were no pavilions or playing fields – the game was played on a field occupied by cows and horses and cowpats had to be removed before every game. The players changed behind the hedge or in a barn or cowshed, and the teas for the cricketers were usually served in the barn by wives or parents. Quoits were played on one of the public house meadows.

One thing we always looked forward to as children was the sheep sales at Hempton near Fakenham. Flocks of sheep would be driven through the village long into the night. They would stop and rest on the church or village green and villagers would give the drovers cups of tea. There was no other means of transport between stations. A fair would come to the village every year and put up its stalls and swings on the public house meadow. We had our many characters – the poachers, the regular drunkards, but no one harmed other people's property; there were pranks but these were harmless.'

OLD HUNSTANTON

'The Hall was the home of the Le Strange family. During summer garden fetes Charles Le Strange and his guests would walk about and talk to the people at the fete and also take part in the games with the children. On prize-giving day he would present the prizes, and at Christmas he gave the school a Christmas tree, gifts and a party. The beach was the property of the Le Stranges and anything found on the beach should have been handed over to them.

The cottages near the church are about the only part of Old Hunstanton that has not changed over the years. The other part of the village is very much changed because of the private houses and bungalows built where old cottages have been pulled down. The grounds of what was Lodge Hotel are now a caravan holiday camp. The Le Strange Arms Hotel down Sea Lane, years ago, was very popular with first class visitors and especially when golf tournaments were held on the 18 hole course. There is also a nine hole course. There used to be three farms, but these have been turned into hotels and caravan sites.

The life of the village was centred around the Hall, farms, blacksmith, hotels, lifeboat, beach, golf courses and public houses, of which there were three. My grandfather worked on the farm and was head herdsman. My father had charge of the farm horses which were used for the launching of the lifeboat when needed.

I can remember standing with my mother holding my hand with my younger sister and seeing a Zeppelin passing over during the First World War, and also hearing my parents and their neighbours saying a German spy had been arrested at the Le Strange Arms Hotel. The hotel barn and some of the cottages were used for billeting soldiers. During the war my mother worked at the hotel; she worked all hours and very hard, often doing the work of men. The eldest of the children at home looked after the younger ones. During this time food was very hard to come by and winters were then very different to those we have now, often snow from

Farm life was also part of village life. Priory farmyard at Aldeby, overlooked by St Mary's church, in 1949.

November to well into March. My mother would trap sea-gulls which she would skin and just use the breasts, sparrows she made into sparrow pie, and she made many meals from offal. Often the chef at the hotel would give her some of the food that had not been used to bring home and always plenty of nice beef dripping. It was while Mother worked at the hotel that she waited at table on George V and Queen Mary.

During school holidays in the summer, my younger sister and I had to take my father's tea up to the harvest fields by four o'clock, we used to walk miles. When we had time to play it was usually down on the beach with jumping poles, jumping large rocks as the tide was coming in. We also liked to watch the inshore fishermen pulling the nets in. Sometimes we would be given some fish, it depended on how many children were there. There was not a lot of time to play as we had to do jobs about our home to help Mother and also help Father on his allotment. We were just as happy doing these things most of the time, but like any children there were times when we would rather be playing with our school friends.'

ROUDHAM HAMLET

'I was born and raised in a hamlet called Roudham in a warrener's cottage, as my father was warrener for the local farmer who lived in the Hall. Rabbits were our chief diet, and plenty of fresh vegetables. Once a year at Christmas the Lord or Captain as he was called who farmed the land brought us a joint of beef, and that was the only time of the year we tasted other meat.

Roudham is seven and a half miles from Thetford and we used to travel there on a road called the turnpike, walking most of the way or sharing a bicycle with my sister and three brothers. We would go to Thetford on a Saturday to climb up Castle Hill and have a picnic, in the summer, and travel back, and that used to fill up our day. On Sunday we walked a mile and a half to church and then again for Sunday school in the afternoon, so our time was always occupied. Bridgham was where we went to school.

East Harling was about three miles away and was noted for its sheep fairs. Tuesday was market day when anything and everything came under the hammer, from livestock to pots and pans.

Roudham had no shop, the nearest was two and a half miles away at Bridgham. There was a ruined church built on a small hill with a round tower and a thatched roof, and eight pairs of chalk and plaster constructed cottages which were dotted across the meadows and down the lanes. Bridgham had two halls owned by the farmers who lived there and farmed the land. There were a post office, two shops and two public houses, the Red Lion and the White Lion. The chalk and plaster buildings were typical of the type found in the Norfolk/Suffolk Breckland area, they had long sloping roofs and windows built into the roof. Another feature was a wooden beam across the kitchen, a remnant from the 19th century when each householder kept a pig. A deal would be struck with the butcher that when the pig was fattened he would kill and cure one whole side for the owner and keep the other side for himself. This would hang on a hook from the beam to make sure the family had food in the event of a long hard winter.

Lighting in the houses was paraffin lamp and candles, and cooking was done by a coal-fired brick wall oven. There was no such thing as a school dinner, we all carried our own packed lunch with sherbet lemonade to drink in summer and in winter a mixture of cocoa and sugar was taken which the teacher would make into a hot drink.

Every morning of the year one of us children would walk a mile to the farm for a can of milk, well, two cans as we brought one for our grandmother who lived at the end of the lane, and we were rewarded with a cup of tea and some home-made cooked goodie and sixpence a week, which was quite a bit in those days. We used to spend evenings knitting ourselves slippers and scarves and also cutting up into strips old coats etc for Mother to make into rugs, and at the end of the day there was a feeling of satisfaction that we had made something useful for ourselves.'

SEA PALLING

'Between the wars Sea Palling had four general grocery shops, two bakeries, two public houses, a butcher's shop, a cobbler, eight farms (five of which sold milk, and some butter, from their own cows), and a post and telegraph office. Telegrams were widely used and the postman cycled in from Ingham twice a day, delivering on both runs. On Sundays in the 1930s the five o'clock bus carried a letter box. There was also a daily parcel delivery service to Norwich on the bus.

Apart from the local shops, several vans came into the village weekly from shops in Stalham, Hickling and Martham, bringing goods ordered on the previous visit. As a fishing village, fish was always available and several fishmongers had their own smokehouses curing bloaters and kippers, which were delicious.

There are still two public houses, but the original Lifeboat was lost in the 1953 floods and the old Cock Inn was demolished for road widening. The village school closed in 1985, and the first village hall, built in the early 1920s, was destroyed in 1940 by an explosion while being used by the army. Several soldiers were killed and much damage was done to surrounding buildings.

The beach was strewn with fishing huts and boats, and we had a good coastguard station with four or five coastguards, who were all greatly respected by the village. They were in charge of the life-saving apparatus but it was manned by local men. It was used to rescue men from boats coming inshore, and was hauled along the beach in a cart by horses from the farms. The same method was used to launch the lifeboat when we had a very busy lifeboat station – as children we loved watching the practice sessions of both, but were kept well out of the way.

People passing through the village were always an event. Just once I remember seeing a huge brown bear "dancing" on its hind legs. It was very frightening to me as a small child. There was also a barrel organ man who came, with a little monkey dancing on top of the organ and collecting money in a mug. Tramps would call at houses for tea and bread and cheese in the summer as they walked from one workhouse to another, and there would be gypsies selling hand-made willow pegs and lace. The scissor grinder man came on a bicycle decorated with horse brasses, while the French onion man cycled round with long poles of onions on his shoulders.

Threshing machines thundered from farm to farm, the boys loving to run beside them, and stallions would be led round the farms, their tails and manes plaited with coloured braids. The ragman came to the school at lunchtime and showed us toys and goldfish we could have if we brought rags to him. I remember one boy taking his father's long-johns from the washing line and exchanging them for a goldfish!

The 1953 floods changed much of the centre of the village, destroying most of the stone cottages and buildings which were the heart of the fishing area.'

AROUND KING'S LYNN

'In the summer of 1920 I was seven years old and lived at Gaywood, then a separate village on the outskirts of King's Lynn. As a special treat sometimes, usually a Saturday, I accompanied one of my aunts to Snettisham where she had a small shop, the Army and Navy Stores. We started early and walked to King's Lynn (there was no public transport) to catch the train which only took about 15 to 20 minutes to reach Snettisham and then we walked a sweet-smelling flower-bordered lane to the market place. My aunt's shop sold clothing (including Army and Navy surplus from the First World War), haberdashery, shoes, household linen, workmen's overalls, children's shoes and clothing, door mats, knitting wools etc, and in summer time when visitors came to the beach, buckets and spades and bathing costumes. Anything a customer wanted, but not in stock, would be obtained from the warehouse in King's Lynn or Norwich on my aunt's next visit.

In 1920 the village had a number of shops and was a busy place. Customers came from surrounding villages and were well known to my aunt. I spent the day wandering round the village, eating buns from the adjacent bakery on the market place and watching the various horses and carts which made up most of the traffic. In the late afternoon the Salvation Army band sometimes played on the market place. By 6 pm my aunt locked up the shop, picked up the takings and we walked back to Snettisham station, caught a train to Lynn and walked home to Gaywood. In due course my aunt was able to buy a cottage opposite the shop and kept the shop until 1971 but became confused by decimalisation and had to give up.

When I was young at Gaywood, a bank holiday was celebrated by a picnic. A favourite spot was Reffley Spring and the time we chose for this was usually about May as the surrounding woods were full of primroses. The spring was a pool, the surface of which had a kind of brown scum so you couldn't see much water. Once a young relative tried to walk on the pool and fell in.

25

Another favourite place was West Lynn. We walked to Lynn and then took a penny ride on the ferry across the Ouse to the fields on the other side where we played cricket, picnicked and then had another trip on the ferry and walked home.

King's Lynn and the area out to Hunstanton was a very quiet place before the war. The railway ran from Lynn to Hunstanton so there was not much traffic on the roads. Most people used bicycles or the train for transport and village shops were busy places. Families and friends often met up "on the hill" on a Tuesday and after shopping took home for tea a few shrimps, a couple of bloaters (a penny each) or a fresh crab (sixpence). We used to crack the claws of the crab on the brick kitchen floor by hitting them with a flat iron.

When the surface of the country roads broke up and pot-holes appeared a van and horse would come and stay in the area and in it a workman would live. He would go round and fill the holes with tar and flints. No one seemed to resurface a whole road – they just patched up the holes.'

WHEN THE FLOODS ROSE

'I was born in 1944 at Wells-next-the-Sea (which in those days was called Wells-on-Sea) in a row of terraced houses which ran parallel with the quay. On the evening of 31st January 1953 we were sitting in front of the fire listening to the radio. We could hear the wind and rain lashing at the front door and I remember my Dad saying, "The

The 1953 floods brought death and destruction to the East Coast.

rain's heavy tonight." Little knowing it wasn't only the rain, but the sea which had risen over the quay wall and also broken through the natural banks along the beach road.

Suddenly there was frantic knocking at our back door, it was our neighbour (an elderly spinster) looking very frightened. She told us about the sea breaking through. Being only eight years old I said, "Oh, let's have a look" and rushed to the front door. Before Dad could stop me I had opened it and in rushed the sea. As you can imagine there was pandemonium. Mum screamed, Dad swore and I was suddenly very frightened. Well it took a while but we eventually got the door shut and laid blankets and old coats along the bottom, but as the sea built up Dad had to put the mangle against the door to keep it shut.

Eventually we had to go upstairs as the water got higher. My last memory that night is looking out of the front bedroom window at the dark sea below.

We were lucky, we had electricity, but our neighbour Miss Judd did not. I loved to visit her when I was a child and she often invited me for Sunday tea, after which she would either light the oil lamp or we would sit in front of the fire and take turns to say what shapes we could see in the red hot coals. The shapes were always changing as the fire died down. She had wooden floorboards and one Sunday teatime after the floods my chair leg fell through the floor, I wondered wherever I was going. The sea water had rotted the floorboards.'

'I was very involved with the 1953 floods, being in Civil Defence. There had been an eclipse of the moon on the Thursday night, then the wind got up. On the Saturday night it was snowing as well as blowing a gale. A friend and I walked down to the cliffs at Gorleston and saw nothing but water where the lower promenade and the beach should have been. An old lady was being rescued from her bedroom window. I went home and offered both my mother's and my services to the police but was refused. A friend with a dinghy on a trailer did the same and was also refused. Later we found out that a neighbour had been trying to set up a rest centre in the centre of Gorleston but could not get enough volunteers!

The Civil Defence soon got organised and for several weeks afterwards we were very busy with food and clothing distribution, assessments for loss of furniture etc. When things were getting back to normal we had a special parade, and who else should come but Lady Clementine Churchill, who was charming and spent quite a long time talking to us.'

'In the 1953 floods my mother and father had to move from our post office at Barroway Drove to my sister's on higher ground, with all the post office stores, stamps and postal orders. As it was getting dark, Mother was horrified to see what she thought were drowned people in the water. They were, thankfully, mangolds from a nearby heap bobbing about.'

NORFOLK FOLK

Norfolk has, of course, close ties with the Royal Family and many of us can recall seeing royalty over the years, in settings formal and informal. But equally vivid in our memories are more lowly folk who made day to day life so rich and full – 'characters' that seem to be missing today.

ROYALTY OUT AND ABOUT

'While staying at Dersingham in the early years of the First World War, I was able to see the Royal Family arrive at Sandringham church on Sunday mornings. My grandfather, who was in the police at Dersingham, was in charge of security for them and used to drive over there each week. I sat between him and a police constable who drove the trap. The Dowager Queen Alexandra, King George V and Queen Mary and all their family were there.'

'I remember travelling on the same train as Queen Mary and George V in 1928. They had their own coach attached to the normal train that day. On arriving at Wolferton station a red carpet covered the platform. The King and Queen stepped from the carriage on to the carpeted platform and through the royal waiting room before entering a royal car to complete their journey to Sandringham.'

'As a schoolgirl in 1936, I recall going into the newly opened Marks and Spencer shop in King's Lynn and seeing Queen Mary, with a lady-in-waiting, buying ladies' undervests priced at one shilling each!'

'At one time during George V's reign the Sandringham estate was open to the public even when the Royal Family were in residence. On one occasion we were in the grounds quite near Sandringham

House, which was just roped off for a few yards, when the King came over to speak to us and asked my father about his occupation.

On another occasion, it must have been 60 years ago, looking down from the promenade at Hunstanton one day I saw Queen Mary with the princesses Elizabeth and Margaret Rose. The children had pretty dresses and straw hats and carried chip baskets and were happily collecting shells. They were quite excited if they found an unusual one and ran to the Queen saying "Look, Grandma" in great glee. There was no sign of protection, only a chauffeur waiting in the car. Queen Mary liked Hunstanton; she shopped there, especially at Sam Marshall's china shop, and visited the garden of rest on the cliff top. Times have changed.'

'For weeks in 1935 our tiny village had buzzed with activity as money was raised for an extension to the local hospital. Now the time had arrived when Queen Mary would come to receive the gifts from all the villages. After much speculation, it was announced that I was the lucky person chosen to present the money to the Queen. What excitement for a seven year old! The night before the big day my mother put curl rags in my hair, which were very bumpy to sleep on.

I had a pretty new dress, over which was a cream velvet cloak lined with shell pink and with a white fur neck trim. Elbow-length white silk gloves with very tiny buttons at the wrist completed the outfit. I felt like a princess!

At the huge marquee erected in the hospital grounds my mother and I took our seats. As my name was called I proudly walked down the long aisle towards the regal seated figure of Queen Mary on a dais. I performed my much-practised curtsey, presented the purse containing the £11 collected by the villagers of Whittington, and backed away. A truly unforgettable occasion.'

ON THE ESTATE

'My father was coachman to Frank Beck, the agent to George V, and had charge of the horses at Sandringham until the war started in 1914, when he entered the Veterinary Corps. When he returned, motor cars had replaced the horses and he was no longer required. He then worked as under-gardener at Park House, which was used to accommodate guests of the Royal Family.

I went to West Newton school, with about 70 children, three teachers and one monitress. Queen Alexandra occasionally visited the school, sometimes accompanied by Princess Victoria, who was around eight years old. They brought lots of small gifts, some of which I still have. Mr Bone, the organist at Sandringham church, gave us music lessons regularly. I won first prize for scripture and was invited to Sandringham House to receive my prize Bible from George V. I was dressed in my best and was escorted in to His Majesty's presence by a footman. I curtseyed and the King talked to me for a while, confiding that he read a passage from the Bible every day.

At Christmas time there was a big party in the ballroom at Sandringham when the King and Queen distributed gifts. The men received a joint of beef, the size dependent on the size of the family. The little princesses would often be helping to give the presents.

In 1937 I became secretary of Sandringham WI when we had 40 to 50 members. Queen Mary was president and she brought Queen Elizabeth, now the Queen Mother, and in time she brought Princesses Elizabeth and Margaret who also became members.'

OUR ROYAL ENCOUNTER

'As I was cycling home from shopping one lovely afternoon in April 1947, I came across a very eccentric farmer friend of mine, who called across to me, "Would you like to come to Felbrigg Hall gates with me, I hear Queen Mary is coming to tea with Mr Ketton Cremer. She will be arriving soon and I would love to see her."

I was thrilled to go and my friend said, "Hold you hard, while I go up to the hall and tidy myself up." I was pleased to hear that as she had been feeding her pigs and was covered in pig muck.

She was soon back, having washed her face and changed the old sack she was wearing for a clean one. This one had Barclay and Pallet stamped across the front of it and was tied up with red binder twine. She had kept on her old-type men's Burberry raincoat, also her size nine men's water boots although it was a lovely day, but this was her normal attire. Her crowning glory this afternoon was her toque-type hat with a black veil over it.

We got on our bicycles and soon reached Felbrigg Hall gates, discreetly parking our bicycles in the hedge. Soon the royal Daimler arrived. The Queen looked lovely in a wonderful shade of blue and was looking interestedly about her when she saw us. She ordered her car to stop, then looked across to us, and gave us a lovely smile and a wave of her hand whereupon my friend gave her a most elaborate curtsy, the sack apron sweeping the ground. The Queen looked delighted, I just bobbed. With another wave of the hand and another smile the car moved on. Such was our royal encounter.'

A NORWICH CHARACTER

'My husband's great-uncle William Cullum was a well known Norwich character. In the spring he would walk miles to pick wild flowers, collecting them in a "frail", the rush basket workmen used to carry their breakfast and dinner. He picked lilies-of-the-valley in woods on the Watton Road, primroses by the Gull at Framingham Pigot, and violets at Bramerton. These flowers he bunched and sold on The Walk for a penny a bunch from a florist's basket with a large round handle. In the autumn he sold hot chestnuts, and in the winter Mr Leach's Cough Remedy at twopence and fourpence a bottle, and cough sweets which he said would "cure the cough, cut the phlegm, good for the old, the young, the weak, the wild and the weary". He also sold the matches which gave him the nickname "Billy Bluelight".

He is probably best known for his summer activities, when for pennies he would race the boats between Bramerton and Norwich. He would stand on the bank at Bramerton and recite: "My name is Billy Bluelight, my age is forty-five, I hope to get to Carrow Bridge before the boat arrive" – and he would be sure to be waiting at the bridge when the boat appeared, even if he had to cadge a lift to get there in time! He is sometimes said to have raced boats to Yarmouth, but my late father in law told me that was a myth and he never ran further than Bramerton.

Billy never could resist a challenge, and once agreed to race a policeman from St Benedict's in Norwich to The Dog at Easton and back again for a purse of £5. They were seen off by a cheering crowd, but when they arrived back, within a few yards of each other, they discovered the lad holding the prize money had vanished!

The only conventional job Billy ever had was in the despatch department at Caley's in Norwich, but his extrovert character demanded freedom and the applause of the crowds. He was much loved by all who met him, and a few months after he died in 1949 at the age of 90 a wooden seat was placed by the river near Foundry Bridge and dedicated to his memory.'

ONE OF THE STALWARTS

'Sixty years ago, my aunt, Mrs Gertrude Reynolds, was the secretary of the WI in Gresham, a small straggling village in north Norfolk. This seems to have been a permanent position, at least until the 1950s, and knowing her, I should guess this was not because she held on to office, but because no one else would do it.

Although she lived at the very end of the long village, everyone came to her for everything from advice to letter writing to officialdom.

31

Even the butcher, who delivered twice a week, would leave all the villagers' orders on her living room table. As the door was never locked, people would come in and help themselves whether she was there or not. The correct money was always left, or a note to say how much they owed her. No one was afraid of pilfering in a small village in those days.

By 1960, Uncle George had retired and they were better off on his Old Age Pension of £3 10s than when he was delivering oil and paraffin to the local villages, out in all weathers on an open cart and with his employer's horse to tend at the beginning and end of each day.

Auntie Gert's flaming hair was a true indication of a quick temper when she was roused, which was not often, but both she and George would do anything for anyone. His war wounds had made it impossible for them to have children, but one winter day their eldest nephew came up from the other end of the village, got snowed in for several days and lived with them from then until he started work in the Civil Service. No doubt his parents with four other children to feed were happy with the arrangement.

My grandmother, who had been a widow for many years, also lived with them in the two bedroomed cottage, with one living room and a scullery. She cooked beautiful bread in a small brick oven in the wall. They were lucky to have a well just outside the door, so didn't have to go far for water. When piped water reached the village, there was at least one inhabitant who still used Auntie Gert's well, as it stood to reason that it must be cleaner than water going through "datty old pipes".

Electric light came just after the war, to succeed the paraffin lamps. The installation was a ramshackle affair and my husband was horrified to discover bakelite fittings on the ceiling and rubber cable baked hard and brittle, ready to set the place on fire at any time. He spent most of that holiday making it safe.

During the war my youngest sister lived with Auntie Gert rather than be forcibly evacuated from London. Soon after the war my other sister joined the Women's Land Army and – yes – went to live with Auntie Gert. She worked for Captain Batt, who was the virtual squire of the village, so, of course, Lady Batt was President of the Gresham WI.

My sister remembers that Lady Batt always brought her replacement Land Army uniforms to the house and would stay to have a cup of tea. It was still a time when people "knew their place" and Gert considered herself a very ordinary country woman and always spoke of her President with respect, but the wreath which Lady Batt sent to Gert's funeral referred to her as "a dear friend for many years". I think she would have been surprised if she had known how many people held her in affection and esteem.'

THE ROMANIES

'I was born in Norwich in the early 1920s, moving out to the Boundary Road when I was three years old. Life was so very pleasant in those days, slow, free and easy, full of joyful events like flying kites, paddling and fishing in the streams, playing hopscotch and spinning coloured tops. But how excited I would be when Dad came home from his job in Norwich and said to Mother, "There's a fine lot of Romany caravans coming our way, heading for Diss I shouldn't wonder."

How I loved it when the gypsies camped in the fields opposite our home. Their beautiful and ornate caravans were brightly painted red, green, blue and yellow, with brass lamps, shining leather and white lace curtains. Running to the Boundary Road I would sit and wait on the then very wide grass verge, which was scattered with dainty white daisies and bright yellow buttercups, pink and white clover and poppies in profusion. As I waited for the gypsies to settle their camp I would make daisy chains and head crowns, or pluck the poppy buds and unfold them to make fairies.

I could hear the laughter and banter as the gypsies slowly unharnessed their horses, and when all was settled I would climb over the five-barred gate to watch the women, girls and young boys make pegs and multi-coloured crepe paper flowers to sell later to the locals. Inching up closer, I would say "Hello". They would stop and gaze at me dubiously, then shyly smile. My attire looked so different to the clothes they wore, me with my panama straw hat held on by elastic under my chin, my Clarks sandals and my short printed cotton dress. The young gypsy girls would be in their very bright coloured full skirts and blouses, with scarves and shawls, and bare feet. Oh, how they fascinated me, with their very white teeth, brown happy faces and laughing eyes.

After tethering the horses, they let loose the many dogs, fetched water and milk from the nearby farm and gathered wood for the fires. I loved to watch all this. They would wash loads of clothes and hang them on the hedgerows to dry. They gathered hips and haws from the nearby woods and searched for anything that might be useful.

My parents never turned any gypsy away, nor tramps. I have known my mother to make them cups of tea and give them home-made cakes. They in turn would tell her fortune by reading the tea leaves left in her cup. One very old gypsy lady said, "Koind loidy, one of your lorvly daughters will marry high." I was one of eight daughters and the only one to get anywhere near that promise

– I married a "Hill".
Boundary Road now, of course, is the outer ring road of Norwich, and the wood where I watched the gypsies is under the Asda superstore.'

CHURCH AND CHAPEL

Sundays were special, set aside from the toil of the rest of the week and with their own rhythm. Going to church or chapel was a regular part of life and children sometimes went to Sunday school twice as well! The compensation came when it was time for the school Anniversary or the outing, always eagerly anticipated.

SUNDAYS WERE SPECIAL

'In our family Sunday was very special and apart from going to the chapel services nothing would be done on that day. My memories relate mainly to the times I spent Saturday nights at my grandparents' home.

Preparations for Sunday would start the day before, with my grandfather cleaning out the pigs, cattle and horses and preparing all their food for the next day, so that on Sunday he would only have to put the food in the yards.

In the house, my granny would cook the joint of meat and boil potatoes, and in the summer months prepare a salad, as Sunday food was always eaten cold, apart that is from the porridge at breakfast. That would have been cooked the evening before, then warmed in the double saucepan on the oil stove. Then Grandfather would add bread, milk, golden syrup and sugar to his. Porridge was for breakfast, whatever the weather, all year round, and delicious it was too!

On Saturday evening before bed it would be into the scullery for the weekly strip-wash, and Grandfather would have his shave, with the mirror close to the oil lamp on the kitchen table. I expect he must have shaved at other times, but it's funny I can only remember it on a Saturday night.

Then on Sunday morning we would cycle the three miles to chapel. Grandfather was a Methodist local preacher, and often he would have to set off really early to cycle to the other chapels to preach. The morning service was at 11 am, after which Granny and

Grandfather would cycle home again for lunch, and I would go to my aunt and uncle's house. Then at 1.30 pm it was back to chapel for Sunday school, where there would be perhaps 20 children, then straight in to the afternoon service at 2.30 pm. After this service, often my grandparents would come to our house for tea (we always had someone for tea on Sundays). With tea over it was back to chapel for the evening service at 6.30 pm, then home and into bed.'

'Sundays *were* special when I was a child in the early years of the century. All clean underwear, Sunday dresses, shoes, coats, hats. In summer we had to wear white cotton gloves, which were very hot and uncomfortable. At 10 am we attended the Wesleyan chapel Sunday school at Claxton, which was a walk of about a mile. We got back home for dinner at twelve o'clock – cold meat followed by cold milk pudding or fruit pie. New potatoes and green peas in season. In summer we changed our best dresses for this. No toys – we hadn't very many anyway – but we were allowed to read books. Then we dressed again to go back to chapel for a short Sunday school session at 2 pm followed by the afternoon chapel service. The singing was good but the sermons sometimes dreary. Then we were back for tea at 5 pm. Tea was rather special: hard boiled eggs and cress, celery, strawberries, stewed prunes, occasionally tinned salmon or anything else which was in season but not plentiful enough for weekdays.

After tea and washing up, in summer we sometimes went for a walk or, all dressed up again in our best clothes, to evening service in the parish church. In winter we sang hymns round the piano, played by my eldest sister. We might be allowed to read again for a time, and so to bed. I don't think we had much time to be naughty on Sundays.'

THE SUNDAY AFTERNOON STROLL

'After church and Sunday roast lunch, still in our Sunday best, we would meet up on Hempton Green with our aunts, uncles and cousins, to go for our Sunday afternoon stroll.

After deciding which way to go, either along Shereford Road or down Green Lane, off we would set, the children running ahead exploring the hedgerows to see what they could find, the women exchanging the latest gossip of the past week, and the men discussing the politics of the day, sometimes arguing their different points of view as we wandered along.

We would often meet other family groups, stop for a chat, then off again going our different ways. We would hear from the grown-ups about their childhood days as we strolled along, picking the flowers or berries, depending on the season.

The weather always seemed to be kind to us, and usually a pleasant time was had by all. We would end up at one of the relatives' feeling very tired but looking forward to the salmon sandwiches for tea.'

PARSONS WERE NOT ALL ALIKE

'We were rather hard up at this particular time with Father out of work, and I know Mother used to worry sometimes as to what we could have with our bread for tea.

It was one of those days that the parson called on one of his rare visits. Mother felt awful, when he looked at us seated round the table (don't they always come at mealtimes!) and said, "Oh, you poor things. Is that all you've got for your tea? I must go and see what I can find for you." Off he went and returned soon after with a large bag. From this he produced several pairs of button boots, some black, some brown, of various sizes, and set them neatly in a row under the couch! Nothing there to eat or to wear, as none would fit us. Then, hey presto, out of his bag he brought forth – a duck – yes, really – a duck, grey flannel with yellow beak and button eyes! My baby brother did make use of that. We've had a few laughs about it since, but not just then!

However, parsons were not all alike, as we found when we moved away, for when Father was taken ill the rector called to see him and from then on, for six weeks until Father recovered, every Saturday morning he came on his cycle to deliver to Mother a large rice pudding and six shillings from his own pocket. We have never forgotten his kindness and generosity.'

CHAPEL DAYS

'One of the highlights of the year at Deopham chapel was Easter and on Good Friday there was a service of song when special four-part songs were sung by the choir, punctuating a story with a religious theme.

From time to time evangelistic services, known as camp meetings, were held on farm land near the chapel and were conducted in a tent by a visiting preacher.

The harvest festival was a lovely time. Taking place in a rural setting made it very meaningful. The chapel was decorated with flowers and garden produce, which was auctioned after the week-night service – a great social occasion. The income went into the Trust Fund which was used for the upkeep and general running costs. The Sunday collections went towards the minister's stipend. He lived at Hingham. Other income was from "Seat money". This was a kind of rent paid for a particular seat which was jealously kept for the member. Seat rents gradually disappeared but as late as 1943 someone paid one shilling and fourpence for one seat for a year.

By 1960 the evening service had been discontinued, but there was still an afternoon service, and the Sunday school still met in the morning. The highlight of the Sunday school was the Anniversary. On that day the children attended three services, in the morning a sermon was preached and in the afternoon and evening the children would sing special songs, helped by a four-part choir. Many hours were spent practising. Children recited poems, commonly known as "pieces". Looking at the length of some of them now I wonder however the children managed to learn them! It was a great social occasion and most of the villagers attended, and on a really sunny day (always in June) the doors were open wide and some of the menfolk sat on the grass outside. The collections were for Sunday school funds and treats during the coming year.

The most important treat was the outing. The first recorded one was to Yarmouth in 1885 when the children were taken by waggon to a railway station in order to go by train. The outing became a regular treat from 1920. It involved nearly all the village children and their parents. The school was closed as the outing took place on a Wednesday. After 1950 it was changed to a Saturday. The only exception to this yearly ritual was from 1940 to 1944. Directly after VE Day in 1945, an outing was arranged to Lowestoft, which was the only place the coaches were allowed to go from this area. It was a joy to see the younger children's faces as they looked at the sea for the first time.

The Sunday school was always well supported and the record year was 1959 when over 40 children were on the register.'

'Sunday school at St Germans was the highlight of the week. Almost all the village children attended regularly on Sunday mornings. This was a mile walk for some of us, but it was a lovely walk down an avenue of trees, huge chestnuts, which met at the top. We walked to one tree and ran to the next, and it seemed no time at all and we were there.

The first Sunday in May was Anniversary Day. We practised for weeks to sing and entertain with poems etc. We all had new clothes and some had hats. The chapel was always packed to capacity. We sang our hearts out and read our poems and went home for high tea, we always had visitors on that day. Then back for the evening performance, all beginning to wilt by then. It was a slow walk home. Next day we went to school, no one very interested in lessons. We were watching the clock, as we were allowed to leave early. We raced home, changed out of school clothes, and off down the avenue again.

At the chapel we were loaded on to two carts, pulled by horses. There was a piano on one cart and an organ on the other, and bales of straw for seats. We went all round nearby villages singing at every stop and collecting for chapel funds. Halfway round we called at the Bridge Inn, run by my grandparents, and were given crisps and pop. Refreshed, we finished the round and went back to high tea at the chapel. After tea we played games and had races.

During the summer holidays a coach was laid on to take us and our families for a day at the seaside. This was a real treat, we took packed lunches and were each given sixpence to spend.

The horses that took us on the rounds were eventually replaced by tractors, and the beautiful avenue of trees was removed to extend the ground for food crops during the war. It became a very bleak and windy walk but is still called the avenue.'

THE SUNDAY SCHOOL FESTIVAL

'When I was a child in Martham during the early 1930s, one of the highlights of my year was the Sunday school festival which was held annually in early July at St Mary's church. Martham church is known as the Cathedral of the Fleggs and is a large and beautiful church with intricately carved pew ends, an impressive setting for a festival.

Preparations for the great event, which involved 30 or so children who attended Sunday school, began on Saturday morning. We took flowers from our gardens to decorate the church. The vicar, Rev Griffiths, had a large well kept garden and it was a great honour to be asked to go with him and help to carry the beautiful roses that he had cut. Wooden forms and chairs were carried from the church room, where Sunday school was held, and arranged in rows in front of the rood screen.

On one occasion a few of us were taken to the top of the church tower as a reward for our labours. This was indeed a special treat as the view from the top of St Mary's church, one of the highest in the Fleggs, is spectacular, looking over the dunes and out to sea in one direction and over the rivers and broads in the other. As we looked down from this perilous height we tried to decide which of the miniature houses was ours.

For such a special occasion we had to be spotlessly clean, so on Saturday evening the zinc bungalow bath was brought into the kitchen, water was heated in the copper, and we all had our weekly bath. My hair was shampooed with Evan Williams Chamomile Shampoo, which came in a green and yellow packet, enough for two shampoos, costing fourpence halfpenny. This was a powder which was mixed with warm water in a white enamel jug.

The festival began at 11 am, the normal time for matins, and the bells were rung for fully half an hour beforehand. All the girls wore new dresses – my grandmother was a dressmaker and had made mine for me – and straw hats trimmed with artificial flowers or ribbons to match our dresses. Our shoes were white or black patent leather and our socks were dazzlingly white without the help of biological washing powders and automatic washing machines.

The boys wore knee-length shorts, long-sleeved shirts with collar and tie, black or brown shoes and their knee-socks almost reached to the edge of their shorts. Their hair was cut short and held in place with a touch of brilliantine, or Brylcreem.

Dressed in our best, we sat facing the congregation. Every pew in the church was filled with parents, grandparents, aunts, uncles, cousins and friends. All were dressed very formally, the women wearing hats and gloves, the men with dark suits and well polished shoes.

As the bells stopped ringing, the organ played and our festival had begun. We sang hymns and songs of praise, well rehearsed, interspersed with readings from the Bible. Those with good voices were chosen to sing solos and duets. I dearly wished to be one of those chosen few, but I needed to sing with the others to keep me in tune.

After the service we went home to a cold lunch and to think about the repeat performance, usually a little more relaxed, at 6.30 pm. The afternoon was spent in suitable Sunday pursuits, nothing noisy, no sewing or knitting allowed, but reading or going for a quiet walk was permissible.

In the evening our friends from the Baptist and Methodist chapels formed part of the congregation. We always felt a little superior to them because they only had Sunday school Anniversaries and we had a *festival!*

I remember all festival days as being perfect summer days with the sun shining from a clear blue sky from dawn till dusk. How unsophisticated we were, and what pleasure we had from such simple things.'

OUR OUTING

'I lived in Diss from 1919 to 1924. On Sunday we all went to Sunday school, the girls in their best frocks. Once a year, one day in the summer, we all went to Yarmouth for the day. A train was hired and children from all the different Sunday schools came, together with people from other organisations and societies. Diss was deserted that day.'

GETTING ABOUT

It is not so long since horse-drawn transport was our only means of getting about – either that or Shanks's pony! The roads were quiet and when we did finally get a motor car, journeys were exciting expeditions. There were the trains, of course, and diesel has never replaced steam in our affections.

HORSE POWER

'For a shopping trip to Norwich from Ickburgh in the early 1920s we used to go by pony and trap, a distance of 30 miles. We sat two facing the front and two facing backwards. I can't remember how long it took us but the pony we had always had to be at the front so he never let anything pass. We drove as far as Earlham and left the pony and trap at a pub where my Dad's cousin lived. We then finished the journey by tram.'

'When I was a girl we lived on a farm at Tunstead. We all went to the Methodist chapel at Sloley, about three miles away. Dad used to take us there in a high cart pulled by a farm horse. The wheels of the cart were iron, so we would go bumping along. When it rained he put a blanket over us to protect us.'

OUR SPECIAL TREAT

'When our Aunt Anna came home to Creake for her annual holiday in the summer, she would give us a special treat and take us out for the day. It was mostly to Holkham beach.
    Mother would first go to see Mr Baker, as he was the village carrier, and as Mother could drive he would let her hire his pony and trap for the day. Once that was arranged Mother and Aunt Anna then made plans for our day out. Hilda was our look-out girl as Mother would tell her to watch for Mr Baker to take his pony off the green where it had been feeding. That meant he would then be getting the pony and trap ready. It seemed ages waiting but as soon as he appeared Hilda rushed in to tell Mother. She then went to fetch the pony and trap. We were all waiting to load up by the time she drove up: Aunt Anna, us four sisters and brother Hardy. By the time we were packed in, the neighbours were out in the lane to wave us off. We were well loaded, but felt so proud riding in the open trap and our mother driving.

Hiram Watson and Kathy Worsencroft travelling by pony and trap near Aylsham, still a common way of getting about in the 1930s.

The pony trotted along the Waterden road and through Quarles. Each time we came to a hill, Hardy would get out and walk along by the pony's head, which he liked doing. Going downhill he would stand on the step. As we came up to the Triumphal Arch the lady living there came out and had a talk with Mother, asking about different Creake people she knew. Further along to the park gates we drove, which were closed. We then had to wait for the lady to come and open them for us, and then another gossip. Aunt Anna would open her purse and pass a coin to the lady, sixpence, and then we were away again, so excited to be driving through the park. There were many partridges and pheasants by the roadside and Mother would several times draw up to let them cross over with their young ones.

When we came to the gates into Holkham village, Hardy would get down and open them. He then led the pony down to the Victoria Hotel where it was stabled and looked after while we went down to the beach. That seemed a long walk and not many people were about on the beach. I don't remember going down to the water as it looked miles away and we were not allowed to go far. So we just paddled in the puddles.

When the time was up for us to return, Mother and Hardy went on in front to get the pony and trap ready. We all loaded up again, Aunt Anna paying the man. He wished us a safe journey home. The pony trotted up to the gates and Hardy opened them, and before he could close them the pony set off running, so Hardy had to run to get in. My word, that pony did not stop to trot; we came home much quicker. Mother would say he knows he is going home. Back home we unloaded and Mother drove back to Mr Baker's. It was not long before the pony was back on the green feeding.

I often think how pleasant it would be to drive round the lanes again in an open trap.'

MY FATHER WAS THE CARRIER

'My father was the carrier for Upton and had horses and various carts and waggons for general work locally. He also had a covered van drawn by two horses with which he used to go to Norwich twice a week, Wednesdays and Saturdays. I was twelve and when not at school went with my father.

We would leave before eight and picking up all orders on the way we went via South Walsham, Panxworth and Hemblington, on to the main road at Blofield, then to Norwich to the White Lion, St Martin's Palace Plain. Here the van was stood down with many others and the horses were stabled behind the White Lion where they were fed and watered. I would then run round the wholesalers delivering the orders for which I would be paid twopence or fourpence, but if I had an order for Looses I would go there first because they always gave me sixpence. I would then return to the van to wait for the orders to be delivered and make sure they were packed in order of delivery, with wood roped on to the roof.

At about five o'clock Father would hitch up the horses and we would start for home. In the winter we only had two carriage lamps to light the way. As soon as we got out of Norwich Father would produce some wonderful sandwiches of harriot lane (corned beef) and new bread.

We were often held up on the main road by 50 or 60 head of cattle with one drover and his dog until they came to a field where they could lay for the night and then be driven on to the various farms next day.

Sometimes Father would go to sleep and I would take the reins, waking him when we got to the next stop. If there was ice and snow Father would put frost studs in the horses' shoes and when we got to Sallow Bush Hill we had to get out and help the horses and keep ourselves warm.

Everything delivered, we would arrive home at about eleven when we fed and watered the horses with short feed and filled the racks with hay. And so to bed.'

'In 1918 Coopers in Diss had a bus. One had to walk to Diss from Scole to book seats on the bus, which had slatted seats, a driver and a conductor. As the bus went along the roadside trees hung all over

Mrs Allen was a familiar figure around Eccles and Quidenham in the 1930s. Tricycles, tandems or ordinary bikes – we used them all.

the top deck and the conductor would shout "Duck", and then later "Sit up again". Canvas aprons were used over the seats to keep dry. I can remember going to Yarmouth, and walking home to Scole from Diss afterwards.

I rode a bicycle then, a tandem with my husband Tom. It had cost eight shillings secondhand. It arrived in Diss by train, and I first rode it on a Monday, during doing the washing! I rode to Thelveton and fell off. I couldn't turn round or get off at first, but eventually we went for miles, including travelling to Lowestoft and back.

To visit Norwich a bus went on Tuesday afternoons from Diss. I went one day with my aunt. It was to be a 9 pm return from the Jolly Farmers and the bus broke down. All the passengers were given a lift in a flour lorry and arrived back at 1 am covered in flour.'

LIFE WITH A MOTOR CAR

'In the 1930s I lived with my parents and two brothers in East Harling, south Norfolk. My father was fortunate to have acquired a motor car, a 1932 model Austin Seven saloon, which was one of the few in the village at the time. This gave us the opportunity to visit places in East Anglia and relatives who lived within these bounds. Memories of these journeys and their traumas remain after 60 years.

Not much travelling was done in the winter months when the cooling water was carefully drained off and the engine wrapped up to prevent damage from frost. Come the spring we looked for a fine weekend to start motoring.

Father driving, Mother alongside and three boys squabbling for seat space in the rear, we set off with picnic hamper and can of petrol on the carrier over the back bumper and in two hours time we were on the sandy beach at Hunstanton. Lunch was beef sandwiches, apple pies or jam tarts and shortcakes (select the one with the most currants). A swim in the sea and a walk along the promenade took until 4 pm when we returned to the car to move on to Docking for tea with our grandparents. Here the problems began as the car proved difficult to start and we boys played or made a nuisance of ourselves on the grass by the pier until action was restored.

Docking was reached in half an hour: it was known locally as Dry Docking as at the time it had only one well, the water from which was pumped by a donkey engine into a horse-drawn tanker which travelled the village daily filling the residents' buckets at a halfpenny a time.

Whilst tea was being prepared my father, aided by several knowledgeable locals, dismantled the magneto, cleaned and reassembled it. Tea at Docking was totally predictable, delicious and always available to visitors arriving without notice. Tea in the best china, samphire in vinegar in season, red salmon, all accompanied by crusty bread from nearby Wagg's bakery. Home-made fruit cake in large portions completed the repast.

Due to the engine problem we left early on the byroads to Swaffham but at Harpley were again halted by engine failure. In time a man in a black Morris saloon from a garage in Massingham arrived, got the engine going once more and charged us five shillings. Ten miles on we were halted again, by a signpost which said "Castleacre 2". I walked there with my father and later the owner of the garage towed us ignominiously to his premises. It was decided to fit a reconditioned magneto which he had in stock but alas, on going to the store cupboard found it locked and the key was with his brother who had gone courting. He returned at 10.30 pm and work commenced by gaslight as we sat in the semi darkness warmed by a welcome cup of tea. In half an hour the engine was fired up and we started the final 20 miles home during which time we boys slept. Next morning we were up early to take part in the George V jubilee celebrations in the village.'

ON THE ROAD

'As a child in the late 1920s, the highlight of a summer Sunday evening was a walk with my parents to the Turnpike, now the A47, to sit on the bank by Postwick chapel and watch the traffic. There could be an interval of 15 minutes between cars, which were mostly Austin Sevens or Morrises, with an occasional Daimler. There were also open-topped charabancs bringing day trippers to and from Yarmouth, with streamers flying and everyone happy, and an assortment of pony-traps and bicycles. Some of the lady passengers in the older open cars wore veils over their hats and faces.

We did not encounter much traffic on the walk, only other strollers like ourselves. My father would comment on the crops in the fields, while Mother and I were more interested in the abundance of wild flowers to be found along the verges, especially the dainty harebells. I enjoyed these walks but when my father met an acquaintance, they would mardle for ages and then I would get bored.

I wonder how many people would take a walk to sit by the A47 today!'

'In 1923 the Ministry of Transport offered grants to district councils for improvement of the better class roads. Smallburgh Rural District Council, meeting at Stalham, decided the Mundesley to Bacton road was qualified to benefit under this scheme as it was called upon to take considerable traffic during the summer months. A survey showed that in one week the following traffic passed along the road: 2,334 cycles, 306 motor cycles, 504 motor vans, 78 motor omnibuses, 15 motor lorries, 70 trailers, 212 light vehicles, 99 heavy vehicles, eleven horse omnibuses, 57 horses ridden or led, and eight handcarts.'

'In the mid 1930s, in the summer months, a policeman called PC Purdy would be on point duty at the junction of Mundesley Road, Cromer Road and the High Street at Overstrand. Overstrand was busy with visitors during the summer. I cannot remember a great number of cars but there were several charabancs visiting the village each day.

PC Purdy was a very kindly man, keeping young folk in order as well as the traffic. One particular memory is that he used to hang bananas on a sycamore tree nearby and led me to believe they had grown there. He didn't convince me, but the bananas were good!'

MEMORIES OF THE PAST

'In the 19th century there were several hundred trading wherries afloat. By the end of the Second World War only one was left, the rescued trading wherry *Albion* built in 1898; she still sails today, taking holidaymakers on river trips and cruises.

At the beginning of the 20th century some trading wherries were being converted to pleasure wherries, with cabins provided for privacy, the hull and sail needing no alteration. Gradually the advantage of building wherries for pleasure was realised, and a great many were built. The Victorians and Edwardians enjoyed the peaceful comfort of gliding on the waterways of the Broads. In the saloon, happy evenings were spent round a five-octave yacht piano, lit by an oil lamp. Comfortably sleeping at night between pillows of softest down and eiderdowns, the only disturbance would be the hoot of an owl, or the sound of a bittern booming.

It was in 1951 that my husband and I, with two sons, came to live in a house by the river in Wroxham. Since 1939 successive bishops of Norwich have sailed by river to the ruins of St Benet's Abbey on the first Sunday in August for a service. It was always one of our great pleasures each year to sail and moor up our "Yare and Bure" with all the other boats to watch the bishop being brought to the abbey on a wherry in full regalia. Choirs from surrounding villages would be waiting on the river bank. The first bishop we saw was Bishop Herbert of Norwich, who came in pleasure wherry *Solace*, privately owned.'

HOUSE & HOME

THE HOUSES WE LIVED IN

So much has changed over the last 50 years in the houses we live in, from those times when oil lamps and candles gave the only light, we cooked over the open fire or in an oven by its side, carpet was a luxury only the rich could afford and we had no labour-saving devices to help us in the home. Were they really the good old days?

GRANDFATHER WALTER

'My grandfather Walter Beck was born in 1860. He and his wife Elizabeth had six children. They lived in Great Walsingham, where Becks had lived for many generations.

Walter was a farm bailiff. In addition he looked after and worked the huge steam engines which helped with the work on the land. He could not read or write, not because he was unintelligent but because education was not available to poor country children when he was a boy. Walter and Elizabeth lived a simple life, dominated by hard work and the chapel. On Sundays the family were expected to attend morning and evening services and in the afternoon the children would go to Sunday school.

After working hard on the farm all day Walter would cultivate his garden and the children were expected to help with this and with Elizabeth's chickens. Cooking was done in an oven by the side of the fire, which had to be lit even on the hottest summer days. On Sunday morning they would take a roast dinner to the bakehouse on the way to chapel, and collect it, cooked, on the way home.

Water came from a pump outside the back door. The children were bathed once a week, in a tin bath in front of the fire, and they enjoyed this. They all used the same bath water but it was topped up with a kettle full of hot water from the fire for each one.

Elizabeth was fortunate to own a box mangle: this was a large box filled with stones, and by turning a handle the box was made to roll along and squeeze water from the washing. Other women in the village paid her a penny to use her mangle.

The lavatory was a brick building, with wooden seats over a hole in the ground, at the bottom of the garden. Everyone had a chamberpot under the bed.

The living room of the cottage was lit by a paraffin lamp, but everyone took candles to light themselves to bed. Their feather mattresses were very comfortable and warm.

In the front parlour they had the luxury of a pianola, though neither my grandmother nor grandfather had much time to listen to it.

My mother and her brothers and sisters went to the village school, which cost one penny per child per week. Walter was pleased to give his children the education he lacked. It was a very basic education, however, and they left school at 13. They had one annual adventure – the Sunday school treat, when they were taken on horse-drawn farm waggons to the seaside for the day.'

FROM TOWN TO COUNTRY

'John and I were two city dwellers – he came from Paisley, near Glasgow, and I was a Londoner. We met at teacher training college after the war and when chance took us to Norwich in 1951 for our first teaching posts, we enjoyed all the amenities that we were used to, although our only assets when we got married were £50 to see us through to our first pay day, a few wedding presents, and our bicycles. Our semi-furnished flat cost three guineas a week and our combined monthly cheque came to under £50, out of which we managed to buy a bed and some items of furniture.

After a year or so we tried to find unfurnished, cheaper accommodation but there was nothing in the city and we could not afford to buy, so we turned our attention to the country. Once again, chance took us to Docking, near King's Lynn, where John got a job in the village school and we rented a cottage from a local farmer for six shillings a week. Our neighbours paid five shillings but he thought, as newcomers, we ought to pay a bit more.

It was a good substantial three-bedroomed cottage made of flint and brick, with a tiled roof, one of a pair, standing in the middle of a field and reached by a dirt track. It was August when we moved in with our few possessions – it took less time to empty the removal van and stow everything away than it did to boil the kettle for a cup of tea on the paraffin stove. I still remember sitting on the doorstep in the evening gazing at the sunlit cornfields beyond the garden hedge and savouring the feeling of having our own home.

Across the backyard, behind the loo which housed the Elsan, and the washhouse complete with copper and tin bath on the wall, ran a single railway line, although by that time only a goods train ran past twice a day.

The cottage had neither gas nor electricity and no drainage or water laid on. Water was brought about once a week to a point at the front of the cottages in a zinc tank on a cart pulled by a horse. Later the farmer had a standpipe installed on the same spot, which

49

meant we didn't have to be so sparing with water but John still had to trudge back and forth with buckets to fill up the butt near the kitchen door.

As the cottage had been empty for some time before we moved in, the garden was completely overgrown with nettles and thistles so it had to be turned over by a horse and plough before we could begin to cultivate it. The previous tenants had kept chickens so the ground was well manured and John grew the finest leeks we have ever had. All our waste water was thrown onto the garden too. Apparently Tide washing powder must have had pesticidal properties because we didn't have much trouble with bugs.

Next door lived a retired gamekeeper and his wife who were the kindest of neighbours. Mr Matthews, whose own vegetable garden was a model of neatness and productivity, helped John in every way he could and in winter, when we came home in the afternoon, Mrs Matthews had invariably filled the kettle and lit the fire in the kitchen range. I did try to use the range for baking but the oven turned out everything black on one side and white on the other, so we gave up and installed a calor gas cooker which was a boon and a blessing, as it not only did the cooking but heated all the water too. We also had a calor gas light in the kitchen but Aladdin lamps lit the living room and we went to bed by candlelight.

People in the village didn't travel very far unless they were the comparative few who owned cars, like the squire, the farmers, the doctor, the headmaster and one or two shopkeepers. The rest of us depended upon our bicycles and an infrequent bus service to Lynn and Hunstanton. It was not possible to get to Norwich and back by bus in one day. On the rare occasions when we needed to get to the station at Heacham, to catch a train or to meet visitors, we hired the village taxi – an ancient and stately Rolls Royce, which the owner treated with loving care and would only start the engine by turning the handle – and travelled in style.

When we had lived in Norwich we liked to go to the pictures on Friday evenings to unwind at the end of the week, but in Docking cinemas were out of reach so we listened to our battery wireless set and soon became hooked on *The Archers*. I can still remember the shock we felt when Grace Archer was killed in the stable fire.

The winter of 1952/53 was our first in Docking and on the night of 31st January, the wind sounded even louder than usual in our somewhat exposed position whilst we were having our bath in front of the kitchen fire. When we opened the back door to try to empty the bath water on to the garden, the gale was so strong it took the strength of the two of us to get it shut again. The next morning, of course, we heard of the death and destruction at Heacham and all around the coast, caused by the terrible wind and surge of the sea.'

FORGE COTTAGE

'After the war, when John and I married, we could not find a small house near the smithy where he worked as a blacksmith, so we had an extension built on to his mother's home, the Forge Cottage. It was quite a large room and as it turned out very, very cold. "The reason is, that you have three outside walls," said a knowing relative.

On winter evenings with "the fire halfway up the chimney" we sat on our hard rexine-covered, so-called "easy chairs" and toasted on one side and froze on the other, as with shiny red noses we listened to the wireless. On Sundays, Max Jaffa and his Palm Court Orchestra, Tuesdays we had stories by the Man in Black, his dark velvet voice filling the room with horror. I cannot remember which night Wilfred Pickles invited contestants to "Have a Go" but best of all was *Saturday Night Theatre*.

I loved our dining room suite, especially the sideboard with its circular carving on the doors. Bonds of Norwich had advertised in the *Evening News*, "The first non-utility suites to have been manufactured since the war" and we could just afford to buy one.'

THE MAJORITY OF COTTAGES

'For many years prior to the Second World War the majority of cottages in small villages such as Little Ellingham were semi-detached and tied, being the property of local landowners, and went with employment on the farm for a very low rent. They were mostly constructed of clay lump and rendered with a lime plaster. About two feet up from the ground level the walls were tarred to help dispel the damp. The accommodation would consist of a front room sometimes known as the parlour, a kitchen and a pantry or large cupboard.

In the kitchen would be a cooking range, highly polished with black lead, or an open fire called a heater stove, which had brick ledges on either side to accommodate kettles and saucepans. All water had to be drawn from a well in the garden. On one side of the kitchen chimney would be a copper which every Monday dealt with the family washing and in many cases Mother took in washing from the more affluent members of the community. The kitchen walls would be whitewashed but sometimes a pale blue colour from the blue bag used to whiten the linen on washdays was added to the whitening. There were always very large nails or pegs on the inside of the back door for the family's caps and coats or father's frail basket (dinner bag made from plaited rushes). The mantelpiece over the kitchen fire supported a small linen line for drying everything from washing to wet clothing.

These tiny dwellings often housed large families. The bedroom furniture consisted of an iron bedstead, chest of drawers, and trunks or large wooden boxes covered with material (ottoman). The small children slept in the second bed in the parents' room, the rest in a smaller bedroom – sometimes at either end of the bed to accommodate them all.

The children would play and amuse themselves all day outside if not of school age. On wet days those old enough would be occupied indoors with various little jobs – such as making spills, which were folded or twisted strips of paper kept in a jam jar on the mantlepiece to supplement matches for lighting candles, lamps and Father's pipe, and for the fire. Then there was cutting squares from newspapers for the lavatory at the bottom of the garden. Worn out clothing was cut into strips for making piece or peg mats. These would probably be the sole covering of all the floors. Children collected cigarette cards and made hanging decorations from cigarette packets. In the summer they would be sent out to gather hogweed from the road verges to feed Father's rabbits and to gather sticks for the fire.

With a wooden box on wheels, with two pieces of flat wood for handles and an old dustpan, boys would collect horse droppings which was plentiful as all farms kept several horses and pony and cart was the usual mode of transport. The vegetable patch was kept fertilised with this and all waste from the house. Boys were always on the lookout to make a penny or halfpenny by opening gates for the more affluent residents. Raising their caps would perhaps procure a better reward. Every property and all fields were surrounded by hedges and entrance gates, always kept closed to guard against passing animals, which were driven from place to place. Transport was mostly on foot or by train, there were very few cars in small villages.'

THE FAMILY FARMHOUSE

'My husband and I married in 1945 and went into the family farmhouse at Deopham when his parents moved out to retire.

It was a long house which stood at right angles to the road. There were two doors in the front and two at the back. We had a "front" room, a living room, the dairy, a store-room and a chemical toilet on the ground floor.

Upstairs were four bedrooms and two rooms used as store-rooms for farm goods such as chemicals, binder twine and animal medicines. We had no bathroom, but each bedroom was equipped with a washstand on which stood a basin and jug. The weekly bath was taken in the kitchen in a zinc bath: the water was heated in a copper using coal and wood.

We had no electricity and used a couple of Tilley lamps and candles to give us light. By the mid 1950s we installed a generator, but although a great improvement on the oil lamps, it had its limitations. I was able to have an iron and a hoover but could only use them when I could find one of the men to start up the diesel engine, which was too difficult for me. (It was a great day when we were connected to the main supply in 1961!)

In the kitchen was a hand pump by the stone sink. We heated rainwater in the copper which was in the corner. The big wash of the week was done on a Monday. The whites were boiled in the copper and the colours were washed in a tin bath placed in the shallow stone sink. I did have a mangle so that helped with the drying, which went outside on a fine day. When it was wet they were draped on a wooden clothes horse round the fire. Washing took all day and ended by washing the tiled floor.

Tuesday was the day for ironing. Until I got my electric iron I used two flat irons. Having heated one on an oil stove, I used it while the other was being heated. This was a slow job, for directly the iron was removed from the heat it gradually lost its effectiveness.

Friday was baking day. With no fridge or freezer, pies and cakes would be cooked and eaten within a few days. In the early days of my married life I had a three-burner oil cooker, with a portable oven which covered two of the burners. The oven was fine for slow cooking but there was always the danger that if the wicks were turned too high the contents would not only cook but also be smoked! From the mid 1950s I had a calor gas cooker which was a great joy, as long as I remembered to have a spare cylinder at hand.

Only the living room had a large carpet, the rest of the floors were covered with linoleum on which were placed one or two rugs. I had no vacuum cleaner; a brush and dustpan were used. The rugs were given a shake. Once a year, at springcleaning time, the carpet was put over the line outside and given a good beating.

We had a car but I was unable to use it freely because it was often needed for the farm business. In such an isolated corner of Norfolk, today, a housewife needs a car to go shopping, but then I had so many tradesmen call at the house. The baker came three times a week, sometimes the bread was still warm. He also carried yeast and flour. A fishmonger came eight miles from Dereham with fresh fish every week. From Wymondham a hardware van brought a variety of goods – candles, saucepans, paint and paraffin, etc. The butcher came twice a week, each time bringing the meat ordered on his previous visit. The grocer brought any goods ordered. Newspapers came every day. I did not need a milkman as we had our own cows. Every two months I had a visit from a traveller who sold tea by the pound, and I would buy six pounds at a time. He also sold bedlinen.

Springcleaning began directly after Easter and I tried to finish by Whitsun. The rooms were worked through systematically, beginning with the bedrooms. Drawers were emptied, the contents sorted out, and fresh lining-paper placed in. I tried to paper and paint one room each year. The last rooms to be done were the living room and the kitchen. The sweep would arrive in his pony-trap: the children stood outside and had to yell when they saw the brush come out of the chimney.

The work in the farmhouse was very labour intensive. I had help for three hours every week. As well as the housework and gardening I reared 400 day-old chicks – 300 pullets, kept for laying and 100 cockerels to be fattened for Christmas. The dairy was part of the house and I had to see to the cooling of the milk and washing of equipment.

They were busy days but very rewarding and there was no time to get bored.'

OUR SMALL COTTAGE

'My husband and I were married in 1950. We rented a small cottage at East Rudham for two shillings and sixpence a week. It consisted of one room up and one room down. We were very proud of our first home.

The one room down was a kitchen/living/dining room. The only cooking stove I had was a black open range with an oven at the side. This had to be blackleaded every day. I had never cooked a meal in my life so I had to set to and learn. My mother had bought me a large cooking bowl and wooden rolling pin (which I still use), and I bought a Mrs Beeton cookery book and that's how I learnt. Bearing in mind we were still on rations I couldn't afford many mistakes, but we didn't starve.

There were two cupboards in the walls. In one I kept all table crockery and cooking utensils, and in the other I would have a bowl on the shelf to do the washing up in, along with two buckets of water on the floor. All the water had to be drawn from a well. We would fetch two buckets at a time. This was another new experience.

We had coconut matting on the living room floor. I would take this up every Friday morning, because all the dirt would go through it. If it was a fine day it would be hung on the washing line to be beaten. Then the floor, which was stone slabs, was swept and scrubbed, before relaying the matting.

There was a little twisted staircase which led straight into the bedroom. This room had linoleum on the floor, with some rugs, so was easy to keep clean. We were very snug.

On Saturday nights out would come the tin bath in front of the fire. What a job to heat all the water!

When it came to having babies, what a palaver. They were born in the home then. Besides all the nappies and clothing to wash and air ready for the big day, there was linen to be cut into about four-inch squares. These were put into a clean biscuit tin. The tin was then sealed and placed in a hot oven to be sterilised. These were the dressings for the baby's cord, kept in place with a crepe bandage. The district nurse would look after us when baby arrived. The only

Fishermen's cottages at Mundesley in the early 1900s, typical of many along the coast.

utensils she had were a large china jug and bowl, a bucket and lots of hot water. I had my first two children this way.

Now we come to the toilet. It was a small building at the bottom of the garden. This housed a bucket, with a seat over it. Each week my husband had to dig a very deep hole and empty the bucket into it. This may sound horrid now, but it was part of everyday life then. It wasn't very convenient to have to run down the garden path at night, or in the winter.

In 1955 we were offered a council house. What luxury! It consisted of three bedrooms, bathroom, flush toilet, dining room, kitchen and living room. Best of all was that we just had to turn a tap to get all the hot and cold water we needed. No more going to the well.'

A FISHERMAN'S COTTAGE

'For my first six years we lived in a small fisherman's cottage at Sea Palling about 150 yards from the sea, at the end of a small row – my mother had been born at the other end of the same row and Grandad still lived there with an aunt. We had one living room and a small kitchen with an oven in the wall and a black cooking range, a small table and an oil lamp on the wall, and a small walk-in pantry. All had uneven brick floors which were covered with coconut matting to stop them turning damp, and peg rugs by the fires.

It was cosy and warm, especially in the evenings when the lamp, with a large white shade, was lit, and before bed we played snap and snakes and ladders, made paper hats and played with our dolls. If it was cold we were all washed by the living room fire, nighties warmed on the fire guard and always a hot milk drink. Then up very narrow winding stairs. Our parents' room was at the top of the stairs and our room was the smaller one at the back. It had a lean-to roof – you couldn't stand up at the outside wall and the window was almost on to the floor. One single bed and a small double bed and a large chest of drawers was all it contained. We went to bed by candlelight, which was replaced when we got into bed by a small Kelly lamp which burned all night on our chest of drawers.

Our drinking water had to be fetched from a pump across the fields, and as my Dad was often away at sea for several weeks at a time, we helped by fetching water in milk cans and jugs. This was then put in a brown earthenware pot in the pantry and covered, but one night some frogs got in through the air brick and into the water! All water was carried away after use into the garden as there were no drains. Rainwater was used for as much as possible, and a vegetable garden was a treasured thing.'

WELL OUTSIDE THE VILLAGE

'Our house was a double-dweller clay lump house, well outside Pulham Market. Our lighting was a paraffin lamp suspended from the ceiling, and candles. The heating was open coal fires. Cooking was done on the hob, in a wall oven or in a paraffin cooker. My gran had a small coal range in her kitchen.

The brick floor was covered with coconut matting and rag rugs. The matting was very hard on the knees when being brushed with a stiff hand brush.

Apart from wooden kitchen chairs we had a sofa and two armchairs, which could be let down at the back by means of a rail which slotted into a set of grooves. In her bedroom Gran had an ottoman, which was a sofa cum blanket box, and also useful as a bed for a grandchild. In her "best" room were chairs and a sofa with horsehair seats, most uncomfortable and prickly.'

OF SMALL STATURE

'My home in Barroway Drove was on the edge of the fens where traditionally people are of small stature and some of our doorways were very low (about five foot three inches, I think). Certainly many of our visitors went away with a sore forehead.'

THE SWEEP TWICE A YEAR

'When it became too hot in the summer time to have a fire it was usual to have the chimney sweep to clean the flues and sweep the chimneys. He would bring his brush and rods and sheet to put up at the fireplace and before he came everything that could not be moved was covered and ornaments all taken away and washed ready to go back clean. Curtains came down and were washed and sometimes the room was redecorated. Usually we needed the sweep twice a year. The sweep in those days at Snettisham was Mr Dodman.'

NEW RUGS

'During the war my mother used to collect all the clothes which were past recycling as garments and cut them into long strips to make a ball. My father made her a frame and on one side the short end of the sacking was attached and the rest was rolled on the opposite side. A blacksmith made her a hook. The balls were sorted into colours and either a design was made on the sacking or the colours were mingled to make a multi-coloured rug. The hook was poked through the sacking and a loop brought through. The effect was much neater than the old rag rugs. This was an essential hobby as floor-covering was rationed and with 24 feet in and out of the house there was a lot of wear and tear.'

BEFORE ELECTRIC LIGHT

'It was not until the 1950s that Northwold had mains electricity so I well remember the daily ritual of cleaning and refilling the oil lamps and the weekly duty of spreading the sheet of newspaper on the table and emptying the melted wax from the candlesticks. This was used for lighting the fire and made for the best blaze possible.'

'As soon as he got home at night, my father would prime the oil lamp. Electricity came to Burnham Market in about 1935. We were glad to get rid of the paraffin lamps. They weren't safe. They hung in the middle of the room and you always had to have a table underneath because if not, you'd bang your head on it.
When the electricity was installed three lights and a plug were free. Any extra lights cost £1 each. My home had five rooms so we paid for two lights. I bought my mother her first electric kettle and electric iron because I was starting to work at the time.'

WATER AND WASHDAY

When water came from pumps and wells every drop was precious. Washday – always Monday – took gallons of it and was a chore we never looked forward to. From the soaking and washing to the drying and ironing, it was sheer hard work! Water 'laid on' has also brought us the blessing of the indoor flush toilet, but those outdoor privies are hard to forget.

FROM WELLS AND PUMPS

'I was one of a family of eight, living in a tied cottage at Bittering. Drinking water was from a well which ran dry in summer, so water during the summer was got from a pond by bucket. This was hard work as the pond was quite a distance away.'

'When I was young we had a well in our garden at Ashill and it was my job to get the water. It was a well where as you let one pail down

Honingham water pump, used every day by the villagers.

another one came up full and it often came up with a toad in it. It was hard work to do, so I just chucked the toad out and took the water in to be used. We never came to any harm that I knew of.'

'We had mains water – there was a tap in the washhouse and another outside where people from the six houses in a side lane had to come to collect their drinking supply. Those nearby came with two buckets each night and one who lived about half a mile away had a tank on the back of a cart which each Saturday morning was hitched to the farm horse and he came for a week's supply.'

'Our water supply at Pulham Market was a neighbour's well, and it was my dad's first task every evening to collect, in pails, enough drinking water to last until the next evening. Water for washing came from the water tanks, placed to catch water from the roof. Gran's water came from a pit and was put through a pot filter before use.'

'In 1947 we moved to a cottage in Honingham and up until 1964 we had no mains water and had to stand ages waiting to cross the main A47 road (especially on Saturdays) with our water pail to and from the village pump. Our only other source of water for washing was from rainwater butts and during the long hard winters I remember my husband loading lumps of ice from the river Tud on to a wheelbarrow to melt and put in the old copper in the kitchen to boil the clothes.'

WASHDAY

'Monday was washday when I was a young child at St Germans. The day began early, when water was carried from a tap shared with a neighbour. Several journeys down long paths were needed to fill coppers, baths and bowls. Starch bowls, blue water baths, soapy water baths and rinse baths all had to be filled. Then the copper was lit and soon there was steam everywhere. Then Nancy would arrive to help. Nancy was an elderly maiden lady, very eccentric, a distant relative.

Nancy loved washday and would beg for more to do when the everyday laundry was done. One lovely spring morning all the clothes were out to dry but there was still soapy water not used. Nancy begged for more washing so my aunt, who was the postmistress, in between paying out pensions decided to take down her gold brocade curtains. Nancy was delighted and went off happily with them. Very soon she was back saying something was wrong with the curtains. When my aunt went to look she had a shock. The curtains were in shreds. Nancy had used the rubbing board.

At that time we had to use coupons to buy material and there were none to spare. The problem was resolved when a friend with a large family did a swap: for some of my good outgrown clothes for her daughter, younger than me, she gave us enough coupons to get curtain material.

Another Monday, the washing was blowing on the line in a field beside the house. A neighbour going home to lunch rushed into the shop to tell us that our horse, Old Jack, was rubbing himself on the linen post. We rushed out to find the post almost down, the washing on the grass and the pig beginning to eat the clothes!

Our lunch on washday was cold meat, with veg, followed by dumplings with raspberry vinegar.'

'The copper had to be filled with buckets of water from the well and the firebox underneath set with sticks and coal before washing could proceed. All the white cottons were put in the copper to boil – everything was either cotton or wool, there were no easy-care sheets. The dirty coloureds had been put to soak in a zinc bath the night before. When the boiling had been done water was taken out of the copper with a scoop or bucket and used to wash the coloureds. Everything was then put through the mangle, an enormous contraption with two huge wooden rollers and a large handle.

Later we were given what must have been one of the earliest washing machines. It was a round tub with a grooved base, and after putting in hot soapy water and clothes there was a grooved board which fitted over the centre pole and was rotated manually. Above this was a mangle with the water falling back into the machine. After the pegging out and drying came folding, and ironing with flat irons heated on the stove.

All the baths and copper had to be emptied with buckets. It was a great help when electricity arrived and an electric copper could be used and even more so with the advent of the twin tub.

There were no school dinners or packed lunches, everyone went home at twelve for dinner so after the mammoth wash morning, Mother was confronted with a horde of hungry faces. We took it all for granted as everything seemed to run smoothly.

Until water was piped to Gayton everyone was reliant on a well or pump and in one very dry summer our well dried up and my father took the lorry to the river and filled big tanks, but of course every drop had to be boiled.'

AT THE BOTTOM OF THE GARDEN

'I think that in the 1930s and 1940s at Thetford, unless you were quite wealthy and lived in the bigger houses, most homes lacked a bathroom and inside toilet; you went outside to use the toilet which was a galvanised pan underneath a wooden seat with a round hole cut in the middle over the pan. These were emptied once a week in the middle of the night by the "Violet Men" as we used to call them, and on Saturday mornings everyone was allowed to collect a bag of disinfectant free from the council – I earned my pocket money by collecting bags for our elderly neighbours. We never had a bathroom, so twice a week our galvanised bath was brought in from outside to the scullery. We had a gas oven in there and in winter Mother used to light the oven and open the door to keep us warm while we bathed. One night was for Mum and the girls and one night for Dad and the boys.

No bedrooms had much carpet, it was lino and a piece of rug beside the bed, and a potty under each bed which was emptied in the morning and cleaned out with a bit of disinfectant.'

'My husband lived with his father and brothers in a small cottage with a large garden. A garden path led from the back door to the bottom of the garden where in a small shed stood the Elsan toilet.

61

My husband tells me he used to cycle to the toilet!'

'The toilet in our garden at Pentney was called a vault type and it had a small seat for the children and a large seat for the adults. We had to cut newspapers into squares and this was threaded with string and hung on the nail inside the toilet wall.'

'My husband's first appointment as headmaster was to a small village school with dry sanitation for children and staff. On accepting the post he had also to agree to live in the school house which was a small cottage attached to the school, with the same form of sanitation and a pump for water in the backyard.

Every Friday afternoon about five o'clock two very old men pushed a tumbril balanced between two wheels past my dining room window. When I first moved into the house I thought they were grounds attendants who waited until the children had gone home from school before tidying the playground. When I realised what was happening and noticed the old tumbril rocking backwards and forwards as they returned a little later, I quickly changed the time of tea. They were the loo attendants!

Later, as workmen renovated the house, a large hole was dug in the back garden to house a septic tank. There was great merriment the next morning as they discovered the large concrete tank floating on water like a boat – they had discovered a previously unknown spring!'

'The outside toilet seemed a long way from the house, especially on dark nights. To add to that, once inside there lurked the largest spiders I have ever seen. Soft toilet paper was unheard of but squares of newspaper were carefully hung on a string. These could be very interesting to read at times but quite annoying if the end of the article was missing.'

'In the late 1950s we went on "the mains" as opposed to having cesspits. This meant the whole road at Sprowston was dug up for the sewer pipes to be laid. Although the water board paid for the installation of the pipes in the road, the householders had to pay for the pipes connecting their property to the road. The old cesspits in the gardens had to be filled in. Attics and garages were raided to find items to fill them in with. Old prams, bikes, clothes, anything was used. I remember peering down one when it was being filled in and being amazed how vast it was, and all lined with red bricks.'

'In the 1920s Sheringham was a quiet, friendly little town, where everyone knew everyone else, and most people were related. We lived in a cottage overlooking Beeston Common, where animals grazed. Our house was one of the first to have electricity, but we had the even greater distinction of being the very first to have an indoor flush toilet. We became known as "them Dennises with a petty on the landing", a great novelty!'

KEEPING THE SOLDIER BOYS OUT

'During the last war I became a baker's assistant, a jack of all trades, call it what you will, at Shirley's the baker's. One of the nicest parts of the job was delivering bread to the villages surrounding Narborough.

West Acre was one village delivery which I still remember with affection. The people were always so kind to me come rain or shine. One lady in her late eighties was almost my last call and the kettle was always on the boil for a cup of tea before the ride home. This lady also had a "little house" down the garden path to which I was often glad to make a visit. This convenience was known as the "bucket and chuck it" type.

The old lady was having to dig a hole far more often than she used to so she decided to keep a watch on the place. To her surprise she discovered that the soldier boys were using it on the way home from The Ostrich in Castle Acre to their camp in the woods at Narford. There was nothing else for it but to put a padlock on the door!

A few weeks later when I arrived with the bread for this lady I found a note pinned to the back door saying, "Please leave bread in wash-house". I went into the washhouse and she had left a lovely bread crock with a cloth to wrap the bread in. On top of the cloth was an envelope addressed to me. Inside this envelope was a key and a message tied to it which said, "Key of the closet". What a thoughtful lady she was.'

SHOPPING AND CALLERS TO THE DOOR

Shopping was a pleasure, sometimes involving a rare visit to town, and most villages had their own shops and traders who would deliver to your door in the days before motorised transport changed our lives. The choice of goods may have been more limited, but we were certainly well looked after!

SHOPPING IN NORWICH IN THE 1930s

'In the 1930s we lived in Bull Close, Norwich. My family consisted of my parents, five brothers and me, the only girl, and I got lumbered with "doing the errands".

Very few people had cars, so shopping had to be carried home. Some shops delivered but my mother was not in favour of this as she liked to see what she was buying, and so shopping the easy way by putting in an order was not for us. I learnt so much from her that by the age of ten I was already an expert shopper.

I remember Thirkettles the pork butcher's in Magdalen Street, where I was sent to buy bacon and ham. This would not be ready sliced, but hanging there would be large sides of bacon and you chose the one you fancied. I would study the bacon and pick the one I wanted, and the next decision was the thickness of the slices. "One pound of long back on number three," was my usual order.

One of the shops that everyone will remember was Price's the draper's, whose very large premises extended into Botolph Street as well as Magdalen Street. As a child I was fascinated by their cash system. There were no tills. Instead your money and bill were put into a small metal container and placed in a tube. These tubes went overhead and led to the cash office. Here the money was removed from the container and the change and receipt put in, and whizzed back to the counter. In the hard times of the 1930s this firm introduced something which they called "Price's Draw". Each participant paid one shilling a week for 20 weeks and was given a voucher with a date on it. If you were lucky you got one of the early numbers and could spend your £1 voucher straight away – hard luck if you got No 20 which meant a long wait before you came to spend it.

In clothing shops of those days you did not help yourself from the racks and try things on. Any attempt to do this would be foiled by a frosty "Can I help you, modom?" Some of the "posh" city shops such as Garlands and Chamberlins employed shop walkers. These rather snooty individuals, always men, would waylay you as you entered the shop with a "Can I help you, modom?" and a look that implied you were not quite the class of customer they were used to.

My favourite childhood shops were in Magdalen Street. Brenner's Penny Bazaar was a long narrow shop where nothing cost more than a penny, small toys etc were sold there and I loved to browse. Near Magdalen Gates was a little Aladdin's cave of a shop that was really my favourite. They sold all sorts of unusual things like kaleidoscopes – tubes which contained bits of jewel-coloured glass, and as you slowly turned the tube lovely patterns would evolve, constantly changing with each movement. There were packets of tiny coloured beads which we threaded on wire to make elegant necklaces, masks, and dolls' house furniture.

One of the specialist foods you could buy in Magdalen Street was "savoury ducks" (sometimes called faggots). These had nothing at all to do with ducks, but were a delicacy much enjoyed by Norwich people. They were made from offal and spices and I don't know what else, but they tasted delicious. People would queue outside the butcher's for them, and while you waited the smell wafting towards you was marvellous. You took your own basin and as soon as you were served hurried home to avoid letting the savoury ducks get cold.

In 1958 the Magdalen Street traders co-operated with the Civic Trust in giving the street a face-lift: repairs and renovations to all the shop fronts were done at the same time and the results were excellent. This was the first scheme of its kind in the country, and people came from far and wide to see it.'

'When I was a little girl living in Norwich, my mother would take me "down the city" on the bus. We always had a bag of chips on the Market, and in the summer an ice cream. To me, "going to the city" is still an adventure.'

VILLAGE SHOPS

'Looking back 50 years one realises how the shops in Burnham Market have changed. Most of the little shops have gone now. When my children were small they always bought their sweets from a little shop on the corner. All the sweets to delight a child were there: long sticks of liquorice, packets of sherbet and raspberry drops. Mrs Beaver, the owner, was a very kind lady who would let them spend ages choosing before they spent their pennies.

65

South Walsham post office and grocery store in 1910, when horse-drawn traffic was the only danger on the roads.

Another popular sweet shop was in the Market Place. It was very old fashioned even in those days, and kept by a little lady called Miss Carter, who also gave piano lessons. She was a very good teacher and had several pupils.

Another small shop sold shoes, both adults' and children's and every make of wool you could ask for. We had several butchers and bakers in the village who delivered their goods by horse and cart.

Mr Hudson brought the milk in a big can from which he would fill our jugs with his measure. His dog Roger, a greyhound, always came with him and would leap over the garden gate and stand waiting for him on the doorstep.

The children loved the cattle market, held every Monday at the back of the Hoste Arms, but sad to say, it is no more.'

'I remember two shops in Terrington St Clement especially well, one quite small, attached to an attractive old pub (now demolished) and run by the licensee's wife, a small rounded lady with a strong local accent and who wore her long hair screwed into a tight "bun" on her nape. There was a very small window on the wall which led to her kitchen and from which she could see potential customers entering, although the bell which jangled loudly when this happened was warning enough. There were large jars of sweets on shelves in the window, with boxes of sherbet suckers, long coils of liquorice, and perhaps some small chocolate bars to deliberate on as we considered the best way to spend our Saturday penny. Everything was weighed from sacks on the floor and sold in blue paper bags, the lard cut and sold from the counter as required.

The shopkeeper's hair had not gone grey but was dark and glossy. This she attributed to passing her hands through it after weighing the lard.

The other shop was much larger and sold hardware and drapery too. There were a number of attractive looking small drawers along one wall behind a counter, which held a wonderful assortment of "goodies", from tobacco to snuff. An employee who worked there in the 1920s remembers someone coming in regularly for two pennyworth of snuff, which was wrapped up in a tightly twisted "blue bag". This shop sold everything needed for the household, from furniture, prams and food, to gunpowder, asked for in tiny quantities, usually in springtime (to sweep a chimney). This was dispensed solely by the owner of the shop and kept in a shed round the back.'

'Our village of Neatishead had two main shops just before the war, but back in the 1920s there were at least another three, each selling sweets, tobacco, paraffin and basic essentials. These smaller shops were run from the front rooms of the cottages.

The two main shops sold all groceries, haberdashery items, chemist's requirements, bootlaces, ironmongery, rubber boots and footwear – indeed, they were general stores. But I cannot remember them opening on a Sunday, and they always closed for a half day each week, so everyone had to get stocked up before the weekend. There were two butchers in the village, both delivered twice weekly. There was no refrigeration but I imagine we did not suffer from any food poisoning! There were two harnessmakers in the village and both used to have facilities for charging the accumulators used for battery radios. They were kept busy making collars for horses, and rush mats for cushions in the carts, and today in the Baptist chapel there is still a rush-made cushion for one of the pews.

We had a market gardener, one of the early ones, who grew cress, cucumbers and tomatoes – I can still smell the cress as it grew in the greenhouses, and the poor old chap if we went to get a cucumber he would say "tuppence"! I suppose he made a living at those prices. He also sold paraffin in the winter months.

Several bakers called in the village. One notable one was Roys of Coltishall: the delivery man had his horse and cart and it used to be said that many a time the horse had to know its way home because the delivery man would be well oiled. During the summer months a local soft drinks firm would deliver weekly, four bottles for a shilling

The Beeston family outside their shop at Bircham in 1911. Village shops provided nearly all our daily needs.

– those lovely bottles with a ceramic stopper and a metal push-off – magic! Ice cream firms would also venture out into the villages – Peruzzi, Walls and Eldorado – a treat in those days.

Living in the village was Blind Bob, a grand old gentleman,

cheerful and independent, and he would know everyone by name, recognised by the sound of their voice. Blind Bob used to be what I would think of as a pedlar, selling goods from a big wicker basket. He would be there on a regular day each week, calling at the houses. He would find his way to the cottage doors, over footpaths, and he was known to take frequent short cuts by using planks over dykes. His basket contained soaps, laces, shoe polish, sweets, chocolates, etc – a strange collection all in one basket, but he sold enough to support himself. In the mid 1950s he went into the Blind School in Norwich, where he spent the rest of his days.'

TO MARKET IN THE 1920s

'My uncle had a smallholding in Brooke and I would spend my summer holidays there. My aunt and uncle would take all week to prepare for a stall at Norwich and one at Yarmouth.

On Tuesday he would kill a pig and every scrap would be used. My aunt had a dairy and made butter, cream and cheese. Uncle kept ferrets to catch rabbits and there were also chickens running about the yard. I would look for eggs, which were sold for one shilling a score. They were taken to market in a large basket, shoppers bringing bowls and boxes to carry them home in. Another of my jobs was to cut flowers for sale, and all the sweet peas had to be bunched into colours.

We got to market very early, our stall just a white sheet laid on a trestle table. Chickens and rabbits were laid out just as they were, and we stayed until it was all sold.

We arrived home very tired but the sheet had to be put to soak, and boiled in the copper the next day.'

NO SHOP IN THE VILLAGE

'There was no shop at Whittington in the 1930s but Stoke Ferry, a mile away, had everything. The butcher delivered, as did the baker. Groceries were delivered from Downham if the order was given a week in advance. Milk was brought by horse and float in a large can with pint and half-pint measures hung on the side. Keeping the milk fresh was always a problem in hot weather and sometimes it had to be scalded straight away before it turned. Milk that was on the turn and beginning to thicken was put in a muslin cloth, seasoned, tied up and hung on a tree to drip to make cottage cheese. Everyone had to be independent as regards vegetables so we all had a vegetable garden, and a large family might have one or two allotments.'

A baker's roundsman setting off with new-baked bread at the Birchams in 1914.

DELIVERED THE SAME DAY

'Milk was delivered to our house in Cromer every morning by the milkman calling out "milk-o" as he came down the passage between the two houses. It was fun to go to the door with the milk jugs and watch the beautiful white milk being ladled from a large steel milk churn into our jugs. The milkman used a smaller steel can to measure the milk into our containers and would chat while he did so, usually adding a little extra "just for you". I cannot remember where his measuring can hung unless it was next to the lid of the churn, which was attached by a heavy steel chain and clanked when he took the lid off.

Shopping was very different from today. When my mother had a large order, perhaps her week's grocery order, she would go to the shop and sit at the counter while a young man in a white coat came to write everything down in an order book. If payment was made the money was put into a little box above the young man's head and he pulled a chain which sent it scurrying along some rails to the office where the cashier emptied the box and returned it containing the receipt. It all seemed very clever and fascinated me. I was very pleased when my sister worked as cashier in the office and explained to me the mysteries of the little railway. The groceries were delivered to our house the same day by a boy on a bicycle.

Alternatively, the grocer would call at the house and while having a cup of tea would write down my mother's order, suggesting any good fruits in season for jam making. One got very attached to individuals in this kind of personal relationship.'

THE PACKMAN

'In the 1920s the packman came to the door at Sparham every fortnight, bringing clothes. He would take payment a little at a time and he said he liked doing it that way as it brought in regular money, and the local people liked it as well because they could get the things they needed without having to wait until they had saved up enough money.'

FOOD AND DRINK

Even through the hard times, mothers managed to provide their families with basic but wholesome food – even if rabbit was the main meal rather too often. In some villages the baker would roast your joint of meat for you, and what aromas there must have been along the village street when Sunday dinnertime came around!

GOOD BASIC FOOD

'Food was very basic but nutritious when I was growing up at Pentney in the 1920s. In the spring my mother made a very special meat dish called lambs' tail pie. The wool was taken off the lambs' tails, then they were singed and soaked in salt water overnight, cooked the next day and mixed with hard boiled eggs and left to set in a jelly.

Rabbit was our main meal. Mother skinned and cooked the rabbit, including the head. We used to quarrel over it because the brains were lovely. Every so often a man came to buy the rabbit skins at threepence each.

Tea time was usually bread and margarine with Flag sauce. It was in a very large bottle. Jam was a luxury. Sometimes we had half a herring and which end we received was often disputed. If you had the small end last time then you should have the large piece next, but it wasn't always remembered by some of the family and arguments would start.'

'In the early 1930s we were still in a depression and money was tight, so food was very basic. My Dad was a good gardener so we always had vegetables and fruit. Mum and Gran made jam and Gran pickled walnuts. If Mum ran out of ideas for our lunch sandwiches we had "potato butter", which we thoroughly enjoyed and filled us. Actually it was mashed potato sandwiches.'

'My mother in law at Feltwell used to make what she called "shituck" with the last of her pastry. She lined a sandwich cake tin, covered it with currants, then put on a pastry lid and pressed it down well. She had an oil stove for the summer time – it took a long time to bake anything but it was always tasty. She always had several Lyons jam rolls in hand and by the time we got to eat them the jam had gone winey – lovely they were. They don't go like that these days!'

'In the summer at Diss we took the weekly joint down to the baker. He cooked joints of meat in his huge hot ovens. This was so the housewife did not have to light a fire in order to cook the joint on a hot day.'

HARD TIMES

'Before the First World War conditions were very hard in agricultural villages such as Corpusty as wages were low and families were large. A shopkeeper said that one mother, being very proud and independent, asked for two ounces of lard to "grease the pram wheels". Another woman had only two shillings and sixpence a week to spend on food and rent: she allowed herself a penny for each meal and had ninepence left to pay the rent. She was given some flour each week by the parish overseers. One family who owned a shop limited themselves to half an egg each, a bloater between three, ham fat on their white bread and a lot of cheese.

Cooking was usually done in a wall oven or in an iron range heated by coal and wood. The cooking implements were mainly large black iron pots and pans, some round with lids and others oval, which could hang from a hook in the chimney. There were hobs by an open fire which could boil kettles and saucepans. Basins and dishes were mainly made of enamel. Thick earthenware pots were used for slow cooking in the oven or storing pickles. Nearly every house had a large earthenware bowl for breadmaking. Knives were made of steel and were cleaned on boards using bathbrick and sharpened on hard bricks. Most large families baked twice a week when bread, cakes, pies, apple rolls and pumpkin pies were made. Potato cakes or bannocks would sometimes be baked to be eaten hot at teatime in the winter. Brown or white flour would be used for making the bread which would be mixed and kneaded and left overnight to rise. Some households took the risen dough to be baked at the bakehouse early in the morning and fetched home fresh bread for breakfast. Home-brewed beer was made with essence bought from the chemist's shop in Aylsham. Housewives preserved red cabbage, onions, and made pork cheeses and piccalilli. They also bottled pears, plums and gooseberries, and made lots of jam.

On Fridays and Tuesdays fresh fish came in by train from Yarmouth and was sold locally from W. Middleton's fish shop. On Saturdays the cockle man from Stiffkey would come round by horse and cart ringing his bell and calling, "Cockles and mussels". He would also bring winkles, samphire and crabs at seasonal times.

In the summer there was plenty of fresh fruit, and vegetables from the garden to eat with cold meat. A tin of corned beef cost fourpence halfpenny and a large tin of salmon, a very special treat, was one shilling and sixpence. In winter the main meal was usually hot – plenty of soups and stews, or meat with onion dumplings. A traditional midday meal at Whitsun would be boiled salt beef with hot vegetables, followed by rhubarb or gooseberry pie with egg custard.

To supplement the meat at harvest time a rabbit would sometimes be given to boys who had helped to run them down as they came from the corn. Some farmers would give the men and their wives a harvest supper after the corn was all safely in. Tables would be set out in the big barn and there would be beef, cheeses, bread rolls, pickles and fruit cake, with beer, ales or cider to drink, then in the evening dancing in the barn to music supplied by the village brass band.

Christmas time meant a turkey, chicken or goose, sometimes given by the "boss", or a joint of beef or pork, followed by Christmas puddings or mince pies.

Most food was bought locally, plenty of fruit and vegetables were grown and most people kept chickens. Sometimes a pig was reared and then killed. There was little waste from pig meat, sausages and brawn being made too. The village was almost self sufficient, there being three local general stores, two bakers, a butcher, a fish shop (wet and fried) and milk every morning from the nearest farm, fetched in a can. This was mainly the domestic pattern up to the Second World War.'

STRETCHING THE HOUSEKEEPING

'My mother told me a story about how she once managed to stretch her housekeeping money to feed her hungry brood. She did it only once and it went against her conscience. A local man at Walsingham

had a large flock of big, fat hens. When it was dark she set off
with a sack and somehow two of the hens got into it. As she was
walking home she met the village constable and her heart nearly
missed a beat. "Good evening," he greeted her. "Good evening,
Constable," she replied as loudly as she could to cover up the
cackle-cackle-squawk that was coming from the sack and she hurried
off as fast as she could. Next day we had a tasty dinner, dumplings,
stuffing and all the trimmings. Mother sent a plateful to the owner
of the former hens and he said it was the best chicken he had ever
tasted. He did not know it was one of his own birds. Mother never
did it again though, the risk was too great. You could go to prison
for stealing. She was a law-abiding woman, but she had to feed her
family.

In the 1920s we were classed as a very poor family. Mother, a
cook at the farm, had married a farmworker and there were eight
children. Father was the breadwinner, but mother was the provider.
I never remember being hungry – dumplings were great for filling
up hollow-legged youngsters and there were always plenty of fresh
vegetables from the allotment. Once I was a real help – a friend and
I went out for a walk on the Lawns and I saw a strange sight. "Oh
look," I called to her. "A poor rabbit has jumped up and caught
his legs in the wire of that fence." We went and got it, being a bit
surprised its feet were tied together. We wrapped it in my coat and
then some people came. Quickly we dropped it and sat on it. When
the coast was clear, we scuttled off home and proudly gave our prize
to Mother. Next day there was a marvellous feast of hare stew, some
being sent to my friend and her Gran. We may have been poor, but
we were so happy. Mother was at home and she kept us clean, tidy
and contented.'

FISH SUPPERS

'For many years before the last war, my father, the late Thomas
Hastings, had a fish and chip shop in Chapel Lane, Hunstanton.
The locals would go in and ask for "a piece and a penn'orth, Tom",
being a piece of fish for twopence and a pennyworth of chips. The
fish would come daily from Grimsby from a Mr Tong. If we had snow
in the winter my father would make runners and fix them to a fish
box so that we could go sledging down the lane.'

'Before the war my father kept a public house at Gorleston. My
mother was very fond of fish, jellied eels being one of her favourites.
A little woman used to come in to the bar with a hessian apron
containing live eels; as well as this apron she wore a flat cap and
she smoked a short-stemmed pipe. Mother would buy some eels and

I can remember seeing the maid skinning them and chopping them up to be put in a double saucepan to be slowly cooked before being jellied.

I can also remember herrings and sprats being soused in large deep meat tins with mutton fat so that when they cooled the fat would seal them from the air. They would keep for weeks like this in the cool cellar, but of course as soon as the fat was cut open they had to be eaten. As a little girl I was soon fed up with them, and no doubt moaned a bit, but the answer usually was, "One of these days, my girl, you will wish you could have some", and I must admit there are times when I do.'

FROM THE CRADLE TO THE GRAVE

We were far more likely to be born, to suffer illnesses and to die in our own homes in the past. In many villages there was a woman who would help out at times of birth and death, although the much-loved district nurse came to take on this task in later years. Most of us trusted home remedies, often passed down through the generations, calling in the doctor only as a last resort and dreading a visit to the hospital in those pre-NHS days.

HOME CURES

'Getting a cold meant the dreaded Thermogene wool. This was a thick, pink, felt-like substance, impregnated with various potions like mentholatum. It covered one's chest and as it got warm gave off strong aromas, and heat! When you realise that at the time a little girl also wore a vest, a liberty bodice (a monstrous thing consisting of a winceyette bodice with twelve small buttons down the front, awful to do up for little fingers on a cold morning), a petticoat, a jumper and lastly a cardigan, you can imagine how rotund we were.

We seemed to have many home-made recipes for illnesses in those days. For coughs my grandmother had her own, or at least her mother's prescription which was held at "Crisps the Chemist" in King's Lynn. A medicine bottle was taken there for a refill. We were also given a little glass of home-made "egg-nog" to invigorate us when run down. This was made by placing whole eggs, shells as well, in brandy for a few weeks until the shells dissolved, and the whole lot was beaten up together.'

'At Hopton on Sea many old remedies are well remembered. For headache, migraine or toothache, vinegar and brown paper was placed on the forehead or jaw. For styes, damp a gold wedding ring and rub it on the stye, repeating at intervals until cured. Warts were rubbed with a snail, then the snail was burned and the wart should disappear. Aches and pains called for a poultice of boiled fresh parsley and bread. For rough hands place equal amounts of glycerine and lemon juice in a bottle, shake thoroughly and apply as required.

A cough mixture was made using black treacle, oil of peppermint, paregoric, white wine vinegar and laudanum mixed together, the dose being one teaspoonful when required.'

'When we had a cold we were put to bed with a heated brick, wrapped in an old jumper, then brought a basin containing a good half pint of onion gruel. Onions were boiled and the juice thickened, with maybe some milk added, and a good knob of butter on top. This was supposed to help you sweat out the cold, and from what I remember it did.'

'I remember that iodine was in use for bad bruises, when I fell down the cellar steps at about five years old, and that the doctor had little to offer in variety of medication other than white bismuth, sal volatile, a red medicine for coughs, and an iron tonic, which was welcome as I found the raw liver which was recommended distasteful. One cure I did enjoy was sulphur and treacle mixed with butter in a little china pot – I was told the fairies had left me fairy jam. This was to clear my skin, and I was young enough to believe in fairies. Other home cures were linseed and bread poultices, to draw out infection and anything from a thorn or sliver of wood in the finger to a painful boil or abcess. A warm shallot in the ear would relieve earache, a clove would numb toothache and the tongue as well. A basin of boiled onions helped a cold and a raw onion, sliced, would heal burns. The warts on my hands were "bought" by being counted and paid for and charmed away by a rough elderly horse doctor, who knew of all the old country cures. My husband, also a Norfolk man, ate fried mice to cure his severe whooping cough when he was a child. A sure and certain cure, but they had to be field mice, not house mice.'

'When my Dad, as a child, had whooping cough, his mother fried a mouse for him to eat. My Mum told me that another cure for whooping cough was to spit the phlegm into a pan of freshly picked nettles, and as the nettles died so the cough would disappear.'

MOTHER COULD CURE ANYTHING

'My childhood memories begin some time after the First World War. My mother's remedies for the family's ailments were endless. Our doctor lived several miles away, and a visit to consult him – by pony and trap – was a rare event. He visited us at home for more serious illnesses.

Patent medicines were few but we were given daily a spoonful of Virol during the winter months. We loved this – it was malty and tasted of toffee. Later, and less popular, was Scott's Emulsion – a thick white concoction tasting of fish. My brother, supposed to be delicate, had to drink daily a tablespoonful of olive oil.

Mother had a shelf in the kitchen cupboard for her remedies. There were small corked glass bottles containing oil of peppermint, oil of juniper and oil of eucalyptus. A few drops were served on a sugar lump, of peppermint for indigestion and of juniper for chills in our waterworks. The eucalyptus oil was rubbed into our chests to help a stuffy cold. We also had two popular drinks to relieve coughs and colds – blackcurrant tea, which was a spoonful of blackcurrant jam in a cup of hot water, and butter, vinegar and honey melted in a saucepan and sipped very hot. Catarrh was relieved by sniffing warm salt water.

Senna pods were soaked overnight and the resulting water was drunk the next morning to deal with constipation. Diarrhoea was stopped by spreading a thin layer of flour on a baking tin; this was baked in the oven until it turned a light golden brown, then mixed with water and drunk.

A "rag bag" contained clean pieces of sheeting which came in useful as disposable handkerchiefs when we had heavy colds. Rag was also used to bind up cut hands and knees, the wounds having been treated with the dreaded iodine. For boils and skin infections bread poultices were the order of the day. Stale bread was folded in a strip of rag and dipped into very hot water. The rag was twisted at either end to remove excess water then placed on the boil or other infection, covered with oiled silk to retain the heat, and everything kept in place with a thick bandage.

Inevitably we encountered nettles and rushed to find dock leaves to rub on the stings. For wasp stings we applied vinegar or blue bag, and for bee stings washing soda.

Every spring we had a course of brimstone and treacle which we enjoyed as it was sweet and sticky. This mixture was supposed to clear our blood of impurities accumulated during the winter.

We knew little of hospitals, and nothing of clinics. When I was six my tonsils and adenoids needed removing. Our doctor and a colleague arrived at our house. The dining table, covered with a

77

sheet, was the operating table, a little chloroform, and the deed was done.

When I developed scarlet fever there was panic. My younger sister was sent away to relatives and I was incarcerated in my bedroom with a sheet dipped in disinfectant over the door. Mother, wearing unfamiliar white hat and gown, looked after me. There were no inoculations available and our parents must have been very worried when three children of a neighbouring family died one week.

Young children feel their parents are all-powerful and I, for one, never worried about illnesses and minor ailments as I always felt that Mother would be able to make me well again.'

SAFETY IN NUMBERS

'Grandad never went to the doctor for his lumbago, preferring to buy a tin of embrocation from the vet for one shilling and ninepence. It took his skin off but cured his back. He also believed in getting all your teeth pulled out as soon as possible as it was cheaper. One tooth cost two shillings and sixpence to be pulled out but the whole set could be done for £5. The family always had bad teeth which is not surprising as we had four or five teaspoons of sugar in our tea, sugar on our cornflakes, treacle on our toast, daily sticky cakes and Victoria sponges. I suppose it was the after-effects of sweet rationing.

When a boy put his fork through his foot one day he was not allowed to go home to be nursed: he was told to undo his flies and use "mother nature's steriliser" – piddle on the wound and the ammonia would prevent infection.

Before the days of contraception, girls knew what to do if they went out with their young man: they put a dozen safety pins all around them, fastening their knickers to their vest. Then, if they got carried away, by the time they had undone them all either they remembered what their mothers told them, or the young man's ardour was quelled!'

BEFORE THE NHS

'We seldom called the doctor but had many a visit from the district nurse, though Mother was very good at keeping us healthy. Mother was secretary of the Nursing Association – people paid in small amounts to support the nurse and supply her with a car. Father was a treasurer of the Hospital League and every year there was a parade with a brass band and a special service held at the school to raise money for the hospital fund.'

'Every year in April an "Egg Week" was held in many villages for the Norfolk and Norwich Hospital, when eggs were given to be preserved for the winter. I remember doing this collection for two years in the late 1930s. Most people at Sea Palling kept a few chickens in the garden for their own use and they were very generous, saving up what they could during that week. The amount of eggs varied from two or three to the odd dozen from those who normally sold to the eggman who came round buying up eggs each week. We packed them in boxes and a laundry basket and this was taken to the hospital. I collected over 300 eggs each year.'

HARDWORKING AND DEDICATED

'In the early 1920s it was decided to set up a Neatishead & District Nursing Association. It started with donations and one or two social functions, and then families who wished to join the scheme paid twopence a week. This entitled that family to the services of the district nurse with no further payment. A nurse was appointed and given the tenancy of a small cottage in Neatishead. How hard-working and dedicated these women were, setting off daily on upright bicycles with basket attached to the handlebars and a Gladstone bag strapped to the carrier. They were equipped to tend people in their own homes. Imagine night visits, for these were the days when the majority of babies were born at home with the nurse in attendance and the doctor would only be called in for the most difficult births. Poorly lit cycles led the way up lonely lanes. These baby delivery jobs would be followed by several visits to tend mother and baby. All mothers stayed in bed for two weeks. For the district nurse this work had to be fitted in with other jobs – dressing wounds, bandaging cuts and grazed knees, etc. People couldn't afford to go to the doctor so readily then. Our Nurse Barham spent her retirement nearby and lived well into her eighties. The coming of the Health Service altered the lifestyle of the district nurse.'

LIFE AS A MIDWIFE

'In 1958 I took up the position of community midwife at Watton. I had come straight from doing my midwifery at Southampton.

I lived in a small cottage which at the time belonged to Watton Nursing Association. I was employed by Norfolk County Council who supplied me with a car. This was a Ford Anglia and the main thing I can remember about it was that the windscreen wipers went very quickly if driving slowly but slowed down the quicker one went! We had a day and a half off a week, other than that I was "on call" 24 hours a day including the night of my day off. I must admit I found this to be a very lonely life. I had no television and could not go out as I was on call.

Home deliveries in those days were common. Many people had no telephones and I was frequently woken with a knock at the door. Before leaving home each morning I would write on a blackboard all the addresses at which I would be if wanted. The board was then placed in the window for all to see. In those days we covered a geographical area and so worked with several different doctors and on my colleague's day off the area doubled in size. We used large wooden blocks to raise the beds to reasonable heights, this sometimes proved quite difficult in an old cottage where the floors sloped. In those days we wore blue dresses and starched white aprons. My outdoor uniform was grey.

The husbands were not then so involved with their wives' pregnancies and deliveries as they are today although I seem to remember that husbands were just beginning to be present at the birth – that was the home ones, of course. Most ladies had their mother or mother in law looking after them and there was always a welcome cup of tea to greet you in the middle of the night. Following the delivery I would visit twice daily for three days and then daily until the baby was 14 days old. In many of these households I felt like one of the family, always welcome, and in many cases have remained friends.'

GOING TO HOSPITAL

'When I was a small child my father was a member of the St John Ambulance Brigade, Cromer Branch, which consisted of a few men who offered their services voluntarily when they had finished their normal work. This sometimes meant a day or night shift. There was one ambulance housed near the centre of the town and the volunteers often lived on the outskirts of Cromer.

When an ambulance was required the first priority was to get the services of a member who could drive (very few people owned cars in those days), then another member to assist the patient and help to carry a stretcher. The only method of contacting members was by the Chief Ambulance Officer walking to the member's home to knock him up, out of bed if necessary. To speed things up he blew a whistle as he approached the house. The memory of the elderly gentleman trotting up the road blowing his whistle often springs to mind when I hear today's ambulance siren and watch it rushing through the traffic.

However, transport was even slower and more hazardous when I was about four, and was sent to the scarlet fever hospital. Scarlet fever was one of the notifiable diseases and isolation considered necessary even from one's own family. I remember Mother bringing in a kind old gentleman who sat on my bed and explained to me what a nice place I was going to and how much I should enjoy playing with different toys and other children. In the meantime my parents would be able to visit me and as soon as all my spots had gone away I would be able to come back home.

I was wrapped in blankets and carried out to a horse and coach. The strange man in charge did not seem very interested, and I remember arriving at the hospital, after what seemed to be a very long time, in the dark. The hospital building still stands and is only about three miles away, but for me the memory remains as one of the unhappiest periods of my childhood. As I was the only female patient for most of my stay, I was a very frightened and lonely little girl. There were two older girls who left within a few days of my arrival. Most of my time was spent sitting in a big chair with a huge teddy bear for comfort. The ward seemed too long to walk down on my own and there were sounds of running water and noises which I did not understand, and although adults came and went at intervals I was alone for most of the time. When my parents came to visit me I made a huge fuss and begged to be taken home. No contact was allowed and visitors just peered through the windows, showing parcels of sweets, fruit and toys, but they were not allowed to pass them through the window. The whole experience was terrifying to me. I was threatened with being shut up in the hay loft if I didn't stop making a noise.'

FIRST AND LAST

'When a baby was born at Pentney in the 1920s, the vicar would call to see mother and baby and half a crown was left for the child.'

'At Barroway Drove, once when an old soldier was ill, having been gassed in the Great War, rushes were scythed from the dikes and strewn on the road so that when the horses and carts passed by they did not disturb him.'

'At Snettisham when a member of the family died they were not taken away, but the undertaker was called and he came and laid the body out and measured for the coffin, and it remained in the coffin covered over with a sheet in a spare room with curtains drawn until the funeral. When the vicar was informed the church bell would toll, five times for a woman, three times for a man, so the village people would know there had been a death. The number of tolls was the number of letters (five letters in woman, three in man). On the day of the funeral everyone dressed in deep black and would have to walk to church behind the undertaker and coffin, which was wheeled on a carrier, and then the bearers would take it into the church, with the flowers placed on top. Later on they did have a glass hearse with black surround drawn by horses. After the ceremony round the grave the mourners walked back to their house for refreshments and the usual reading of the will if there was one. Mr Lincoln or Mr Chambers were the undertakers in those days.

A christening was quite a big event too. The baby would have a lovely long white gown, probably made by one of the family, and shawl. The godmother and father were selected and a special service arranged with the vicar, and then a special tea after. The usual thing was to have *winkles* for tea, so at the table a large pin was placed beside each plate. Of course after the winkles came jellies and christening cake and the baby was given the presents – silver mug, silver bracelet, silver cross and chain, or in those days possibly a gold half sovereign or a sovereign, which was a lot of money. Usually the baby was named after the godparents.'

'I worked in the draper's shop at Burnham Market in the 1930s. If there was a death the relatives would come in to buy their mourning clothes. The order would be placed in Norwich and arrive the next day. They just used to send two or three frocks and people seemed to be quite satisfied. You didn't get all the picking and choosing you have today. It was the done thing to go into mourning for at least six months, a custom that continued till well after the war.'

CHILDHOOD &
SCHOOLDAYS

A NORFOLK CHILDHOOD

Growing up in the country, or in country towns, we were familiar with the farming year and wildlife and able to wander freely without fear. There was little if any traffic to disturb us, and we walked miles and stayed away from home all day! Life for many was hard in those inter-war years, but we have memories of secure and happy childhoods, growing up in Norfolk's unspoilt countryside.

A NORFOLK FAMILY

'My husband, who is 81, was one of a family of 14 children, ten boys and four girls. His father was a farm labourer and they lived in several tied cottages in Norfolk, staying on average about two years in each location until they came to Wootton Marsh, where they lived for most of my husband's schooldays.

His father was a man with a quick temper, and many a time the boys were sent to bed by their mother to escape a good hiding after he had discovered some of the mischief they had been perpetrating.

There was 25 years between the oldest and the youngest, so the older ones had left home before the younger ones were born and the whole family were never living at home all at once. My husband was number ten so he came in for an easier time than the first five or six, as the older ones used to help with the finances when they started work. Two of the boys went into the Navy and one in the Royal Marines in the First World War, and they were also called upon again in the Second World War.

There was no family allowance then, so they must have had a struggle to feed so many hungry mouths. His mother was a good cook and they had lots of soups and stews, and rabbits were in plentiful supply. She often told me that she never made up less than 14 pounds of flour at a time into pastry and cakes. Even so, the boys were not averse to helping themselves to a few turnips from the fields on their way to school in the village of North Wootton, a walk of one and a half miles.

The school had only two classes and was typical of the times, 1920 to 1930. Lessons were not very interesting, and the boys were only too anxious to escape into Wootton Woods with their sandwiches of bread and dripping or cheese in their dinner hour, which often meant a furious chase back when the bell rang for the afternoon session.

When they were not at school, they spent a lot of time on the marsh babbing for eels which involved threading worms on a strand of wool, which was dangled in the water of the creek. When the eels took the bait, their teeth became entangled in the wool and they were hauled out and taken home to be cooked, a tasty meal indeed. They also had to gather samphire when it was in season, and wash it, then take it around the houses in North Wootton village and sell it for a few pence.

During the winter in the dark evenings time was spent making rag rugs. The children had to cut up pieces of old coats and trousers into strips about two inches by one inch, which were then pegged into hessian sacks, washed and opened out flat. Designs were mostly traditional, with a border, a square or diamond in the centre of a plain colour, then the background filled in with mixed colours. Sometimes a new rug spent a winter as an extra bed cover before being put down on the floor.

My husband's eldest sister, when she was 95, told us she could remember the death of Queen Victoria and the end of the Boer War. She recalled her uncle being given a hero's welcome when he came home from South Africa at the end of hostilities. He arrived at Swaffham station and was pulled on a farm cart by men from the village in a triumphal procession to his home in Great Cressingham.

It says much for the way they were brought up that they all survived, and none of them got into serious trouble but grew into responsible citizens. There are only five of them left now but I think they can look back on a happy, if hard, time when they were all together.'

A LITTLE THATCHED COTTAGE

'As a child I lived in the village of Bressingham in a warm little thatched cottage with kitchen, living room and two bedrooms. There were six of us, all girls, you can imagine how we slept on feather mattresses, the younger ones were in Mum and Dad's room. Dad was a lengthman working for Norfolk County Council mending roads, he had a little cart with a scythe and a hook. In snowy weather he could spend all day clearing the roads using horses and a plough.

Mum was a very good needlewoman. People have said to me since, "You Flatman girls were always well dressed", but it was only because Mum was good with her needle. If someone gave us a coat, we would sit in the evening and unpick it, Mum would make one of us a coat from it and the odd bits would go for making rugs. She always made shirts for my Dad and my grandfather as

Many Norfolk children enjoyed a donkey ride on Sheringham beach in the 1930s.

well. Sometimes Mum would buy some material from Diss market or from Newbolds.

Our cottage was owned by a farmer and we girls used to do odd jobs around the farm sometimes, not for money but we would occasionally be given something to eat. We regularly went to another farm to collect milk in a can and on the way home we had this game where we swung the can by its handle very quickly and if you were lucky the milk didn't come out. But if it did, we would go back to the farmer's wife and say tearfully that we had fallen down and lost some of the milk and how cross Mum was going to be with us, and the farmer's wife would tell us not to worry and top the can up again with fresh milk. Mum never knew. We never split on each other.

For entertainment, we used to amuse each other. My sister used to give us what we called a Shanny Halfhour and we laughed and laughed. We played ludo, dominoes and draughts etc. When my eldest sister got a boyfriend we acquired a gramophone. I think Dad got it from one of the sales. It was one of those with a big horn, our first record – a big one – was *Bells across the meadow* and we played it over and over again. The next one was *Albert and the Lion*.

At harvest time when I was a girl we used to go to the farm to take the men's "fourses" up the fields. We'd sit and watch them have their break and if we were lucky we might have a piece off a meat pudding or something.

We had a village policeman called PC Poulter. There used to be an old fellow in our village who loved to cycle in to Diss to one of the pubs and have a lot to drink and a talk with his friends, and one night he was biking home and the village policeman caught him without a light. In those days you had to have a front light, but not a rear light. Anyway, this old fellow had to appear in front of the Diss Magistrates and when he was asked why he hadn't shown a light on his bike he said, "Well, it's like this here. I didn't need a light – I had the moon!" It amused the people in the court so much that they paid the fine for him. Biking without a light would probably have been a five shilling fine.

Another tale I heard was of someone cycling without a light back from Diss to Bressingham when a voice in the dark said, "Look out, old Poulter is up the road." This person said, "Oh, thanks" and hopped right off his bike to be met by PC Poulter himself and he was booked.'

BY A COUNTRY LANE

'On a sunny June day I think back to another sunny day – in June 1926 – when our family moved from Norwich to a new house in Cringleford. Cringleford was then a compact and closely knit village

87

on the edge of the countryside. The road going past our home was a country lane and I don't remember much traffic – indeed we children would run helter-skelter down the lane and over the crossroads to watch the trains go by, throw crumbs to the ducks and sometimes wander on the marshes, pick flowers and have a picnic or perhaps a bathe in the part of the stream known as the "shallow" pool and the "deep" pool. There were very few houses on our road; the ground opposite sloped steeply and was ideal for tobogganing in the wintry weather.

At that time there was only one small shop in Cringleford, but milk was brought round by horse and cart, another man came with vegetables to sell and yet another one came round with sweets – he was very popular and was known as "Yum-Yum". One of our jobs on Saturday mornings was to take the household washing round to be done in one of the cottages, and we also had a large mangle which was housed in a shed still known as the laundry.

As there were several of us we made our own amusements and we used to run "sales of work" in the summerhouse and act little plays – there was no fear of boredom. In 1931 the Guide Company was formed and we made many friends through this movement.

Nowadays the "country lane" is quite difficult to cross because of the traffic, there are many more houses and the population must be many times greater than when we came – but still we regularly enjoy walks down to the level-crossings, the old trees are there, and there is a country feel about what is still a village community.'

NO ANGELS

'I was brought up in the inter-war years in the tiny village of Tatterford. Our family was at that time the only one with school-age children in the village. My three brothers were all altar boys at Tatterford church, but were by no means angelic! One summer the two youngest boys, Ted and Bob, went for a walk by the river. The fine sunny afternoon clouded over and a heavy storm broke. Mother was, naturally, very worried, not only for their safety but also concerned that their clothes would be soaked. Imagine her surprise, therefore, when the boys returned home after the storm wearing dry clothes. "Where did you manage to shelter?" she asked. "Oh," came the reply, "when the rain started we took off all our clothes, hid them under a bush then sat in the river till the rain stopped!"'

GROWING UP AT THE INN

'I was late starting school at six years, being undersized, and after only six months it was discovered by the school doctor that I had

Six year old Beulah Fisher of Ludham loved her new parasol so much that she ruined her mother's solo in church by parading up and down the aisle.

tuberculosis and so became exempt. So from the age of six until 15 I missed formal schooling. Nevertheless I had lessons, first with the infants teacher and later with a retired teacher, and I did not escape the dreaded visit of the School Inspector to find if I was keeping up to standard. I remember being tested on such words as helicopter and gyrotiller, which were becoming everyday terms in the English language at that time.

My parents were publicans and came to the King's Arms at Ludham in 1922. I was born in 1923 and was their second daughter, my sister being nine years older. I did have childhood friends, despite being termed as infectious, but most of my pursuits were out of doors as were many of my meals. Fresh air was the only known cure for TB in 1929 and many children went to the sanatorium, often through drinking infected milk such as I had. There were no tuberculin tested cows on farms till much later.

My parents were persuaded to let me run free of restriction, so I often preferred bare feet to shoes, and being thin, started rumours of ill-treatment! Actually I enjoyed the freedom, climbing the tallest trees and making myself friendly and gaining much entertainment in the next-door saddler's shop, where, obtaining scraps of leather and borrowing small tools, I would chase patterns and help to stuff horse-collars with straw and to my joy get taken in the sidecar of the motor cycle to deliver supplies and repaired harness to surrounding farms and villages. The blacksmith would allow me to pump the bellows and throw water on to the furnace to clear it of flames. Heating the horseshoes and hammering to fit the waiting horse – what a smell of singeing hoof!

The carpenter in the adjoining shop would explain his work in detail and I saw cartwheels being made, from the wooden spokes being inserted into the hub to the metal trim made by the blacksmith on the outer rim. Again the hiss of steam as it was fitted. A lot of my time was spent on farms, among the animals and workmen. Horses to ride, bullocks and chickens to feed, and calves to teach how to suckle, using one's fingers and warm cows' milk from a pail.

Womack Broad used to freeze over more often than it does now and most of the men were proficient skaters. We children were content to slide, and shrill voices would proclaim our enjoyment. There was an occasional mishap of ice near the edges giving way, but other than wet feet and legs no one seemed concerned that anything worse could happen. Children did wait for the expert opinion of adults who tested and examined the ice before anyone ventured on, and woe betide anyone seen throwing sugar beet on to the ice to get embedded in the following frost and spoil the clear run of skating enthusiasts. The sugar beet would be awaiting wherry transport to Cantley. I even rode my bike on the frozen river, not without mishaps – cuts and bruises on my bare knees.

Living in a public house, I got entertainment from watching bowls matches on our two bowling greens and meeting people who came by car, coach and boat. They needed refreshment, relaxation and entertainment, and the first was provided by packets of biscuits and crisps, music by visiting pianists and jolly singing inside the green room while I played with their children outside. If they were in need of real nourishment there was the fish and chip shop opposite our public house and the other one, a beer house, The Bakers Arms, and one could buy for one shilling and sixpence a substantial cod and chips. We children could have crispy scraps of batter for nothing. There were three fish and chip shops at one time and of course the rivalry was too much and not enough trade for all, so the longer established shop won the day.

My parents were well liked and popular. Father had served long term in the army and had risen to Sergeant Major; he was easy going but strict enough not to allow bad language or behaviour, and was respected for it. Mother worked hard too, but enjoyed the company of our customers and the humour. Having a powerful singing voice she was often asked to perform, and by this time I could accompany her as pianist. Everyone seemed to know the ballads she sang – *The Holy City*, *Bless This House*, and *I'll Walk Beside You* were favourites, but I confess that the song *God Send You Back To Me* used to send me into tears when I was younger.

Mother, my sister and I were all in the choir at one time. On Sunday night the locals would grow impatient waiting for our return from evening service, before Father could unbolt the door and let in the rush of men eager to begin the serious drinking and games of darts and cards. In the summer, Sunday evenings brought in wives with their husbands, dressed in their silks and cottons and the husband in his best cap and suit, and buttonhole of a summer rose.

It was cold in parts of our large house in winter, but having TB until I was 15 heat was not recommended for me. We had coal fires in the public rooms, but the counters meant only the customers could feel them, and some certainly meant to, judging by the comments of those who could not!

Our bedrooms had no means of heating, no sockets for plugs. Lino on the floor meant the shock of cold feet if one missed the bedside rug. My bedroom sash windows were open most of the time and crossing the floor to find the switch by the door I met a sprinkle of snow or a puddle of rain on more than one occasion. No bathroom either, just the usual washstand in each bedroom and matching jug, bowl and toilet set, and a jug of hot water had to be brought upstairs for washing purposes.'

'I am 78 now but this takes me back to schooldays when I was eleven. In the village where I was living a farmer had two farms, one for cows, the other was arable with horses. The same farmer had a few other farms around Norfolk and he employed his own blacksmith, who cycled from one farm to another, shoeing horses and mending implements. The blacksmith visited the farm in my village on Fridays and Saturday mornings. Each farm had its own forge with bellows, also an anvil. On Saturday mornings the blacksmith used to allow two of us boys to fiddle around in his smithy. At a quarter to nine he used to pop over to the farm foreman's house for a cup of tea. He left us, one smoking a pipe in the back of a cart and the other working on the anvil making a false link. I usually ended up at the anvil hammering away. People round about could hear the anvil's ringing noise, little did they know it was not the blacksmith making the noise: he was far too busy drinking tea.

My dad was a cowman and took great pride in his job. He never walked behind his herd, he taught the calves to follow him, he never used a stick. Sometimes on a Sunday afternoon we would go down the farm and give Dad a hand to get done.

There were 38 Khaki Campbell ducks at the farm. They would be on the pond, but as soon as they saw Dad they would come round the buildings in case he left a door open, then they had a feed. They always walked in single file and if Dad left a door open the front one would go quack, this went along the line then they would go into the building, leaving one outside to watch for Dad. Inside were bags of peas. One would be open standing about three feet high; one duck would jump on top and scrab the peas for others to gather up, they took turns at being on top and scrabbing them out. The sight or sound of Dad was signalled with a big quack from the one outside and they were soon on the pond.

When I went to school at Mulbarton we used to spend virtually all year making a big bonfire on the common ready for Guy Fawkes. We would cut your fence, clear your rubbish and take anything to burn. The garage gave old spoiled oil and grease and shops had a clear out for us. A number of grown ups used to help us on the night, it was a big thing and very well organised, the village turned out in strength for the occasion.

One year it had been raining all week and it was difficult to get it to burn. In those days when they cut hedges and trimmed the sides of trees, they bundled them into bunches called faggots. The first year they would stick the peas and beans with them, then they kept them to get sear (dry) for kindling. As the fire would not burn, a man helping said to some of the boys, "Can't you pinch a couple of faggots to give it a start?" Instead of pinching they went to the man's house and said, "Your husband sent us for two faggots," and his wife told where they were. They took them back and the fire got under way. The man said, "Is there any more where you got them? If so get them, they will not miss them." So the boys cleared out all his faggots. He had a great time burning them and learnt of his folly the next day.

Harvest time on a farm used to be something special. Parents got a few extra shillings, children had good fun. The women used to take their men hot dinners at noon and fourses at 4 pm. Sometimes the women would have to look for them, as they could be in another field. One day a couple of us boys were walking along and in a gateway we saw a lady eating a hot meal. She said, "I've been hunting for my husband everywhere, the dinner will get cold so I am eating it while it is still hot!"'

THE ROADS WE WALKED

'I remember walking to school along Church Lane at Stanhoe twice a day as no school meals were provided in those days. The high banks were covered with wild flowers, alas no longer seen, and a mass of wild roses grew in the hedges.

We would stop by the blacksmith's pit and watch as the horse-drawn water-cart was being filled by a pail-sized cup or ladle on a long wooden handle. Later on, when a hand-pump was erected, we thought life had been made much easier for the person who had spent his days carting water to cattle and sheep in the fields.

In the autumn, a time would be spent getting beech nuts from the row of trees that grew in the "Patch".

Perhaps we would meet the Rev Black, who would always ask us to "Smile, please". One day we even saw the R101 airship going overhead, or perhaps it was the R100?

In those days there were three classes in the school and about 60 children attending. In the playground at the rear of the building was a row of lime trees and over in the far corner were walnut trees, a temptation to the older boys whose hands would often be inspected to see if they were covered in brown stain. The outer shells of walnuts leave a brown stain that will not wash off.

The cricket and football pitches were on another part of the pasture and here were two large horse chestnut trees set close together that formed a pavilion for the players.

On our return walk down Church Lane in the afternoons, we would sometimes be lucky enough to see Mr Goodman and Mr Farmer shoeing a wheel, which involved a large fire made mostly of hawthorn hedge cuttings which heated the iron band

Mr Wick and his daughter at St Germans siding. Children always loved a ride on the gentle work horses.

that made the tyre for the cart wheels. Perhaps another day they would be shoeing horses, the smell of hot iron on hoofs is a never to be forgotten smell.

Perhaps I would meet my father returning from ploughing and would be hauled up to sit in front of him on those great cart horses and have a ride round to the stables at Church Farm.

In the winter we would skate or make slides on the blacksmith's pit, which would be lit by the stable lamps, as we called them, otherwise known as hurricane lamps. In the summer we would be fishing for tench in the same pit, the lucky few with a cane rod and hook and others more often with a long stick and bent pin.

We spent a lot of our free time in the farmyard, a much safer place in those days with hardly any machinery. Sometimes we helped the pigman to chop the mangolds and turnips by turning the iron wheel on the turnip grinder and watching the chunks fall into a large basket called a bushel skep, which looked like a chunky pineapple. Perhaps, if we were hungry, we would eat a slice of turnip, peeled with the pocket knife, or shut-knife as we called it, that every boy carried in his pocket. We might even search amongst the large heap of cattle food in the corner of the barn for Koshy Tosh, as we called it, or a great delicacy, a piece of locust. This was a kind of bean that looked like a piece of dry leather but was very sweet.

In the spring, we made whistles from hazel twigs, again using the pocket knife and resulting in many a cut finger, or a pop gun which was made by taking the pith from the middle of a stout piece of elder and making the ramrod from hazel wood.

At this time, a great many turkeys were reared on the farm and one particular year they were housed in what was known as the "Boxes" up the farm track opposite the Kennels on Bircham Road. One night a dog attacked these turkeys and the next day Alfred Jakes and I, both about nine years old, were sent to scare off the dog if it came again. We spent all day there and were rewarded with sixpence each. We did not see the dog!

During the better weather the farm horses would be put on a pasture for the night. After their day's work they would be fed then let loose to run up to the pasture by the Kennels. It was our job to run ahead and open the gate. There would be about 16 large horses galloping along and they knew exactly where they were going and in those days we had no fear of them, although I should not like to do it now.

Another great event was when the steam ploughs came. They would stand one at each end of a field and a plough would be pulled backwards and forwards between them, always fascinating to watch.

In the 1930s we had a Scout troop and a Brownie pack run by the Rev Banister and his wife. The Brownies met in an attic at the rectory once a week and this was greatly enjoyed. The Scouts met in the old chapel. Both came to an end when the Banisters left the village.

I can remember walking in 1933 or 1934 with other families one Sunday afternoon to the end of the Creake Road opposite Barwick House drive to see a combine harvester at work. I believe this was the first one to be seen working in Norfolk and was on the Shammer Farm. In those days the harvest was still gathered by horse and binder which had huge wooden sails to push the corn onto the knives. These sails would often break and many times we were asked by my father to take them back to be mended by Mr Bone in his carpenter's shop at Church Farm. Many an hour was spent by the children living at Church Farm in this shop which was always full of the smell of wood shavings and sawdust, as nearly everything used then was made of wood. Mr Bone was kept busy repairing waggons, gates, hurdles, cattle troughs, etc. There was also a paint shop next to his shop and as this was always kept locked it was our delight to craze him to open it so we could nose about amongst the tins. Why, I don't know, as it only contained tins of paint, mostly red and blue.

In the early 1930s the road past the farm was tarred for the first time. A steam-driven tar engine was used and the chippings were rolled in by a huge steamroller. This resulted in the first good surface we had known and led us to play many more games on the road. For some reason these games were always seasonal and would last for a few weeks and then we would start another game.

We had iron hoops made by Mr Goodman and then as the evenings grew lighter in the spring, out would come the tops, which we would lash with a whip to hit them up the road where they would land and spin; perhaps we would chalk patterns on the tops so that we could see them better as it grew darker. During the summer we would play hopscotch, again chalked out on the road, or perhaps skipping and jumping over a rope stretched across the road. All these were possible as there was no traffic.

One of the highlights of the week would be when Mr Giles from Docking came round with his horse and cart, selling hardware and sweets. His cart would be piled high with tin pails and baths hanging from the sides. We would have a halfpenny each to spend and this would usually be spent on liquorice laces or sherbet dabs.

Some days we would see the shepherd, Mr Rayner, moving his flock of sheep. The road would be a mass of sheep, all controlled by two dogs that seemed to know where they were going. Often we would stand in a gateway to stop the sheep entering.

In the spring the sheep would all be gathered together and the sheep shearers would arrive and the winter coats would all be shorn by hand. The shearers were a gang of men who travelled for a few weeks from farm to farm by bicycle and sheared from daylight to dark, probably sleeping in a barn for the next day's work.

During the school holidays we would often go for long walks, looking for birds' nests, gathering blackberries or conkers and nuts, depending on the season. In those days we could walk the green roads and by-roads wearing just shoes; alas, we now need wellies to traverse the by-roads and the old green roads are becoming impassable apart from tractors which have aggravated the problem by cutting large grooves in the surface.

Sometimes we would beg Mr Seaman to let us ride his tricycle. If you are able to ride a bicycle this is very difficult as it is almost impossible to steer a straight course!'

ON GRANDMA'S FARM

'The joy of rising early and going to fetch the mixed herd of cows in for milking with the help of Toby the collie; the cows, used to the routine, did not need much encouragement as I opened the gates. All milking was done by hand, my two uncles were quick on the job with their caps on back to front sitting astride their three-legged stools. I had my own little stool and was allowed to have a go. The farm cats sat waiting patiently for their bowls to be filled, getting the occasional squirt to tease them, What a delight to have my own enamel mug of warm milk before it was put through the cooler in the dairy. In the summer with the dew still on the ground Grandma and I would take our baskets and collect dandelions which were at their best for wine making, this was mostly consumed at harvest and festival times.

All the neighbours helped at harvest time knowing at the end when all was gathered in we would have a harvest supper. The fields of corn had to be hand scythed all around the edges to make room for the horses to pull the binder which went round in decreasing circles. This was the part I did not like as the rabbits and wild life were sent scurrying and the men shot to fill their bags.

The men all took their dockie bags full of nourishing home-made bread, cheese, pickles, and apple pies, sitting under the haystacks to have a break. Grandma and I would often take them a billy can of fresh tea or a flagon of home-made wine. Very often I was allowed to stay and watch, returning home with my uncles, sitting side saddle on one of the cart horses. Grandma always insisted side saddle, as sitting astride gave one so small a sore bottom.

Sometimes, past my bedtime, I was allowed to carry the lantern and go down to the stables to check and shut up for the night. I would hold my uncle's hand tight as we neared the Dutch barn as so often the barn owls would glide past with a ghostly flap of wings and wee beasties would scamper amongst the straw. On the way back he would tell me all the names of the stars.

In my bedroom a little oil lamp burned until I fell asleep, and in the corner was a door which led into the attic which always seemed to be stocked with pumpkins and various fruits all laid in rows, while from the beams, on big hooks, hung hams in net bags from which came an aroma that one never forgets.

When the butter was churned I was allowed to turn the handle and make my own little pat of butter. The delight of collecting the chicken eggs whilst they were still warm, often the reluctant hen sitting tight and giving a peck not wanting to part with the fruits of her labour.

From Grandma's farm on the Norfolk fens in the 1930s, how clear the vision of horse brasses gleaming, sitting by an open fire, listening to the radio, or forever winding the gramophone and singing along with the records, the home-baked bread with jam or cheese followed by milk pudding for supper.'

THE SUN DID NOT ALWAYS SHINE

'I was about six years old the day our school at Blofield Heath was flooded in 1946. It was July, the weather was hot, the atmosphere heavy and sultry. At about 3.30 we heard the distant roar of thunder. The sky darkened and the clouds were rent by a terrific flash of lightning. It was as if the heavens had opened the way the rain beat against the large panes of glass in the window. The water gushed and gurgled off the field, swept through a door at the back of the school, flooding both the classrooms. The brown tide of muddy water quickly rose around the legs of the desks and we had to climb on to the lids of the desks and sit there. I cannot remember any panic, we must have thought of it as a game. Some of the boys floated sweet papers made into little boats on the surface. My mother arrived to take me home. Luckily she had her rubber boots on so was able to help carry the children out of the classroom. We started down the hill for home. Riverlets of sparkling water rushed frantically down the hill. A man riding his bike up the hill called to Mother, "You haven't half got a lot of water at your place, Mrs." We soon found out what he meant.

Our bungalow was at the bottom of the hill in a dip. The rain had rushed from the road and the field, breaking the bank of a small spinney as it passed and emptied its load into our garden. What a sight. Fortunately the house stood on slightly higher ground than the garden so the water had not gone indoors. My mother, coping as usual with the situation, put me indoors and waded through the water to the goats' house which was deep in water. The youngest kid was standing on his back legs looking over the half door. The water was up to his neck. There was only one thing to do. Mother brought the kid indoors. By this time I was sitting in front of the blackleaded cooking range crying. "You can stop that now," said Mum. "There's enough water about already without you adding to it." She pushed the kid in front of the fire and gave me a rag to wipe it dry, while she went back for the two adult nannies.

As you probably know goats will eat anything and three goats in a small back kitchen is a catalogue for chaos. They started by eating my drawings I had done earlier on brown paper. They nibbled the strings on Mother's pinafore. Hanging from the ceiling was a sticky flypaper. Up on a chair scrambled one of the goats, grabbed the flypaper and down it went flies and all.

Five times that month the storms came, no sooner had the water subsided than it was back again. It came across the meadow like the sea washing on to the beach. It washed anything laying about along with it. The garden broom and brushes ended up in the field opposite with an accompaniment of assorted rubbish. Once the fire engine came and pumped us out, but it soon filled up again. My brother punted along the garden path in the tin bath but I was not big enough to join in the fun. All I could do was watch through the window. The damage to the harvest must have been very bad.'

'Like most children born in the war years I was without a dad, mine was away serving with the Royal Norfolks in Burma. Dad came home the day after my fifth birthday and we started to get back to a normal family life. I remember playing for many a happy hour on the bomb sites in Norwich making secret dens from the bits and pieces we found there.

Learning to sew with the elderly lady who lived a few doors away in our terrace is something I shall not forget. She had me hemming fine muslin squares for milk jugs and sugar basins and when the small hems were finished I was allowed to go through her bead box and choose four brightly coloured beads to sew on the corners. She seemed to have boxes for everything, nothing was thrown away during the war years and it was hard to break the habit.

In 1953, Coronation year, all the children at school were given a book and a tin of toffees. I remember being taken from Wensum View school in a coach to the cinema, the Ritz at Costessey, to see the film of the Queen's coronation. Few people had a television in those days. My parents didn't hire one until 1957.

I left school at 15 and went to work in a tailor's shop, Greens of the Haymarket, where tailors sat cross-legged on tables like little garden gnomes. As an apprentice it was one of my jobs to shrink the cloth with heavy gas irons; we had electric ones but with water the gas ones were safer. My wages were a grand £2 2s 3d for a 44 hour week.

Times were changing and young people in the late 1950s were no longer dressed like younger versions of their parents, they wanted their own fashions. Mother wasn't pleased when I wanted a pair of trousers with ten inch bottoms (drainpipes) with zips at the ankle so you could get them on. Mum just wasn't with the fashions of paper nylon petticoats, disposable paper knickers, stilettos and winkle-picker shoes, rock and roll music and of course Teddy boys, young men who dressed in mock-Edwardian style.

I loved to jive and joined a formation group called the Norwich Jivettes, six girls and boys; we practised at the Industries Club, a working men's club in Oak Street, Norwich. I spent my teen years dancing most evenings and giving demonstrations – it was a great time.'

AWAY FROM HOME

Families were often large but they stayed close, in spirit if not in location, and grandparents and aunts and uncles were favourite destinations for many a Norfolk child at holiday time. Sometimes it gave us a glimpse of a completely different way of life, or took us back in time to Victorian days. Sometimes, too, there were other, more famous, people to meet.

FAMILIES STAYED CLOSE

'I was a country child and often think how lucky I have been for that very reason. In those days families stayed close together with grandparents, aunts, uncles and cousins all around, either in the same village or close by. We all knew each other well and didn't have to wait for a holiday before we could "go to Grannie's". I have such lovely memories of all four of my grandparents at Corpusty and the pleasant times my cousins and I spent in their gardens among the sweet-smelling old fashioned flowers. How precious to us were the freshly fallen petals from the roses adorning the bower and the florets that fell like snow from the snowball tree. We gathered them gleefully and painstakingly threaded them on to cotton to make bangles and necklaces. The scent of the phlox reminds me of the days when I would help Granny Gay gather armfuls of pink rambler roses, marguerites, phlox and yellow sunflowers with which to trim the waggon for the Sunday school Anniversary, when we children all had a "piece" to say. One year little Jack, halfway through his piece, stopped suddenly, clapped his hand over his ear and announced, "There's suffen in my lug!"

Grandfather Gay had a large vegetable garden with apple and plum trees. He used to give Mother a large basket of bullaces for jam. We loved that on our bread and squabbled over who had the most "cobbles". Grandfather also kept goats and chickens in the "goatyard". We often had a drink of goats' milk. Granny wore a white apron when she milked the goats, sitting on her three-legged stool while they stood quietly on the bench, munching away. Grandfather used to cut bundles of "furrers" from the "furrer" (furze or gorse) bushes on the common just across the road. He chopped it up for the goats, using a contraption he'd made for the job. I believe he also used this to grind cockle shells for the hens. He was very clever at making gadgets and made beautiful clothes pegs to order as well.

Granny was midwife to the village and its neighbourhood, often walking several miles, day or night, to make a delivery. I have known her bring a baby home to care for while the mother spent time in hospital. If we had a nasty cough she would make us a goose grease plaster to wear next to the skin, on our chests, until the cough eased. Another of her "cures" was a drop of eucalyptus oil taken on a sugar lump, and each springtime she dosed us with a concoction of sulphur and treacle. She made golden eye ointment from celandines and pure pork lard, and I've watched her make cinder water for babies in her care by placing a small hot cinder in a saucer of water – probably for wind or hiccups, but I couldn't say for sure now which it was. I do know that the doctor had doubts about the survival of a very young baby with whooping cough, that Granny pulled through with spoonfuls of a jelly made from boiling together linseed and liquorice.

She used to tell us to eat "sour-gogs" (a kind of sorrel) saying they were good for us. We'd often gather some and tuck in on our way home from school. We ate them from a bunch, unwashed of course. There was no pollution then. It wouldn't do to eat from the roadside today. We also used to eat the tender young briars of the wild rose, peeling them first. Besides this "sweet briar" we also enjoyed young blackberry briars and the opening buds of hawthorn which we called bread and cheese. We liked, too, to eat the young green seed pods of mallow, which we called "pick-cheese". We used to dawdle home from school searching for these "goodies" in their respective seasons, and often arrived home with our footwear covered in marl which the roadman used to bind the stones when he mended the potholes. On Saturdays at the right time of year we would go in a little gang to Long Meadow, taking an old broken knife, to dig for ground-nuts. We amused ourselves for hours doing this, scraping away round each plant to reach the nut which we then scraped and ate there and then, taking the biggest we could find home for Mother.'

A LAYING DOWN OF FORMALITIES

'Lady Margaret Douglas-Home, sixth and youngest child of the sixth Earl Spencer, has lived in Burnham Market for many years. Until very recently she played *Jerusalem* for us at WI meetings in Burnham Market village hall.

She was born in 1906 and as a child spent all her summer holidays at the family house called the Shooting Box in North Creake. She says, "It never entered one's head that we would go anywhere else. For us North Creake was a tremendous laying down of formalities. I adored it."

The long train journey from the great house at Althorp in

101

Northamptonshire was undertaken in a special railway carriage loaded with an immense amount of paraphernalia, which included musical instruments and two ponies, and with a considerable staff of servants. A joyous sign that informality had taken over was the appearance on the platform of the solitary footman who accompanied them, wearing a rather gaudy tweed jacket on top of his livery trousers.

The Althorp staff "heads of department" stayed at Althorp so there was a lightness of heart amongst the younger servants, but Lady Margaret's father, a handsome, elegant man famous for his exceptionally high collars, always brought his own valet, Mr Martin, "so that he should get up looking right". He made no concession to heat or holiday clothing, continuing to wear his usual rough black suit. During the First World War, presumably as a gesture to the grave situation, he abandoned his high starched collars and replaced them with a scarf carefully wound round his neck to look like a collar.

Lady Margaret's mother died at her birth, and her father remained a forlorn, withdrawn figure. There were no other children to share her holiday with her. Her elder brothers and sisters came to stay at the Shooting Box, but they were grown up and mostly married. She spent most of her time with kind and loving servants. "I was the only child left, and they thought the world of me, as if I was their own." Every day she went out in the waggonette, attended by Mr Marsh, the groom, often for picnics. "However alone we were, he always wore his livery with his black top hat . . . and usually it was only me."

The beach didn't play a large part in these holidays. She only went to Holkham Beach "when my brother came, and it was such a bore. You couldn't get within half a mile of the sea." Her greatest pleasure was bicycling. "I can see myself now getting my bicycle out of the stable yard and going really what I thought was miles, rather *fast*, and all by myself. Absolute bliss." She also adored going to Fakenham. "That was the arch treat."

Lady Margaret remembers her clothes changed very little. "The same old skirt came out, and always black wool stockings and "useful" shoes. There was a thrilling moment when I was allowed to take my socks off. The weather was very hot, and I'd been fussing an awful lot so the governess said, very reluctantly, "Well, take your socks off." We were in the waggonette, and I was told to hide the socks under the seat."

The Shooting Box was demolished some time after the war, to Lady Margaret's regret. "We all loved it. I can't think really what made them such happy holidays. Perhaps it had something to do with the smallness of the house. It was different, and yet

it was tremendously traditional because we'd had it ever since
Sarah Jennings (the Duchess of Marlborough) bought it."'

THE AUNTS OF ACLE

'Grandfather owned an engineering works in Acle and I was born
in the house attached to it. Because my mother was an invalid, I
spent most of my school holidays with Norfolk aunts, travelling by
train in the care of the guard. The field by Acle station was full of
meadowsweet and kingcups. I once squeezed through a wire fence to
pick some and sunk into the most unsavoury mud you can imagine.
Acle was full of my aunts, but I generally stayed in the house where
I was born.

You went through the works and up a path, passing a strange
sort of water-pumping device which has now been reassembled in
a museum. The stairs faced you as you went in, carpeted with
shiny brass stair-rods which were cleaned every week. Crossing
the landing you could step into the maids' quarters which had only
lino, and a flight of very steep wooden stairs led to a door into the
kitchen.

My bedroom had a huge carved four-poster bed with drapes and
curtains, a feather mattress which took two people to shake and a
little stool to climb into bed. There were oil lamps with chimneys
downstairs, but I had a candle. My aunt told me that Grannie had
died in the room and on the night before, as she was going up to
attend her, a huge black dog with flaming saucer eyes had rushed
down at her. She had been found in a faint at the foot of the stairs.
Of "Ole Shuck" there was no trace.

On my washstand stood a ewer, a toothbrush holder, washbasin
and soapdish, all with a rose design like the chamberpot which had
a chamber cupboard by my bed. By candlelight the curtains swayed
into strange shapes and the lip and handle of the ewer looked like a
face and I was always very frightened at night. A brass can of hot
water was brought to me in the morning, but the cold water in the
ewer was pumped from a well in the scullery. This water came into
the sink full of nasty little wriggly things and I didn't like washing
in it, so used to pretend I had used some by tipping it into my
chamberpot.

Drinking water came from a tap outside and people used to ask
if they could short-cut through the garden to fetch it. Over their
shoulders they had a yoke and so carried two buckets at a time. A
slype or passage divided the walk-in pantry from three outhouses,
for wood and a couple of what were called "petties". One had two
circular holes cut in the well-scrubbed wood and the wooden front
on which I used to drum my heels unlatched so the Night Cart

103

men could remove the buckets. Carefully cut newspaper squares hung from a nail and there was a tin of pink powder to sprinkle afterwards.

There seemed to be no safety regulations in the engineering works and I wandered freely round the foundry, now rebuilt at Gressenhall, watching the sparks fly in the smithy, the huge fan belts drive machinery and, my great joy, the molten metal hissing in the moulds. I don't recollect any protective clothing other than overalls, but the moulder who smoked a hundred "fags" a day was walking his dog across the fields to Fishley at the ripe old age of 90.

Two other aunts shared my care. One had married a wealthy gold prospector and had a large house with peacocks, croquet and tennis parties on the lawns. She had a parrot, cases of stuffed exotic birds in the hall, and a boat moored down the boat dyke where the Hermitage now stands; but more important to me were the strawberries, raspberries and white and black currant bushes in the kitchen garden and a sort of icehouse where ice cream could be made.

The other aunt's husband farmed cattle on the Acle marshes where will o' the wisps danced at night, and also grew oats and later sugar beet. There was always a farm cart to hitch a lift on and I used to take "beevers" and big jars of weak beer to the harvesters. The dairy was fascinating but the churning was too much like hard work. I learned how to "hear" when the butter was coming. My job was to stamp the logo on to the butter which was patted into shape with wooden paddles.

I think I was a lucky child with my aunts and very sheltered life. I never heard any bad language until much later and that was when a government official came to explain about sampling Uncle's sugar beet for sugar content. He had grown excellent beet for years and he reckoned without any blank-blank inspectors and, he added irrelevantly, he always paid his tithes!'

ALL OUR HOLIDAYS

'My first three years of life, during the First World War, were mostly spent at The Willow, Witton Bridge, North Walsham, with my Marshall grandparents, as my father was in the Royal Flying Corps. My mother paid the rent of our London home for several months at a time, and came here. I can remember trenches along the roadside which froze over in the winter and children sliding on them.

My mother helped my grandfather with the harvest, passing the stooks of corn up to him. I, though only three, thought I was leading the horse (it didn't need any leading) and shouted "hold yu" when we moved off. My granny used to bake in a wall oven, and she used

Paddling in the sea at Gorleston in the 1920s. We were well covered up when we went anywhere near the sea!

an iron with heated metal inside. When she fed the free-range hens she called out "Boys, boys". After the war and after my sister was born all our holidays, even into my teens, were spent here. We lived in a flat in London and were always being told to be quiet and not disturb the neighbours. When we came here we would run down the field shouting at the top of our voices with no one to tell us to be quiet.

We got water from a well and soft water from a water butt. There was barbed wire along the front wall to prevent horses on the way home after work from rubbing against it and damaging it. I once saw a donkey feeding on the common roll over and over in the dust on the road. My grandfather had two horses besides bullocks, one was a working horse and the other a driving horse. When he was working about a mile away and started for home the driving horse would neigh. My granny would lay the table for dinner as she knew my grandfather was on his way home.'

WE DIDN'T TRAVEL FAR

'My grandmother was the first in the family to have a television and as she lived just up the road from us at Sutton, we went up there in the evening. We thought it was lovely, although it was black and white and quite a small screen.

One of my grandmothers took all her grandchildren to Yarmouth every summer. We caught the train from Stalham, went on the amusements and always had a lovely meal in a store called Arnolds. That was usually our only outing of the year. We used to get so excited. I remember going to London on a coach trip, that was like going abroad for some children in our village. We just didn't travel far.'

BORN AT THETFORD

'I was born in the small south Norfolk market town of Thetford in the late 1920s. I arrived six weeks early – just as my grandma was cooking steak and onions for lunch. I was very small and not expected to live, so I was put in a wooden blanket box to keep me warm and the same grandma fed me sips of sugared water and I lived to tell the tale!

Gran was a tall, elegant lady. It was sad that she died when I was only three years old. It was she who took me in to Jenny Lind Hospital, Norwich when I had a large abscess in my neck. I can still recall things that took place while I was there. I was so unhappy – no visitors were allowed, the cot was hard and I hated the fact that boys and girls had to bath together! I still have Gran's violet silk handkerchief sachet with her name "Ella" on the front and inside one of her lace handkerchiefs.

Grandpa died a year after Gran. He was a happy-go-lucky soul who in his youth had ridden a penny farthing cycle. His main means of transport used to be a pony and trap and he found it difficult to get used to cars – his driving was erratic to say the least! Grandpa used to take us for walks along Green Lane to show us all the birds' nests and to look at the eggs but not to touch. He bought me a tiny blue teddy bear from Clarkes in King Street, which I loved dearly.

My other grandparents lived at Great Yarmouth, how we used to look forward to our Sunday visits. Grandfather used to walk to meet us along the Acle New Road. You could see him miles away, he was an old sea captain and had a rolling gait. He kept me happy with tales of his travels around the world. Sometimes if the tide was right he would row us out to Scroby Sands in his boat *Peggy* to see the seals.

Grandmother was a gentle soul – she always had a house full of family summer visitors. She wore granny-print dresses and black stockings and gold-rimmed glasses. She used to cook us wonderful Sunday lunches in her black-leaded cooking range. Her Yorkshire puddings were the best that I have ever tasted. We had fresh pink shrimps for tea in a large glass bowl and on leaving for home were given half a crown and some home-baked sausage rolls in a large paper bag.'

VICTORIAN THROUGH AND THROUGH

'Granny Green was a Victorian through and through. In fact as a little girl and until she died, I didn't think she had legs. She wore her full length widow's weeds winter and summer alike, the only difference being in winter she wore a battered black felt hat and in the summer what I always thought was a white lace doyley on her head. She was as strict as any Victorian could have been.

My paternal grandparents in Norwich had owned the timber yard in Garden Street, H. J. Green and Sons, and true to the name, every bit of correspondence was carried out in green ink. You could approach Garden Street from King's Street, passing by the Steward and Patteson or Bullards or Morgans breweries. Those wonderful smells, and to this day I still enjoy the smell and taste of beer. The only drawback to approaching from King Street was that Thorn Lane which we had to come up was very dark and spooky, particularly in the winter. Or we could come down from Ber Street. All those terraced houses, shops, bakery and timber yard were razed to the ground to make way for Rouen Road.

Granny Green was very strict and didn't particularly like little girls, much preferring boys, my brother being the only one. On arrival on a Friday afternoon after school, I had first to play her the piano. (Nearly 60 years on, that same piano made from our own timber graces my home, the kick marks having been lovingly eradicated by diligent polishing.) Then if I passed muster (which wasn't often, hence the kick marks) a cup of tea in a willow pattern cup and a ginger snap were the order of the day. I wore a short gymslip and can still feel the prickles of the horsehair sofa. Then, and only then, was I allowed to go across to the timber yard with the *Eastern Evening News* for my uncle. I always received a big welcome from the men in the yard. Looking back I shudder to think what the safety inspectors of today would have thought about the huge unguarded saws, machinery etc. The pit was where huge trees were sawn, the sawdust being one enormous soft sweet-smelling mattress, where I was allowed to wallow. I adored the men and they me. Of course there was always the frantic cleaning down before crossing back across the street to Granny, who had forbidden me to go anywhere near the men and machinery. I'm sure she knew! How those men moved the trees; no fork lift trucks etc, just block and tackle and pure muscle power. How I loved that yard.

Granny Green had a brother, my Great Uncle Jim, who was as naughty as she was severe. I can hear her now, berating him roundly when he arrived complete with a pint of freshly cooked winkles. I loved them, but before I was allowed the first taste, the winkle black ends had to be plastered all over my face as beauty spots. She would get really angry with him for spoiling me rotten, but he always won her round.

My cousins, who were numerous on my mother's side, were allowed the *Beano* and *Dandy*, but Granny would only let my brother and me have the *Children's Newspaper*, which we hated. She also gave us pocket money. One Christmas, I had seen a diary in Jarrolds which cost sixpence, one whole week's pocket money. I dearly wanted to buy this for my father as a Christmas present. The man in Jarrolds promised he would put it on one side until I came back with the money. Hot foot I ran back to Granny asking her breathlessly for my pocket money. That week, no pocket money, as I had asked for it!'

HOLIDAY TIME

'From the age of eight or nine onwards I used to go and stay in a lovely old red brick rectory, standing in a considerable area of land. It was crenellated and there was a lion couchant either side of the big stone-lined porch. A large stone-flagged hall and at the end a beautifully curving staircase – but no electricity, water from a borehole, and a cesspit. Not that I was conscious of these last three – it was great fun going to bed with candles, and seeing the huge shadows we made as we went upstairs. My friend slept in the blue room and I was in the adjoining dressing room.

I lived in Norwich so one of the delights as I woke was the cooing of the woodpigeons in the trees outside the window. Breakfast was in the spacious dining room, all panelled, with big brown shutters, behind one of which was a tiny secret cupboard. There was nothing in it, but I wondered what might have been hidden there in years gone by. Another thing that fascinated me was the hatch – a huge circular affair with a central division, which rotated. You could not see through to the kitchen, but the food came through from the unseen cook, Laura. After breakfast, chairs were put back round the walls and Laura and the other two maids came in for a short reading from the Bible, then everyone turned and knelt at the chairs for prayers.

There was lots to do for two little girls – a long rope suspended from a tall oak – an island in the middle of a large pond – mushrooms to scrump from a neighbouring meadow. There were swamps to be traversed in our wellingtons, and who dared to go in deepest? I lost a boot once, and got even muddier retrieving it, but luckily was greeted with laughter when we got to the back door. In the walled vegetable garden was a metal bar for somersaults and the like, inherited from older brothers. And also in the garden, dear old Mr Lacey, a real Norfolk character with white hair and beard and a battered old trilby. He came each day on his tricycle. As I was born a Geordie, it was from him I learnt the real Norfolk dialect. It was he who pumped the water each day for use in the house, except Sundays. When we grew bigger and were able to reach the long metal handle we were occasionally able to help when the boys were not there.

The rector's wife spent quite some time each morning cleaning and trimming the lamps used all over the house. (What have we done with the time saved, now that these tasks are no longer necessary?)

At autumn half-terms we went to Yarmouth on the Saturday or Monday and saw the herring boats in their dozens and the fisher girls working on the quay. In the afternoons we were left at the roller skating rink while my pal's mother, a keen Red Cross member, used to go to the depot and bandage the fisher girls' sore, cut and salty fingers with what these Scots called "wee clouties".

How old the rectory was I have no idea, but when I read Jane Austen some of her characters would fit so well into the sunny morning room, and also the big drawing room with its elegant wallpaper, not often used unless to do piano practice or on a parish "occasion". I seldom went into the rector's study except to say goodnight, and it was difficult in the lamplight to see what was there apart from the book-lined walls and the desk full of papers.

On Tuesday morning we piled into the car, picked up two girls from a nearby farm, and drove along the turnpike to school in Norwich. What a change from suburbia; and yet when the reverse visits happened there were other school friends near and handy, fireworks in November, cinema visits occasionally, and sometimes a theatre trip: just as magical a weekend for the country girl as were my visits to the rectory. At least, so *she* thought.'

'Family holidays as such didn't happen but we did have long-suffering aunts in Norwich, London and Kent who would invite two or three of us at a time to stay. They would take a lot of trouble in entertaining us.

In Norfolk we had a great-aunt who lived at Morley St Peter and we did stay there before, during and after the war. She was very Victorian and was disgusted that children should be wearing dresses above their knee! We lived in luxury there as she had maids, and hot water was brought up to the bedroom every morning. There was a bathroom but water was only pumped up and heated for that once a week. In a shed was an engine for making electricity which provided the lighting. She and her husband were keen bridge players and played croquet so we were able to enjoy both. Bridge (a simple version I think) was often played in the summerhouse and when meals were ready the gong was banged. My first taste of crab-apple jelly was there and now I make it for the grandchildren. My aunt had her own sewing room where we would often sit and make dolls' clothes.

For driving around locally a very early Ford would be used and most of the locals would know to keep their distance as half the time Aunt was patting her golden retriever in the back! On Saturdays the Armstrong Siddeley came out of wraps and was driven to Norwich, which was an even more hair-raising experience, although the dog was left at home. Uncle would give us each two shillings and sixpence and we would have a wonderful time in Woolworths buying presents for those at home. For lunch we would go to a restaurant, upstairs, in the Haymarket. Luxury indeed!'

GREAT FUN

'In 1934 when I was four years old I went to stay with Grandpa and Grandma Leeds in East Dereham. My mother was busy having a new baby in the neighbouring village of North Elmham. Grandpa was the manager of Stead and Simpsons shoe shop in the market place, and a strict Methodist. They lived in the house over the shop, people remembered him for years as he had a beard – unusual in those days.

It must have been a WI summer garden meeting that we went to. Grandma wore a longish navy dress with tiny white flowers and a large all-enveloping cloche hat. I can remember sitting (or squirming) on the grass under and around her chair. I cannot remember any food, but the demonstrator showed all the ladies a new way to cut a loaf – starting at the top crust and slicing horizontally down to the bottom. I thought this was such a good idea (why?) and was most disappointed that Grandma continued in the old way when we got home. There was a competition, all the ladies had to sew on a button behind their backs – great fun!

It was dusk when we walked home. The excitement was not yet over. I encountered my first toad, sitting on the pavement. I was allowed to take him back and keep him in a tub – until he escaped. This was much more thrilling than that new baby sister!'

SIR RIDER HAGGARD AND GEORGE BALDRY

'I first met Sir Rider Haggard when he was about 60 years old and I was a small child aged six. I saw him on one or two occasions after that around Bungay but it is the first meeting which remains in my memory. I was visiting the house with my aunt who was calling on one of the daughters, when we were met in the drive by an old man (or so he seemed to me) who was very busy "spudding" daisies from the gravel with a long walking stick. He asked my name and suggested that I should stay and talk with him in the garden, and he let me use his stick! When I tired of this he took me into the house to show me his treasures. The hall and staircase were hung with trophies from Africa – spears and shields, carved heads and multi-coloured masks – my memories of them now are very hazy, but I know I had nightmares for some time afterwards.

My brother, who was six years older than me, was an avid reader of the Rider Haggard books so from a very early age I was able to borrow them and read all he had written, together with those of Jules Verne, Henty and Alexandre Dumas. I was particularly delighted to read *Montezuma's Daughter* because the first chapters were set in the Bath Hills, one of our happiest childhood playgrounds.

My father was a country-loving man and introduced us to the delights of boating on the Waveney and walking on the common and marshes surrounding the Haggard estate; we fished and paddled in the pools and played at the foot of Bath Hills, running up and down the steep "Target Hill" – so called because the local Volunteers, until about 1910, had used the Hills as a rifle range, the butts being situated on the Ditchingham side of the river whilst they shot from

111

the common. My grandfather, my father and his brothers were all members of this association and were all good shots, holding many trophies – their well-loved commander-in-chief was Colonel Hartcup, a relative of the Haggard family. My father told us that when he was young the social life in the Bungay area was very good, and winter balls were held at Ditchingham House, Ditchingham Hall, Upland Hall and Earsham Hall, at which the local band played (the Lancers being their favourite dance) and that the band men and boys were given wonderful suppers in the servants' hall, waited on by the butler and the maids.

We kept our rowing boat with George Baldry's boats at Mill Cottage. He was a fascinating old man, now known to thousands through his book *The Rabbit Skin Cap* edited by Lilias Rider Haggard. His knowledge of folklore and country crafts was very wide, and it was a joy to listen to him. He was a courteous man, one of nature's gentlemen, and as I grew older I came to appreciate his knowledge more and more. I spent many hours listening to his arguments and ideas on his pet theme of perpetual motion, and he would show me the hundreds of gadgets he made and used for his experiments.

In later life I returned with my own son and his many friends to row on the river, and George would always come to meet us, raising his hat in a grand sweep as we approached. Now this hat was a great source of amusement to the children, and lasted many summers. It was a straw hat with a large brim, and had evidently once been a lady's pride and joy, had been worn by Mrs Baldry, and then passed down to George. I forget at what stage the crown disappeared, but for several boating seasons the hat was just a large brim, with George's head and hair as the crown. Long before we got within sight of the Mill Cottage I would lecture the boys, and threatened them with dire consequences if they so much as tittered on seeing George, but as soon as they saw him raise his hat they flung themselves into the undergrowth and through the hedge, stuffing their handkerchiefs in their mouths, whilst I was greeted by George and conducted to the boats with all his wonderful old-world courtesy.

Those boys now have children of their own, and one of their greatest regrets is that they cannot take their youngsters rowing on the Waveney in George Baldry's boats, gliding in and out of the sunshine under the trees at the foot of the gardens of Ditchingham Lodge, past Lilias's riverside cottage which she wrote about so often in her *Norfolk Notebooks*. Sadly, George Baldry's Mill Cottage has disappeared along with all his boats, and only those who knew him know that the odd bricks remaining in the grass, the clumps of snowdrops in spring or the rose blooming in the thickets were once his cottage and garden.'

GAMES, TREATS & CHORES

Games went in seasons, and we all knew when it was time to put down one toy and pick up another. We played in the roads, more often than not, and were easily able to avoid the occasional car or pony and trap. Our treats were simple, from the Saturday penny to helping in the harvest fields, and most of us had chores to do at home before we could expect to be let out to play.

GAMES IN SEASON

'In the spring at South Creake out would come the hoops and skipping ropes; we would skip going to school and back home, also in the playground and any time we played around. We also had marbles in little draw-up bags and rolled them along the dusty road as we went to school. That often made us late! Again we played with them in the playground and on the way home, sometimes ending up with a full bag, or an empty one. Spinning tops and whips came out as well, and we would spin and whip them as we went to school. The boys were always good with theirs and would race one another, boasting who had the best racer. Their whips usually had an old leather bootlace which made a cracking noise as they whipped the tops.

In summer time we still ran around with the hoops, the girls having wooden ones and the boys had bigger iron ones and iron hooks with a wooden handle. When going nice and fast they then held them by the hook. We would bounce a ball going to school and back home, in the evenings playing tip-catch-out. We also played hopscotch and hide and seek, calling out "cocoo".

Autumn was the time for conkers; everyone played with conkers! There were plenty of these in the village. They would be well dried by the fire or in the oven before use and then we'd see who had the best hitting one. Then we had pop guns made from a piece of elder branch. For pellets we collected acorns and with one at each end when the stick was pressed, they made a lovely popping sound.

It was chestnutting time as well. The "planten" at Leicester Square was full of chestnut trees. As we came out of school, we would run up to the wood and fill our pockets and bags, and again at the weekends when our parents would go as well. That was a lovely pastime.

As winter drew near we still ran our hoops, and when the snow and frost came we played snowballs and made snowmen. As soon as the pits froze over and the ice was hard enough we went sliding, seeing who could make the best slide. The best pits were the Parsons Pit, the Horse Pit, a little pit in the corner of the Pleasure Ground, and Bugs Mire on Sug-gate (or South-gate). The boys would make the sparks fly with their hobnail boots and make candles on the ice. It was nice just to watch them. Only the older boys and young men were allowed on Bugs Mire. Sunday afternoons parents went and some would join in the fun.'

'The girls at Pulham Market played a ball game called "Donkey" against a wall. This began with seven straight throws and catches, then six different movements, then five of another and so on down to one. We also had different games with skipping ropes. In late summer Dad made us pop guns from an elder barrel, burnt out with a red hot poker, a hazel candle and acorns to shoot. There were also bows and arrows from willow wands and string and dead stalks as arrows to fire. Because we could easily hear the few cars coming from a good distance, we were able to whip our tops along the road.'

'Playground games were seasonal – hopscotch and skipping any time but marbles in the better weather, when a hole could be scooped out of the dried mud, and top and whip when the roads were dry and dusty.'

THE SWEET MAN

'One of my happiest childhood memories is that of the Saturday morning "sweet man" calling in our road at Cromer with his donkey and cart absolutely laden with everything imaginable. He looked, to us as children, a small, wrinkled and rather bent old man. He was quite cheery, but didn't stand a lot of nonsense from the children who crowded round his cart jostling each other to get a peep at all the goodies inside, deciding how they were going to spend their saved-up pennies.
    The cart was packed with jars containing every kind of sweet to delight children. Having made a choice, finally, for it was not an easy thing to do, the sweets were carefully weighed or counted out into little pieces of paper which the old man deftly twisted into cones. He seemed a magical person as we watched him. Our halfpennies could buy quite a lot if we were choosy. We could buy two big gobstoppers which changed colour as we sucked them (one at a time!), or ten aniseed balls was another good buy. A "treat bag" consisted of a variety of misshapen sweets in a sealed bag and cost a penny, but was well worth it if you were lucky enough to get a chocolate

114

in the bag. Sherbet fountains and long liquorice bootlaces with an interesting bobble-sweet on the end were strung around inside the cart like decorations.

As well as sweets there were brightly coloured marbles and miniature toys. There were also boxes of household necessities: floorcloths, soap, scourers, needles and cottons. It was like Aladdin's cave and we longed to look inside and fiddle with everything – poor man, what patience he must have had with us children. On the outside of the cart hung saucepans, pots of all shapes and sizes, cans, garden tools, and paraffin cans ready to be filled as required. The metal things made a lovely tinkly, metallic sound as they jostled together when the donkey and cart moved off.

The old man always seemed to be walking beside the donkey, leading it rather than riding, perhaps he thought he would be too heavy for the poor animal with such a full cartload.

It was a sight and sound that we all looked forward to every Saturday and I am sure our parents used the "sweet man" as a bribe occasionally during the week.'

THE COUNTRYSIDE WAS OUR PLAYGROUND

'What a wonderful stretch of the river Bure we had for our playground. The water sparkled so clear (so good to drink) that you could see trout and crayfish basking on the bottom, and sticklebacks darting in hundreds. Our time was spent, on those hot days, in the river or on it in a canoe made by our fathers. We shared our river with dippers, kingfishers and otters, which would slide with a splash into the water a mere 50 yards or so upstream, quite unconcerned by our laughter.

Not too long ago I visited our swimming pool. What a sorry sight, now reduced to just a few yards wide, thrusting its way through weeds and rubbish, and what a colour! No otters splashing, no dippers or kingfishers and no flowers decorating the banks. Nothing left but happy memories.'

'We would be up bright and early, full of excitement, looking forward to a lovely day. Our mum would do us a packed lunch, usually jam sandwiches and lemonade, we would gather up our baskets and off we set, calling for our friends on the way. We hurried along, eager to get to the woods nice and early. It was quite a walk from Hempton, but we didn't mind – and what a sight when we arrived. It would take our breath away, it was like looking at a carpet of blue as far as the eye could see.

We spent all day in the bluebell woods, playing our make-believe games, climbing trees and picking the flowers. When it was time for

115

lunch, the jam sandwiches tasted wonderful. Then we would fill our baskets with flowers and make our way home, tired out but very happy after our annual trip to the bluebell woods.'

'A vivid childhood memory of mine comes from the early 1940s. My grandfather and uncle worked on a local farm at Holme Hale and they would get permission from the farmer to allow my mother, aunt, cousins and myself to invade his ditches for primroses. This happened every Good Friday. Directly after breakfast we would all set off complete with bottles of cold drinks, hot cross buns, baskets and wool.

Excitement grew as we approached the yellow banks of primroses, each one trying to get to them first. After they were gathered and tied into small bunches with the wool, they would be carefully placed in the baskets and taken home, there to be placed in bowls of water until the next morning when we would take them to church, complete with small potted-meat jars which had been saved for this purpose. There we would present them to the ladies who were decorating for Easter Sunday. They would be placed on the window ledges and around the font. How proud we were when sitting in our pews on Easter morning and gazing at those little yellow bunches which had been picked with love and care.'

'Harvest time and holidays in the 1950s are very clear in my mind. Harvest was magic! My younger brothers and I were allowed to "help" with the harvest. The corn was cut with a binder – no combines – and later on it had to be threshed. The corn sheaves were stacked together in groups and made lovely hideaways for us children. Rabbits ran as the corn was cut, so that ensured a few good dinners. Of course the picnic lunch with sandwiches, home-made cake and Corona (preferably ginger beer) in the flip-top bottles was looked forward to and formed an important part of the day. Tractors and grandfather's horse and cart worked side by side.

My holidays, usually the whole six weeks in summer, were spent with my widowed grandmother who lived in Hunstanton. The days seemed endless. I had to amuse myself and provided I returned on time for meals Gran was quite happy for me to wander by myself. It was safe then. Sixpence lasted a long while on the slot machines, especially if I found an odd penny or two.

Depending on the tide I would walk the shoreline playing and paddling in the rock pools as far as Old Hunstanton, then walk back along the cliffs to Gran's and tea. Wherever I go I still like walking along a shoreline but it doesn't have quite the same feel.'

116

WONDERFUL PERFORMERS

'Professor Woods lived in the North Walsham area. He used to visit the schools, and he often pushed a strange cart on which he brought his cages of white mice.

The children all brought a penny each to see his menagerie. The mice were wonderful performers.'

IN AND OUT OF SCHOOL

'My earliest recollection is of starting school, which was Cavell infants of Lakenham; there with my friends we enjoyed all the usual games with a ball, or skipping ropes, either singly or with a girl either end and one jumping in the middle, till one was caught in the rope and then had to take a turn in turning the rope. Also we loved marking out numbers on the ground whilst kicking a slate and hopping on one foot.

Once home from school we would play in the road with our spinning tops on the top of which we had drawn pretty patterns with chalks. We'd hit it with string tied to a stick and see who could keep it spinning the longest. We'd play hide and seek and many other games and pretend not to hear when our parents called us in for tea, as we knew soon after tea it meant early to bed.

When the schools closed in August we'd take sandwiches and bottles of water and spend all day on the park or places near by. My best memory is of Scotchies meadow and Lakenham Cock Green. We'd go dredging in the river, two of us holding a sack between us catching the tiny fish, which we proudly took home in a jar (if a naughty boy didn't tip them out first). We'd also go tadpoling near the Lakenham swimming baths. Scotchies meadow (which was just past Lakenham Cock Green) was our favourite place as the concrete bridge stanchions were used as slides. We'd run up them and then slide down, wearing holes in our shoes and knickers, much to our poor mothers' despair. We'd paddle and splash around in the reed-covered river and then play hide and seek in what to us then were hills and dales, and gather pretty flowers to make daisy chains.

In the Easter holidays if the primroses were out we used to walk for miles to gather them and proudly took them home. I remember once seeing a young courting couple and the young man asked if he could buy mine. I promptly said yes when he gave me a shilling (a fortune to us in those days) and he lovingly handed them to his young lady. I was admonished by my Dad when I got home and excitedly showed him my shilling and told never to accept money from a stranger again – especially for something that I had gathered for free.

My brother would sometimes let us ride on a trolley he'd made (consisting of two planks of wood with four pram wheels on it and a piece of string to guide it with). We flew downhill using our feet as brakes but had to walk up the hills. We also used to get him to make us pop guns out of willow and put potato pieces in and shoot with them, or a catapult.

Summer always seemed long and hot to us in those days and we were seldom bored and all too soon had to start back at school in September again.'

ALWAYS SOMETHING TO DO

'When I was a lad in the early 1930s we had no electricity or wireless so we had to make our own amusement, but we would always find something to do.

There always seemed to be ice and snow in January in those days. Most of our time was spent sliding on the village pond or playing snowballs. In the long winter evenings we would amuse ourselves looking at old comics that we swopped with other boys, or making something to play with the next day or sometimes playing with model farm animals or toy soldiers. It was surprising the fun that could be had with a little imagination.

When the snow melted the village ponds would be full and the ditches running fast. Just right for sailing our paper boats or tin lids or anything that would float. Next would be the March winds, for flying our home-made kites. Another thing to do was primrosing and bird nesting and as the weather warmed up we would be tiddler fishing with a jam jar on a piece of string and paddling in the ponds or chasing butterflies and bees in the hay fields.

Then would come the long summer holidays running rabbits in the harvest fields, little boys with big sticks. Sometimes we even caught one. After harvest would come collecting blackberries and mushrooms, wild plums and crabapples along the farm hedges. Next would be the time for collecting hazel nuts and acorns, to be made into home-made pop guns. Horse chestnuts had to be collected and dried ready for playing conkers. There was very little traffic on the roads in those days, just horses and carts and the odd car, so we would spin our tops and run our hoops on the road in safety.

When the leaves began to fall we would gather them up for our bonfire on 5th November. We might even have some fireworks. Soon it would be Christmas and the village shop would have its show room open in the evenings with the Christmas goods on show. We used to spend hours looking and hoping but money was very short, so it was mostly all in vain. Christmas over with its joys and disappointments, we were once more back with the ice and snow. There was always something to do, the days were never long enough. We didn't have time to be bored.'

WE DID ENJOY OURSELVES

'There were two sets of twins in my family in a year and a half and we lived in a "one up, one down" at Walsingham. We did not have much money to spare but we did enjoy ourselves. Christmas was the best time of year. I had a rag doll, an orange, an apple and some nuts in my stocking. We did not have a Christmas tree, but when we came down on Christmas morning there was a holly branch all decorated and shining.

I liked the summer holidays too. We had a long walk to school in term time (no school buses then) and the poor old tramps from Thursford workhouse would be sitting at the side of the road chewing their hunk of bread and drinking out of a billycan. I took my Dad's tea to him in the harvest fields, a hot shortcake and sometimes a meat pie. The men let me ride in the waggons and this was great fun.

When we moved to a larger house, Sundays were special too. On that day only, we were allowed to go in to the front room. Mother had four whatnots with more than a hundred ornaments on them so we had to sit still and be careful. There was also a gramophone; you had to wind it up and fix a tiny silvery needle into a screw and lower the arm on to the record. If you were at all clumsy, or jogged, the record was scratched and would then stick, repeating the same bit over and over again. Records were so easily broken. I sobbed when *I've never seen a straight banana* was sat on by an uncle. I loved the *Laughing policeman* but for some reason that was not considered suitable for Sundays.

For the chapel Sunday school treat we used to go in waggons to Wells and on to the beach; my Mum packed up a picnic and we had winkles from a stall, or whelks from the whelksheds. On the way home we were given a packet of Lucifers, a sort of match which we struck and threw into the road to light our way.

The only time I had new clothes was for Sunday school Anniversary; patent shoes, white socks, a flowery patterned dress and a straw hat to match. I felt a fine lady, but when I came home I had to change at once into ordinary everyday clothes.

There was an annual visit of the fair to the Square by the Knights Gate, and Mum gave us a penny, or if she had it to spare, tuppence and it went quite a long way. There were rides, fairings and humbugs. I had plenty of enjoyment when I was a child.'

EARNING MONEY

'We were not given pocket money except for one Saturday penny sweet money but we had various ways of earning it. We kept rabbits which we looked after ourselves – feeding and cleaning – but our father would take them to the buck and to market for us. This was purely a commercial operation for us and there was great disappointment if the doe only produced two or three babies. Every day food had to be collected and at the weekend two days' supply. We would come home with the sack balanced on our handlebars.

Another job was collecting jam jars from the dump at Whittington, washing them outside in a big bath, and selling them for a halfpenny each. For weeding the cobblestones at Stoke Ferry House we were paid twopence an hour but there was a bonus here as we often came home with several pounds of strawberries.'

'On our way to school in the mornings at Ickburgh we delivered milk to people who lived in the almshouses as they had their own cans, but in the afternoon after school we used to deliver milk from a two-gallon can by the measure which hung inside. We carried the can on the handlebars of our bicycle, a bit tricky sometimes in the winter when the roads were slippery, but I can't remember ever spilling it. The milk used to cost a penny halfpenny a pint or a penny a half pint in the summer but went up in the winter to twopence halfpenny or twopence.'

'On Saturday mornings the older children would have their weekly tasks, taking the various jobs in turn. The least popular job was scrubbing out the petty (privy), and other jobs were washing down steps, cleaning cutlery etc. Pocket money was earned by running a small paper round and running errands.'

NO TIME FOR PLEASURE

'I was the second child of seven, five girls and two boys. We lived in a small village, Rockland St Mary, and went to the village school. No time for pleasure, always looking after brothers and sisters, being the oldest girl.

When I was about ten years old, during playtime at school I had to go to the headmaster's house (quite near the school) to make up the fire and get his mid-morning drink; after school I would go back to do the washing up!'

WE DID IT FOR ENJOYMENT

'When I was ten years old my father managed a country garage and he used to go out to the various farms and smallholdings around Stanhoe to repair cars and farm vehicles. Often he would let me go with him and I have many happy memories of the times the farmer's wife, who was always around, would take me to see the animals and chickens, then we would go into the kitchen which was always so welcoming with smells of things cooking on the range. In those days many people kept a pig and had it killed for the house and used to have hams hanging around the kitchen walls; there were no fridges. Often we would go home with a pork cheese, some pigs' fry or some butter, and it always seemed to give them pleasure to give you a little treat like that.

We had two three-week holidays from school, not six altogether like they do today. The first was when the fruit was ready for picking, and as most of the smallholders grew strawberries we used to go to help. We picked in four-pound chip baskets which were emptied into wooden trays to go to the factory for making jam.

The second holiday was later in the year when the potatoes were ready for picking. They were ploughed out and we were given a piece called a retch, between two sticks, to pick up. You just filled a basket and left it and the men would come along with a horse and cart and empty the baskets into the cart and take them to the end of the field. They were piled up into what is called a clamp, then covered with a layer of straw, and then this was covered with soil to keep the frost from the potatoes.

We received a small payment for the work but it was quite incidental as we really did it for enjoyment. At the end of the day we were given a ride home in the cart – this was the highlight of the day.'

OUT FOR THE DAY

Holidays were few and far between for most children, and outings were great expeditions for many of us, perhaps the only time we saw the sea or travelled far from our homes. How many today remember the Crippled and Poor Children's Outings from Norwich?

THE CHURCH SCHOOL OUTING

'Early one sunny July morning in 1926, a mercurial bunch of 13 year old boys was assembled at the corner of The Chantry and Chapel Field East, in the city of Norwich. I can recall that day most vividly, I was there. I remember the tall trees of the Chapel Field, ringed by those sturdy lance-pointed iron railings. The times too when I had scaled them to effect a short cut of such minimal advantage as to label the exercise "showing off", a short cut to the iron-studded porchway door of my school St Peter Mancroft.

I had risen early that July morning, washed briskly in the open air at the communal water tap, I'd even scrubbed my neck. The night before I had collected my pay from Cockrels the draper's where I worked after school hours. I'd wrapped my pay safely in a piece of rag, as my shorts no longer held small objects, and here I was waiting for a charabanc to arrive. Most of the other lads in the group had white plimsolls on their feet, but one poor lad had wellingtons. I had black "plims" borrowed from a friend. Many of the boys had shaven heads, these haircuts by the generosity of the "the nit nurse's chit". Others had hair nicely groomed, no free haircuts for them.

The Rev Saberton was our shepherd for the day. He was an exciting figure and drove an open tourer, usually full of Scouts. I had often secretly yearned for a ride with him, still here we were all going together to Great Yarmouth, sponsored by the Reverend himself. It was to be my very first ride in a motor and my first trip to the seaside.

It seemed as a dream when this beautiful blue coach rolled up. It had several rows of bench type seats, upholstered in deep blue leather. Each row had doors at either end and these were entered by a running board which ran both sides of the charabanc. A black canvas hood was neatly folded back. Its fittings were of brass polished highly, and they glittered in the sunlight. The delay to board was prolonged while the names were being called, and

122

the boys in the meantime had somehow without intention sorted themselves into two groups, those neatly dressed from the posh homes, and those from the deprived homes.

The school of St Peter Mancroft Boys had a complement of a hundred or so lads from the age of seven to 14 years. These pupils were divided according to their age into three classes, and a much smaller class called the seventh-X had for its pupils those in their last year at school; a few of the brighter boys leapfrogged into this class. The headmaster, Mr Grimble and later Mr Lyon, taught this class. They were certainly kept in check with a firm hand, often containing a short cane.

On various Saints days in the ecclesiastical calendar, when falling on weekdays, the pupils of the school would attend their namesake church of St Peter Mancroft and take part in the service of communion. The seventh-X would occupy the choir stalls and this they considered a great privilege. We couldn't sing very well but we made all the right noises in all the right places, at the right time to the priest's chanting (The Rev Canon Meyrick). The catchment area for the school included some of the most deprived areas of the inner city of Norwich, such places as Hudson's Buildings of Coburg Street, parts of Pottergate, and the alleys, yards and courts of St Stephen's and St Benedict's. Many of the school's pupils, thanks to the Great War, were of one parent families.

The Reverend Delanoy Saberton was the curate of St Peter Mancroft. He was a kind and understanding man, and very much liked. By sponsoring this one-off outing, he in his way was trying to redress a little of this deprivation. He chose those for this outing from all the boys from the deprived homes and a sprinkle of the others too.

So here we were on that sunny July morning sitting in this wonderful charabanc like kings on a throne, bouncing our way down Theatre Street and sweeping around the bevy of trams in Orford Place and down the wide Prince of Wales Road before climbing the Thorpe Rise. We were on our way. It was only then that I had time to study my fellow trippers. It seemed the poorest of the lads were sitting at the back and those from the posh homes at the front. Now this had come about without any planning, we had automatically divided into two camps and that proved not to be a very good thing.

The very young looking Reverend, dressed in his light clerical grey and wearing what must have been very daring in those rigid days of protocol in the 1920s, a white open shirt, was sitting next to the driver. Suddenly pandemonium! An impish lad from the back had rolled his lunch wrapper into a hard missile and aimed it with splendid accuracy, catching a well groomed head a sharp blow. Soon bodies were clambering over the backs of the seats and fist fights

123

spilling everywhere. The driver brought the charabanc to a halt and the Reverend, much alarmed at this flare-up, read those present the riot act and threatened that the bus would turn back if the fighting was repeated. This brought calm to the rest of the journey, broken only by a few snide remarks from both sides. This wonderful ride to a new world for me continued. One knowledgeable lad (he wore glasses and could always be seen with a book in his hand) who admitted to being a seasoned traveller said the smell of ozone was getting stronger. This remark was derided by many with none too pleasant remarks to do with bodily hygiene being directed at the unfortunate lad. I thought the smell corresponded with the aroma of fish-paste sandwiches someone had eaten for lunch, but this thought I kept to myself, not wanting to show ignorance of nautical smells.

The charabanc, despite the absence of modern spring technology, responded to the road imperfections wonderfully well, due mainly to the splendidly lush, heavy leather upholstery. We jolted with decorum the Acle stretch, the flatness of the landscape none too impressive, but the thought of future revelations paramount. I can recall too my sweaty hand grasping tightly that gold mine of coins, in a grubby piece of rag, my passport to pleasure. I also remember vividly the well proportioned knees and thighs of the boy sitting next to me, and comparing the pallid texture and skinny legs I was showing.

Reaching the outskirts of Great Yarmouth we all sat up with interest, all friction gone. I had gone as far east as I ever was to go, unless of course Kelling Sanatorium, where I was to spend some time in my early adulthood, had a distinction more easterly. We pulled into Great Yarmouth's Market Place, where the lads streamed from the many doorways of the charabanc and soon were surrounding a pea and chip stall. There I experienced some of the most delicious chips and peas I've ever had the pleasure to taste. The memory of that taste and flavour is more securely fixed in my memory than any other episode on that virgin trip to the sea.

The charabanc had to be left on the Market and we had a very long walk to the promenade. How near we were getting could be gauged by the thickness of the layer of sand strewn on the pavements. I was amazed at the crowds of holidaymakers. The beach was crowded and we had a long sliding walk to the sea front. I was slightly disappointed – the sea wasn't as blue as the picture books, but the disappearing horizon certainly impressed me greatly. Soon our plimsolls were off and we were paddling and larking about and the inevitable happened, these two groups from different backgrounds furnished their own robust play which ended with trying to push as many in the water as was possible. The melee culminated with several of the lads falling in the sea. The Reverend dancing around trying to restrain the boys gradually brought sanity to the group and all was quiet.

We moved away from the ocean higher up the beach where we joined a band of Garibaldi people who were organising beach games. This quietened our gang for but a short period. Someone mentioned the Pleasure Beach and with a few coins still jingling in our pockets, before the Reverend could give his blessing we were off. The prices soon reaped their toll on the pocket money and before long Rev Saberton walked us off to a beach hut restaurant where he had arranged for us to have tea and buns, all paid for by that kind man.

The time was fast approaching for us to leave, and at the instigation of Mr Saberton, much to his later regret, we went to have a last peep at the sea. I ask you; buns all eaten, money spent, a recipe for impetuousness to run its race. Old scores and new had a field day. The good Reverend trying to calm the fun, because that's all it was, fell full length in the North Sea and his light clerical grey suit darkened perceptibly. I felt sorry and ashamed, as I was truly one of the instigators, but the excitement of the occasion outstripped my powers of restraint.

The following Monday at school a few of us were invited by Mr Lyon the Head into the cloakroom where we were caned. This was after a lecture which included a history of the part played in monetary terms by the Reverend Delanoy Saberton. I must admit too, that the black eye I displayed was paraded with as much pride as my scaling of the Chapel-in-the-Field iron railings had earlier provided me with.'

THE CRIPPLED AND POOR CHILDREN'S OUTING

'How well I remember as a child in the 1920s and 1930s the Crippled and Poor Children's Outings. These took place each year in the summer from Norwich. All eligible children were selected from schools and homes in Norfolk, first the crippled children then the poor, and believe me, there were a lot of very poor children in those days.

What a wonderful spectacle those outings were. My parents would take us from Boundary Road to Chapelfield Gardens to witness the occasion. Business people and the better off with cars would give their time for this special treat, and often decorated their vehicles with balloons and ribbons and depictions of characters from nursery rhymes, flowers, animals and birds.

One year in particular when I was ten years old, it was a lazy, warm summer's day when we walked to Chapelfield Gardens pushing the two youngest girls in the big family pram, with our food for a picnic stowed in the well of the pram. After watching the happy, excited crippled children get into the first cars, then the poor children eagerly took their turn to climb aboard. Most drivers were dressed up in amusing outfits – some of the very rich would send their chauffeur-driven Rolls Royces or other splendid cars and these did not get "dressed up" too often but were truly majestic in their own right. The streets in the area of Chapelfield Gardens were lined with hundreds of flag-waving families and friends, no one wanting to miss such a grand sight.

We waved and called out to the crawling vehicles as they passed us, and oh how I wished I was eligible to go with them, but after Dad explained to me what it was really all about we all carried on into the gardens for our picnic and a play on the swings and roundabouts. Sometimes we would still be in Norwich when they returned from their day in the country, most looking mucky and tired but happy, but some tearful and glad to see their parents.'

SCHOOLDAYS – THE BEST YEARS OF OUR LIVES?

Slates and inkwells, wet clothes steaming by the classroom fire, children from five to 14 taught in the same room, long walks to school – memories common to all of us educated in rural schools. Norfolk children have never been slow to stand up for their rights, as stories of school strikes show, but many will have cause to thank teachers who struggled to give us a basic education.

LARGER THAN MOST

'We were fortunate at Claxton in the fact that our school was built to serve four villages so was larger than most village schools, and we had five teachers, at least two of them college-trained. The Head's wife had the infants, some of whom started school when three years old. Standards one and two each had an untrained teacher who also taught needlework through the school. Girls and boys alike learned to sew and knit up to Standard two, after that the boys did drawing and painting and the girls still did needlework. We also learned grammar (parsing and analysing sentences), geography, history, scripture and arithmetic. Later on the boys did gardening, having acquired a small field which was divided into plots, two boys to each plot.

Almost all the girls wore starched white pinafores over their dresses in the early 1920s. Boys wore knickerbockers buttoned below the knee and stiff white collars over their Norfolk-type jackets. Boys and girls almost all wore heavy boots with hobnails and metal heel and toe caps. Our roads were very heavy on footwear, mostly being made up of broken flints, and there were many cut knees. Being without boots was an accepted reason for not attending school. The attendance officer was a very busy man.'

CLOSED IN 1922

'The school at Sparham was built in 1850. All the children were taught together in one room but the tiny playground was divided into two parts, half for boys, half for girls. The schoolroom was heated in winter by a coal fire; the price of coal in 1922 was 18 shillings and sixpence for ten hundredweight. School holidays in summer time were regulated by when harvest started, as so many children helped on the farms to earn a little money.

In 1903 Mother was teaching at the school when there was a loud banging on the door. Mrs Bidwell shouted out that she wanted to see her son Harry. He was sent out to her, she gave him a real hiding and said, "I'll teach you to forget to post a letter, I've had to walk up here and do it myself." When he came back into the schoolroom, Mrs Dack the headmistress said, "I wouldn't have let you out if I'd known!"

The last teacher at the school was Miss Barbara Samples, she cycled every day from Hindringham (twelve miles each way) to teach the last five children at the school. I remember Miss Samples very well, she had a lot of black curly hair. Some mornings the mist she had cycled through all clung in her hair, it looked lovely. Other mornings she arrived at school absolutely soaking wet and had to hang her clothes on the guard in front of the fire all day, so they were dry enough for her to go home in.

After the school closed some of the children had to walk to Bawdeswell or Lyng. Mr Billy Millet the blacksmith of Main Road, Sparham, took the ones that couldn't walk far to Lyng school with his horse and cart. The last entry in the school log reads as follows: "APRIL 12TH 1922: This school closes today for Easter. It will not reopen as instructions have been given to parents of the children, to send the latter to Lyng."'

SCHOOL STRIKES

'I can remember the Burston School Strike. The central characters, Mr and Mrs Higdon, were close friends of my parents and visited us regularly in Norwich. I remember Mrs Higdon particularly. She had a very soft voice and always found time to talk to me. I found her fascinating. She was rather eccentric. She always wore a man's felt trilby hat with the fold knocked out and a leather belt buckled round for trimming. Once when my father was pleading for support for the Higdons at a meeting of the local NUT Mrs Higdon fell to her knees and called on the Lord to strike the vicar dead! This surprising action did nothing to help the Higdons' cause.

In 1914, villages were ruled by the squire and the rector and the Higdons did not fit in with their expectations of how teachers at the local school should behave. Mrs Higdon was the head teacher and her husband her assistant. She believed that lessons should extend beyond the Three Rs and interested the children in other general subjects. She also taught some elementary French and I think she taught one girl shorthand and typing. This was to help the children have expectations beyond domestic service and farmwork.

Eventually, relations between the Higdons and the hierarchy deteriorated so much that a complaint was sent to the Norfolk Education Committee and they were dismissed, although they were not given the opportunity to defend themselves. The village children and their parents refused to accept this and came out on strike.

It was the longest strike in English history and lasted 25 years. What was so amazing was that the whole of England joined in the dispute. Money came in from individuals and trade unions from all over the country. The Higdons continued to teach on the village green and in a carpenter's workshop.

Mundesley schoolchildren in about 1920. Pinafores were still commonly worn by girls.

With the contributions it was decided to build the Strike School and in 1917 the teachers' union agreed to pay them, backdated to April 1914. The school closed in 1939 on the death of Mr Higdon and Mrs Higdon's poor health, but it still stands as a memorial to the spirit of a small, remote village in Norfolk which would not accept injustice. Outside the building are plaques let into the stonework with the names of the committee formed to fight the cause and I am proud that one of the names is my father's. The school is now a museum and every September a celebration is held and attended by many hundreds.'

'In 1921 there was a movement in the country against corporal punishment and some of the pupils at Hevingham school had staged a strike. Now some of the older girls and boys at Corpusty school decided to register their disapproval of corporal punishment. About 20 of them did not return for afternoon school one day but assembled behind the "pop factory" until the rest of the school were inside. They then made their way up Heydon Road and kept away all afternoon. Next morning came retribution: everyone had one stroke of the cane on the hand, boys and girls.'

FELT SLIPPERS

'Children in the 1920s wore lace-up boots to walk two or three miles to the school at Burnham Market every day. The Women's Institute members made felt slippers (kept in a specially made red slipper box at the school) so that children could change from their wet boots and so sit with dry feet on wet days.'

HORLICKS AND THE THREE Rs

'The Three Rs were uppermost in the curriculum at Little Ellingham, with sewing for the girls and crafts for the boys, and poetry and singing. As well as a hymn to begin the day, grace was sung before and after dinner. There was drill in the playground every morning following assembly and the register being called. A Horlicks Malted Milk Cabinet consisting of trays of mugs bearing nursery rhymes, a large tin of Horlicks and a copper urn were supplied to the school by the firm. At playtime pupils enjoyed a mug of Horlicks for one halfpenny. This payment was sufficient to purchase further tins of Horlicks as needed.'

ONE LARGE ROOM

'The school at Sea Palling had one large room which held two classes – no division between them until later years, and an infants' room. Both were heated by coal fires, which never managed to heat the iron pipes around the room. Oil lamps hung from the ceiling but as we came out of school at 3.30 in winter and 3.45 in summer, they were never lit. The playground was made up of very large rough stones which were hard on the hands and knees if you fell!

The only way to wash was under a pump outside and this froze up in winter. The water was undrinkable. A jug of drinking water was brought from a nearby house in later years, but no one was brave enough to ask for it! So we had no washing facilities until Lifebuoy soap came to our aid. We all had to wash our hands at home with Lifebuoy soap for two weeks. Each day we were given a star to stick on our cards and at the end of this the school was awarded two metal washing stands, bowl, soap dish and water jug, and a metal framed mirror with a lifebelt painted round it and we all had a "clean hands" badge, but of course we still had to use the pump. No dinners at school unless you lived a very long way from school, or in very bad weather. Then sandwiches were eaten in the porch. So we walked several miles in a day and slept like logs.

The playground was divided by a tall black fence – girls and infants one side, boys the other. The girls' playground was in Waxham, the boys' in Palling, the boundary stone being halfway along the road wall. We lined up and marched into school and were not allowed to talk in school unless told to. We had prayers and a hymn first thing and sang prayers each afternoon before going home. Empire Day was always celebrated with lessons about these countries, and a display of labels and wrappers from food and fruit from the empire which we collected for weeks beforehand. St George's Day was also celebrated. On 11th November, Armistice Day, we were always reminded why it was held and observed one minute's silence. Any important day was talked about.'

LEATHER BOOTS AND KNICKERS

'We went to the village school in Pentney and the girls all wore clean white pinafores over their dresses. Apart from the normal lessons the girls learned to cook and the boys learned woodwork. Some boys wore brown linen hats with a drawstring, issued by the "dicky nurse" who came every six months, because they had ringworm. We used to walk nearly three miles each way to school. I wore leather boots with strong soles.

The cane was frequently used at school, and when we got home and Mum found out about it we went to bed without tea.

On one occasion coming out of school a man was standing at the gate handing out goldfish for old rags. I wanted one of those fish very badly so I went back into the school and found an old sock. I went home very proud of this prize and showed the fish to my mother. Knowing I had no rags to do this exchange she promptly turned me upside down to discover if I still had my knickers on or had I given them as rags. I am pleased to say she found me correctly dressed.'

WE HAD TO BE THE BEST

'Watton had two schools in the 1930s, senior and junior. I enjoyed school. The academic timetable was rigid, but we did craft work on some afternoons – no painting, but bead-weaving, canework, marbling etc, and also knitting and needlework. I could "sew a fine seam" by the time I was seven. I remember turning up the hem of a nightdress the wrong way. The headmistress wasn't very pleased with me, nor with my teacher. I was lucky to escape being caned. This was the norm for the children who couldn't attain the standard of excellence required. Even the country dancing team had to be the best. If we dared to come second at the County competition at St Andrew's Hall we were made to feel that we had let the school down.

Sadly, my father died when I was nine. No support services in the 1930s, but when, at ten, I was awarded what was then called a Junior County Scholarship, there was no question but that I should take it up. My friend and I left our homes at 7.30 am to walk to the station to catch the "Crab and Winkle" at 7.50. On our first morning we were given a lift in a milk-float – a jolting ride, rather like the old cakewalk on the fairground. School finished at 3.35 pm and we had a prep period until five, when we walked to the station in a crocodile for the 5.30 train. Home by 6.30, then tea and more prep. By that time we should have been too tired to watch TV had it been invented! At great personal sacrifice my mother saw me through Thetford Girls' Grammar School, as it was then, and on to teacher training college. In those days you could have a loan from Norfolk Education Committee, which was deducted from your salary when you started teaching. You were obliged to teach in Norfolk until the loan was paid off. Grants were a post-war innovation.'

A VERY HAPPY EXPERIENCE

'School in the 1930s was a very happy experience at Whittington. We had two teachers, Miss Dora Prouton who lived at Swaffham

Playtime at South Walsham school in 1935, a typical village school hardly changed from their parents' time.

and drove an Austin 7 and Miss Hind who lived in the next village at Stoke Ferry. Having started school at three years (nearly four) to keep up numbers, my school life spans several years. The age range at the village school was four to 14.

Cowrie shells were used for counting and we traced our letters. Miss Hind had a pack of cards which had the letter on one side and a picture on the reverse. We ran through these every day. After learning our letters and how to build words we advanced to double letter sounds on a word board. When we could read, a reward for finishing our work was choosing an Enid Blyton Sunny Story.

There was a cupboard which housed a large selection of wooden puzzles, all in chocolate boxes or similar. These had been made by the "big boys" with a fretsaw in their handicraft lessons. These were used in the afternoons as was Matchbox meccano and plasticine. We wove baskets and sewed National Saving Thrift cards as well as trying our hand at knitting. The very young had boxes of coloured

132

bricks of different shapes and sizes which had to be fitted back into the box each time. This was a maths experience of the greatest order especially for a four year old. Most afternoons we sang nursery rhymes, danced or did group reading.

The icing on the cake was the school concert which was held every other year in the next village. This was a treat for everyone. "Concert dresses" came out of mothballs, were measured and passed on to the next-in-line – luckily we were all girls – ten of us and I was fourth in the line. The dressing-up box at school always caused great merriment as it was sorted out, and some parents, especially my mother, helped with the costumes under Miss Prouton's guidance. There was a whole evening's entertainment of sketches, songs, rhymes, dancing and the "big play". Having a set of redundant top hats at home my mother made the horse's head for "Widdecombe Fair" with an old tweed coat. He had great big teeth, big eyes and a tongue hanging out. A school bench padded out with sacks of straw and covered with a horse blanket made the body. I remember the audience clapped and clapped. The morning of the concert, a Saturday, we would walk to the hall over a mile away (with our hair in rag curlers tucked under a beret) for a rehearsal. There was a bucket toilet partitioned off in the changing room.

When we were seven or eight we progressed to the big room which was divided from the little room by a glass screen which could be folded back. When the doctor came to examine us the screen was curtained over as examinations took place in the little room.

Apart from covering the basics Miss Prouton introduced us to all sorts of interesting things such as papier maché, oil painting on cork mats using a stencil, weaving, leather work and fretwork for the boys. The girls did knitting, sewing and embroidery. We learned sword, country and morris dancing in the summer. The Red Cross was covered too as we learned how to do the various bandages and how to make a sling. The older girls joined up with other children for cookery lessons in the next village.

Miss Hind unfortunately had to leave as she couldn't afford to live on ten shillings a week (not being qualified in the accepted sense) and a young teacher who could speak French took her place so French lessons were introduced. In the summer we were taken on nature walks, the highlight being the fen walks before the fens were reclaimed during the war.

When war broke out we converted a cave in the neighbouring farmer's field into an air raid shelter where we could carry on our lessons. The school expanded during this period, for a short while, as several evacuees arrived in the village.

Each Christmas there was a party with each parent contributing something. While we went home to change into our party gear the tree would be hung with presents for all of us, bought by Miss Prouton and her assistant. What excitement!

During the year we put our odd pennies into a blue National Savings book to help towards the annual school treat to Hunstanton. All the parents came but I remember one year when Miss Prouton took charge of us as another baby was imminent. This was the only time we saw the sea so it was a real treat. My memories of this are associated with biscuit tins of hard boiled eggs, new potatoes, and bright red apples. These outings of course finished when war broke out in 1939 but there were compensations as we went round the village collecting old iron as part of the war effort.

In the dark afternoons the hanging lamp would have to be lighted as school finished at 3.45. The caretaker was responsible for filling it with paraffin and cleaning the wick, as she was for lighting the fire in the corner of the classroom. When it was very cold we took turns sitting in the seats near the fire after doing some warming-up exercises.

When the dentist visited he parked his caravan in the farmyard opposite the school. It was a great privilege to be picked to help the dentist. The duties entailed mixing the fillings and emptying the pot holding the extractions!'

WARTIME SCHOOLDAYS

'West Bradenham school was closed in 1993, and as the building stood forlorn and empty waiting for a buyer to give it a new lease of life I took one last wistful wander through its now silent rooms which surely still echoed with village voices of – could it really be? – half a century ago.

It was during the years of the Second World War that I first entered that school at the tender age of just three years. Infants were taught by Mrs Slegg in the little room and those pupils of about eight years old moved on into the big room to be taught by the headmistress Miss Chambers, or "Polly Fluff" as she was always known outside the school premises, a nickname obtained when she first came to the village and wore an overcoat with a fluffy fur collar. There were just two classrooms, divided partly by a frosted glass panel which in 1993 still bore the imprint of the criss-cross paper stuck to the glass during the war to prevent splintering during bombing.

About 20 pupils attended the school, roughly divided between the two rooms, so there were never enough of us of any one age group to play any team games. Our PE lessons took the form of "drill" which consisted of various leg and arm exercises and manoeuvres using wooden hoops. In summer we also did country dancing, morris and maypole dancing to recorded music played on a portable wind-up

134

gramophone. When the gramophone needed rewinding the music became slower and slower and consequently so did our dancing.

Along one wall of the little room was mounted a long blackboard in front of which we infants pulled up our chairs and drew pictures. I can still remember how difficult a procedure this was as one could never make enough room for knees *and* lean forward to draw on the board. Another project of the infants was for us each to make and embroider a linen napkin to place on our desks when we had our morning milk. We each, boys as well as girls, had to hem-stitch the edges of a square of linen after which Mrs Slegg would draw the outline of an animal in one corner for us to chain stitch around. I had a pink dog on mine and my brother a black panda face on his – this was the emblem of a group of Polish soldiers billeted at West Bradenham Hall at the time. Another infant occupation was "fraying". We would each be given a small piece of material which we had to fray out into single strands; this was to be used by Mrs Slegg to stuff a mattress and pillow for a dolls' cot for the infants to use during play sessions, a project never completed during my time at the school as we couldn't get enough scrap material to fray and other stuffing material was unobtainable during the war.

Both morning and afternoon school sessions started with a hymn or grace and an evening prayer was always said at the end of the school day. I recall I was always pleased when Miss Chambers announced, "We will sing the doxology" – as a child I never knew what this meant but was only too thankful that it was a short hymn.

There was no electricity or running water in the village so the classrooms were lit by Tilley lamps and the outside lavatories, or offices as they were called, were across the unpaved playground. Anyone falling over in the playground and having a grazed knee, as often happened, would have the wound washed in cold water drawn from the pump after which iodine would be painted on with a small brush kept in the First Aid tin. Oh, how it did sting and the iodine stain remained long after the wound had healed.

Both the schoolrooms were heated by open fires – one in the little room and two in the big room, one at each end. When the weather was particularly cold the biggest boys would move our desks into a semi-circle around each of the fires so we could get a little extra warmth.

At Christmas time we children made paper chains with which to decorate the classrooms and the two teachers made large decorations with our wooden PE hoops. The hoops would be bound with coloured strips of crepe paper and attached to them would be about six lengths of coloured wool threaded and knotted through circles of coloured paper cut and crimped around the edges – again a wartime expediency. In a further effort to combat wartime shortages both our teachers made stockings for themselves. At each playtime and at any spare time before lessons began both Mrs Slegg and Miss Chambers would knit these intricately patterned stockings on four needles with very fine fawn coloured thread wound on a large spool which they would tuck under one arm while they knitted.

The education we received was very elementary but very thorough, especially the Three Rs. Looking back I would think it very similar to the education received by a Victorian child as our teachers were certainly trained during that era but were always very thorough, very strict and very fair.'

'When I went to school eight miles away at Downham Market we went on the service bus and had half an hour wait after school for the bus home. Some children had a cycle ride of several miles before catching the bus and on a route of ten miles there was no bus at all and the children cycled. No one complained.

We had a super staff at school. Parents were never seen at school but they did get a report each term, which they had to sign. A London school was evacuated to the area and we shared the school with them. We had it in the morning and in the afternoon had our lessons in various buildings and huts in the town. No one seemed to suffer – well, perhaps the staff did as they had to move round for lessons in all weathers.

Always starving, when we came out of school we would buy bread buns, which were not rationed, for a halfpenny each and with one in our pocket would surreptitiously break off a piece and eat it. No one would ever be seen eating or drinking in the street.'

POST-WAR SCHOOL

'There was no luxury of being driven to school at Bradenham by car or bus, we always had to walk whatever the weather. Consequently on rainy days we would arrive at school with soaking wet clothes. These would be draped over an enormous fireguard around a closed-in solid fuel stove where they steamed away all day in an effort to dry them.

In very cold wintry weather the crates of small bottles of milk which were left outside in the snow would be brought into the classroom by the children at morning break. You could always be sure that the top of the milk would be frozen so that the cardboard milk tops were always standing above the bottle necks on "ice columns".

On Pancake Day the teacher brought her primus stove and enough eggs, flour, milk etc for all the children to mix and cook their own

136

The country dance team relaxing after their performance at Sitfield primary school in 1952.

pancakes in the classroom one at a time. What patience she had and what fun we had. I don't think the authorities would look kindly on this hygiene/fire hazard today!

During primary school days we were always read an Enid Blyton story at the end of a Friday afternoon, and a pin could have been heard to drop as we listened to the stories of Mr Pinkwhistle and his friends. I remember walking home feeling that everything was all right after listening to such gentle innocent stories.'

RURAL SCHOOLS IN THE 1950s

'I must be one of the last people to have attended an "all-age school". Most pupils arrived in the infants' room of Stanhoe school aged five years, progressed to the big room of the long low building at seven years, and moved up through the desks until they left at 15.

The infants' room was small and cosy, with two large alphabet boards on the wall and an abacus for counting. There was also a harmonium. The big room housed the school piano, with a map of the Holy Land on the back, used by the rector on his visits for

137

scripture lessons. The juniors sat at one end of the room, in desks with fixed seats, and the seniors further up the room, with desks with inkwells. There were two iron stoves, one in the middle and one at the far end. This room also housed the library for the village when the Library Service started and villagers could borrow books for their own pleasure. There was one teacher in the infants' room, who had been there most of her working life. The big room was presided over by the head teacher who taught everyone from seven to 15 years, except when a student teacher was available, who would take a group by themselves.

We seemed to spend a lot of time reciting tables as a class, doing sums, drawing and scripture. But innovations did take place. Part of the playground and part of the field were dug up to make gardens tended by the big boys. We played games on the field too – netball and rounders, and we had a sports day with races, sack races and egg-and-spoon races.

I have vivid memories of sitting outside on the gravel at the front of the school in the sunshine, where the big girls taught me to knit; of going for nature walks down Church Lane as an infant; and of the coming of the telephone. It was black and sat on the mantelpiece, and every day one pupil had to take a turn to ring through to the next village to pass on the dinner numbers. I hated it, and to this day hate making phone calls!

But this idyll was not to continue. Two things broke it up, firstly the opening in the early 1950s of the secondary modern school at Hunstanton (now Smithdon High School) where pupils moved at eleven years of age, and secondly the eleven-plus examination. I was one of the few pupils to pass for the grammar school and spent the remaining years of my schooldays travelling to Fakenham, ten miles in the opposite direction to my village friends. It was a more divisive move than anyone could ever have known.'

'Sprowston Junior School was situated on School Lane and was a considerable contrast to the infants school when I transferred there in the 1950s. Whereas the infants school was a modern building, the junior school had been built in 1860. There were still outside loos that backed on to pigsties, so you can imagine what the smell was like.

Miss Read was in charge of the top class and also ran the girls' netball team. She drove a pale blue Austin A30 and she used to drive the whole of the netball team (seven of us) plus a reserve to the away matches. There would be three on the back seat with two on their laps, and two more on the front passenger seat with one on their laps. It was a good job we were never stopped by a policeman.

When Norwich City had the great FA Cup run in 1959 there was great excitement at the school, in part because one of the players,

Poringland primary school, 1935.

Bobby Brennan, had a son there. The replay of the semi-final against Luton Town was played midweek and one of the teachers brought in a wireless so we could listen to it. We were all very sad when Norwich was knocked out in the replay 1–0; they had to wait 30 years before they reached the semi-final again.

About this time rock and roll became very popular. My oldest sister was in her mid-teens at the time. I can remember my parents being very angry with her for wearing tight jeans. She was also banned from visiting a cafe that had a juke box!'

THE WORLD OF WORK

ON THE LAND

Farming was the backbone of Norfolk's way of life, many of the farms small family concerns where everyone from children to grandparents helped out. For those brought up to farm work, the life was hard and rewards few – and even going on strike brought little relief – but these were skilled workers who took a great pride in their abilities.

A FAMILY CONCERN

'Can your memories go back to the early 1950s before the by-pass was pushed through? Can you walk in your mind from Honingham village along the Hall drive, past the Red House on your left, the old Farm House on your right, round the corner between the chestnut trees and up the hill, where primroses and violets grew on the banks, so thick that you couldn't walk between them? You climb to the top of the hill, through the woods and down towards Old Honingham Hall standing to your right, in springtime with its backdrop of rhododendrons. Turn along the water fence, then up again past the bluebell-carpeted woods, climbing Hilly Holey up to Breck Farm, in those days a complete working farm, built in mellow red brick. A Norfolk barn with big double doors on both sides, to allow the air to blow through. Bullock sheds, a bullock yard, stables, tack room and cart sheds. Also, facing one another across the gate to the bullock yard were two brick cottages.

My grandfather, Mr Richmond, hired Breck Farm from the Estate, and it consisted of 112 acres. One cottage was occupied by my aunt and uncle, Mr and Mrs Rackham, and the other by Mr and Mrs Norman and their son, Alie. Mr Norman and Alie both worked for my grandfather. There was no electricity or piped water to the cottages; it was oil lamps and well water, with the washing done in a copper in the outhouse.

The animals fared better; their drinking water was pumped from a borehole by a petrol engine and taken in water carts to the field tanks. Quite a task in hot weather to keep up with their drinking. Our shire horses were kept at Breck Farm. When I can remember there were only two, Prince and Smart; even then they were outdated, superseded by the tractors and combine standing in the barn, and when one died we sent the other to Norwich Brewery to become a dray horse, so that he wouldn't be lonely.

J.B. Watson and his faithful dog Jip, with other harvest workers. Hand tools still took pride of place on many farms.

My grandfather farmed pigs at Breck Farm, running them out on the sandy breckland, before it became fashionable to do so. His pig huts were sturdy wooden sheds, built on skids, so that a horse or tractor could pull them to fresh ground. Not the lightweight Nissen huts of today. It was not all pigs. We employed six men on the two farms, Breck Farm and Village Farm, where we lived.

Sadly, Breck Farm is no more. Just Easton Estate field numbers. The old buildings were pulled down and only a water tank over the borehole can now pin-point the spot. But some of us can remember where once a working farm stood and, if you close your eyes, still stands, ageing in the Norfolk sunshine.'

'When my grandmother was expecting and ready to give birth, only the midwife was present. Grandad went milking as usual, he had a herd of 35 Jersey cows. Granny gave birth to a little girl she called Margaret and the midwife was ready to leave when Granny said she thought she could still feel a baby inside. The midwife checked and had to agree. Forty minutes later my mother was born, and was called Doris. When Grandad was told the news his heart sank for he could ill afford two extra mouths to feed. His father said cheerfully,

"Don't worry, bor, perhaps one of them will die!" They didn't, but had to put up with being put to bed in two drawers for there was no money to buy them cots.

Grandad had had to leave school at twelve because the First World War broke out and the masters went off to fight. His first job was as a milk boy in Wisbech. He went out with a pony and trap, ladling out the milk from churns into pots provided by customers. There were two rounds daily and one on Saturday afternoon. One lady never washed her jug and used to put her coins in it to pay for the milk.

On the farm there were many animals around apart from the stock. Four or five cats lived in the barn to keep the mice down. They were not fed except for a daily pie-dish full of stale bread soaked in milk which was put down for them with a shout of "Here cats! cats! cats!" Being semi-wild they could hardly be called "kitties". They were always fighting amongst themselves and producing endless kittens.

The pigs on the farm had no names except for the boars. There were always two: Big Charlie and Little Charlie. Big Charlie did all the siring and Little Charlie was to be his replacement if he should suddenly develop a weakening of interest in his work. If Little Charlie grew rather big and was still not needed he would go for bacon and a new Little Charlie would be kept aside in case of need. You cannot be sentimental on a farm.

The dogs too were of the utility type. They kept the rat population to an acceptable level. Winkey and Binkey were Jack Russell terriers, so was Sting who was not supposed to be a pet but won the heart of my mother and her twin sister, who used to dress up the dog in dolls' clothes and push it around in a pram.

Grandad had an old sheepdog called Jip who followed him everywhere. One morning he went to Fakenham to the ironmonger's and got talking to the owner. Jip had been told to sit outside and wait. After a couple of hours, Grandad went home to his chores. At five o'clock the owner of the shop noticed the dog sitting there and recognising it rang Grandad to come and collect it. He had left the shop by the back door, completely forgetting the dog sitting at the front. His regard for Jip increased tenfold.

The farm had Elsan toilets which were emptied once a fortnight and always at lunchtime. The man who carried the pails out always ate a jam sandwich while doing so. Despite this lack of hygiene he was never ill and lived well into his eighties.

During harvest my mother and her twin sister would be given a job. A long and narrow net would be set up at the end of the field, and armed with a stick each they would wait for the reaper to come their way, flushing out rabbits and hares which would then get caught in the net. Their job was to "finish them" with the sticks.

144

Other children would be doing the same at the other end, and dogs flanked each side to steer the quarry into the nets. You could get a dozen rabbits in a day. These would either be sold to the butchers or put on a train to London. Grandad sold all his strawberries that way too. They would be picked by gangs of ladies who had to be careful to pick with the stalks on, putting the fruit into punnets made of thin woven wood strips.'

FLITTING DAY

'In the late 1920s to 1932 I lived in East Lexham village, about four miles from Castle Acre where I was born. My days as a small child in that delightful village were happy times, the little village school where I started my schooling we could walk to in minutes. In the springtime the pastures, dykes and banks were adorned with many wild flowers not seen by the children today. A river ran right through the centre of the village through a swampy pasture-ground that used to be a mass of yellow king-cups. This was just across the road from the house we lived in.

At Michaelmas each year you or your employer might decide you were to "flit" – this applied mainly to the farming fraternity. Your parents would apply for a new job and 11th October would be the day for you to leave your present home and move on to the new address, or new village. Your china and valuables would be packed in large teachests, everything carefully put away ready for the day of the move. The night before, all the beds would be dismantled and we would sleep on the mattresses on the floor of the bedroom, ready to get a very early start the next morning. The reason for this was because your furniture and all your household belongings were transported to your new destination by horse and waggon: your outside things like garden tools etc were packed on to a tumbril (a smaller version of the waggon) which was also horse-drawn, and as you can imagine it might take quite a few hours to reach your new home. The waggon was always loaded so as to leave a space at the back for mother and children to sit and ride as there was no other transport.

For me this story relates to around 1932. I would then have been about nine years old. Along with my two brothers we left East Lexham to arrive at a little hamlet between Stanhoe and Burnham Market, in the region of 20-odd miles away – it seemed the other end of the earth to us. The waggon with its two horses, a harness and a trace horse, usually travelled in front, with the tumbril following on behind. Well, the horse that was pulling that was quite a lively character, his name was Trimmer. Frothing at the mouth and snorting he insisted on being right up near the waggon, frightening us all as we sat there not being able to move, and because we were so terrified the driver decided to give him rein and he took off at a considerable speed for a cart horse, causing great havoc to the load he was transporting, resulting in the chest of drawers and goodness knows what else being strewn in the road. That was a memorable flitting day.'

THE WORK WAS HARD

'I lived at Flitcham and at 14 years old in 1924 started work at Brereton's Farm and was put to scaring crows. My wage was five shillings a week. I lived with my mother in a cottage with no running water. This had to be drawn from a well nearby which served all the neighbouring dwellings. There was one fireplace and when money was very short we resorted to an oil stove and some kindling collected from the forest. Coal was only a shilling a hundredweight. The rent was £3 18s a year. To augment the meagre wage, I went poaching regularly, catching pheasant and rabbit which, with vegetables grown in the garden made a good nourishing stew. Dumplings were added occasionally from flour and yeast by the local baker for a penny or two. I paid two shillings and a penny into the Odd Fellows each week which gave us ten shillings a week if a doctor was needed.

Work started at 6 am, a break called nineses with bread and jam and cold tea, then more work until midday – half a loaf of bread with meat or cheese, a slice of fruit cake and an apple, followed by a Woodbine cigarette (a penny for five). Work finished at dusk and I went home to a hot dinner.

The work was extremely hard and I learned to manage the three horses, how to plough, threshing, stacking, and cutting turnips. Three horses and a waggon took corn, barley and wheat to King's Lynn, some to be taken by train and some by boat, which I had to tip into the hold from sacks as a hand levelled it in the boat.

As a Christmas present I received two shillings and sixpence which was then taken back for having Christmas day off! There was no transport in the village so a bicycle was essential for work and the occasional visit to a public house.'

'Work was mostly hard where I was brought up at Claxton, but that was an accepted thing, as was the fact that some people had to work all their lives for very little reward while others did not work at all. Most men worked on farms. Some served apprenticeships and were qualified blacksmiths, carpenters, bricklayers etc. A premium had to be paid for an apprenticeship, which usually was four or five years, during which the apprentice was bound to work for very little in

146

return for learning his trade. Even after that his wage was not very high, but higher than the farm labourer who might get no work and no pay in bad weather.

Girls usually went into domestic service and were prepared to work very hard. Their children were mostly well brought up and their homes well kept. Married to farm workers, they managed their low income with great skill and very hard work – washing, cooking, mending and cleaning. Perhaps large families living near one another made for happiness.'

'The horseman's day on our farm at Titchwell began at 5.30 am, in the stables feeding and grooming the horses and harnessing them ready for work in the fields at 6.30. The men would take food with them for breakfast, which was eaten between 8 am and 8.30, and dinner, 12 noon to 12.30, eaten under a hedge, and then back to work until 4.30. After taking the horses back to the stable, feeding, watering and cleaning them, he would go home for a hot meal, then back to the stable at 6.30 to rack up for the night, spreading clean straw in the stalls and seeing the hayracks filled and giving the horses another feed.

Saturday was a half day but the horses still had to be seen to in the evening, and twice on Sunday. The horseman had to be skilled in the use of all horse-drawn implements such as reapers, binders, haycutters etc.'

Harvest time was the 'crowning of the year', when the whole family worked together in the fields, as here at Caston in 1928.

147

WHEN WE WENT ON STRIKE

'When the depression in agriculture occurred just after the First World War, farm workers' wages fell by ten shillings a week to 36 shillings for a 50-hour week. During 1922 wages dropped to 25 shillings a week for 50 hours, but when in 1923 farmers wanted to make a further cut in wages and increase hours to 54, the Farm Workers Union called the men out on strike. This was mainly confined to Norfolk and the men were to stay out until wages were maintained at 25 shillings for 50 hours' work. This meant great hardship for the workers who were down to six shillings a week strike pay. Fund-raising marches were held all over the county.

In Corpusty and Saxthorpe nearly all the farmworkers were out on strike. A body of men marched to a farm on the outskirts of the village, Holly Heath, to protest to the masters. They were met at the gate by one of the owners carrying a shotgun. He threatened to fire if they entered the yard. One or two ventured nearer, so he fired just over their heads. As one worker present said: "You should have seen them turn tail and run, their hats flying off in the wind." One foolhardy youth, Jack Keeler, was about to go and tackle the farmer and grab his gun, but was pulled back by an older man, Albert Platten, who said, "Leave him be. He is an old man and you have your life to live."

The farmworkers were very bitter as they felt they had been badly treated. The strike lasted about three weeks and the workers went back to work for 25 shillings, the farmers having been hard hit too for lack of workmen. Some of the men were given menial tasks to do when they did return to work.'

STRAWBERRIES AND PEAS

'Strawberries were the main crop grown on the allotments in the 1940s at St Germans. All year, people looked forward to the picking time, which lasted about three weeks if the storms didn't ruin them. The senior school pupils had to have half of the summer holidays to help pick the crop. No good saying you didn't want to go, the headmaster always knew if you missed a day. Those summers were boiling hot with thunderstorms most days. Many times we had to carry prams, cycles and the trays of fruit from the fields and along lanes on to the main road: tractors got stuck in the mud and I once saw a cartload of trays of strawberries topple into a dyke of dirty water. Some of the allotment holders took great care of their plots and kept them clean, others were full of thistles and nettles which made the work even harder. We all had "the strawberry walk", bent double, painful legs and thighs and a lot of sunburn.

One person stayed at the end of the rows to weigh the fruit and keep a check on each individual picker, and would also amuse the babies and children and give drinks etc. An old shed was shelter from the storm and it was a squeeze to get everyone in plus strawberries and prams. If it had been a good season one employer hired a coach for his pickers and families and sent them to the seaside for the day as a thank-you.

Pea picking came next and families all went along and children had a lovely time romping in the empty stalks.

The allotments have now been taken over by farmers and used for cereal crops, and there are very few big strawberry growers locally. All the jam factories are closed and most of the canning factories are gone too.'

HARVEST TIME

Harvest is a time most people look back to with great nostalgia. For those few weeks of the year it was essential, for the sake of the harvest and for the family budget, that everyone pulled together to get the harvest in, and even the school year was organised around harvest time. Horse power was still the norm on Norfolk's farms then, and many a young child proudly led these gentle giants to and from the harvest field. Later in the year would come threshing day, another time of great community interest. The coming of the combine harvester changed more than just a way of working, it heralded the end of a way of life.

THE CROWNING OF THE YEAR

'The word HARVEST stood out in all our minds in block capitals. It was a goal toward which the farming community at Caston had been struggling for months, ever since the seed corn had been planted. If all conversation did not consist entirely of harvests past and present, they all held some reference to it, and not just between farming folk, but the butcher, the baker and the postman too.

"The barley is looking well this year."

"Will the fine weather hold?"

"Barnham's don't look like being fit for another fortnight." So it went on.

It was a matter for congratulation to be the farmer who started

Threshing at Erpingham in the 1920s.

cutting first, but to be the last to finish was a disgrace too great to be borne. Everyone worked like mad to get the last stook to the last stack, then they could say triumphantly, "We've finished, all is safely gathered in."

Preparations were made for a smooth start. Scythes were made razor sharp, the sailer-reaper was dragged from a dark corner of the barn and all moving parts liberally smeared with cart grease. This came in a large can and looked and smelt like dirty lard, which I suppose it was as it was one of the products of the knacker's yard.

The kitchen came into its fair share of activity too. Home-brewed beer would be in great demand from the thirsty men in the fields. I remember one day Mother got out a large bread pot. It was the colour of mellow bricks, rough on the outside with a smooth glaze on the inside. In this she placed a muslin bag of malt and hops and poured on a quantity of boiling water. Yeast had to be added, but not till the liquid had cooled somewhat. Mother was in a hurry, so she decided to hasten the cooling process. She drew two pails of water from the well and fetching down the zinc bath that hung on the outside wall near the back door, placed it on the kitchen floor and poured in the icy water from the well, then lifted the heavy bread pot and its contents and placed it gently into the bath. Almost immediately there was a sharp report. We watched helplessly as the pot slowly parted in two and golden liquid mingled with clear water. It was no laughing matter at the time, all that lovely beer wasted and a good pot broken.

It was a colourful scene. The sky was bright blue, without a cotton wool cloud in sight. Trees darkened into the distance, and the cornfield was a biscuit-coloured sea that quivered gently in the heat. Here and there was a flash of scarlet as a poppy shone through. Everyone carries in their mind what to them is the most perfect picture. It could be a rose, a sunset, or a bird in flight. But to me a field of standing corn is the most beautiful sight in the world.

At last the wheat was declared fit to cut. The fields had to be "opened" which meant that they had to be mown round by hand to give passage to the sailer-reaper.

Father had taken his scythe and made a wide path round the field, mowing with rhythmic motion. Like all things done well, it looked so easy to the spectator. Every so often he had to pause to sharpen his scythe. He would take a carborundum, or rub as we called it, from his pocket and with every swing of his arm it bit into the steel blade, making a sharp swish, swish, that could be heard fields away. Then once more he bent to his task and the corn fell before him like a defeated army.

All was ready for the sailer-reaper. No ship on her maiden voyage was ever launched with more excitement than was felt for that well worn machine as it sailed through the gateway to cut our first field of corn. Two horses pulled it round the field with Harold sitting on a very uncomfortable looking seat, while the cut corn spewed out behind them in a never-ending ribbon.

Father gathered the cut corn into sheaves with his hands and making a kind of rope with a twist of straw, gave a deft tug, tied a knot and threw down a neat bundle that was a sheaf of corn. This he continued to do round the field. His shirt was dark with sweat and his hair clung to his head in damp curls. Jack and Sidney then stood the sheaves up in stooks or shocks as we called them, to dry in the sun. A shock was two rows of sheaves, about ten in all, standing head on to form an archway.

This made a lovely little tent for a child to play in if there were no thistles in that part of the corn field. Little girls didn't wear slacks in those days, which was a great pity.

Mother arrived with a large basket which contained the fourses. A very welcome break. We all sat down in the shade of a hedge with the exception of my brother Harold who was still seated on the reaper. I was glad to sit on an old sack by the wooden stand where the cutter bar was sharpened. The stubble was cruel to my short legs and they were red with scratches.

Dozens of tiny flowers were exposed to view now the corn was down, scarlet pimpernels, blue bird's eyes and of course, plenty of poppies and white cockle. There were patches of thistles on the headland, these must have been very unpleasant for the men

151

handling the sheaves.

Mother handed out food from her basket. Shiny golden brown home-made bread, spread with farmhouse butter, apple rolls sweetened generously with brown sugar and thick shortcakes. Everything tasted wonderful. Gyp sat as close as he dared, watching with anxious eyes for fear he should be left out of the feast.

A ladybird crawled over my boot. I studied it with great interest. Its scarlet wings with tiny black spots shone in the sunshine. "Ladybird, ladybird, fly away home, your home is on fire and your children are gone!" No, I didn't care for that old rhyme.

"Bishy-bishy-barny-bee,
Tell me when your wedding be.
If it be tomorrow day,
Take your wings and fly away."

That was much better, it held happier implications. But the little insect didn't fly away, but crawled under the sack to join its relations.

Mother picked up the empty basket and went home to collect the eggs.

The men continued to work in the corn field with the reaper going round in ever decreasing circles. There were cries of excitement as a terrified rabbit rushed out and made for the shelter of the hedge. Harold on the reaper could clearly see several more as the area of standing corn got smaller and smaller. His shouts could be heard over the clack, clack of the machine.

Then all at once the frightened creatures made a bolt for safety. It was the best thing they could do, for the enemy couldn't attack them all at the same time. But several met their deaths from blows from sticks. The bag was about a dozen rabbits and a hare. Mother and I hadn't the stomach for this kind of sport, so we were usually absent when the last rounds were cut.

My father and brothers came home tired and dirty, but the horses had to be fed and the pigs were shrieking their heads off. All the animals had a belated meal that night.

Father hulked the rabbits, giving the guts to the ferrets. The cats and dogs helped themselves, there was plenty for all and to spare. The rabbits were laid on the cold dairy floor, all were in good condition, but wouldn't fetch much money as rabbits were plentiful when farmers were at harvest.

The harvesters drank their cocoa and were so tired they almost fell asleep before their heads touched their pillows, to awake next morning to another day of toil.

The fine weather continued and each field fell to the reaper blade. Of course there were occasional stops for repairs, with Jack crawling under the machine with a spanner making the necessary adjustments. Jack was the mechanic of the family and was at his happiest with machinery he could take to pieces and with luck, put together again.

The waggon was pulled out of its resting place, the ladders put on its sides and as the corn ripened on the shock it was carted into the stackyard to await the thatcher and the threshing tackle.

A ride in an empty waggon was a thrill. I was lifted into it as it left the stackyard and returned to the corn field for another load. The waggon bumped over the rough ground and I bumped with it, standing on the floor of the waggon with chaff and grains of corn shuffling under my feet. The harness creaked as the horses plodded on and the dry smell of straw pervaded my nostrils. Father sometimes put me on Beauty's back but I didn't like it much, I was so far off the ground and the horse's back was hard and damp with sweat.

Sidney was the boy who "halloed hold gee". He sat on the horse's back as it pulled the waggon from shock to shock. There was one man on the ground passing sheaves of corn with a pitchfork to another man on the load and as each shock was gathered up, Sidney called out "Hold gee" to the man on the top of the waggon to let him know they were moving on, for he was in a very precarious position as the load got higher and higher and could have fallen off if caught unawares as the horses started with a jolt to get to the next row of sheaves.

And so the harvest was gathered in as a brilliant August made way for a golden September.

Wheat and barley realized about 16 shillings a coomb that year.'

HOW GEE OR HOLDYER

'Until the farms had tractors the farmworkers were paid for the harvest, not by the week, so the quicker they gathered the harvest in the more money they had. When I was nearly eleven years old I used to go in the field behind my father, when he mowed round the field before the binder came in. I gathered up the corn he had cut and tied it into shoves [sheaves]. After the corn had been cut by the binder we went with the men to set the shoves into shocks. There were six wheat shoves or ten oat shoves or ten barley shoves to a shock. When they started carting the corn I rode as a "holdyer boy", holding the horses still while the shoves of corn were being placed onto the cart. When my father put the thatched roof onto a stack he had me up there to help as I was lighter than the men. When the harvest was over we had a day out at the seaside, usually Great Yarmouth.'

153

'My father was a farmer around Bradenham and every year I looked forward to harvest time when I could be "how gee" girl. This would entail riding on the horse's back and driving the waggon from one shock to the next. The waggon was quite long and there would be two men on the waggon and two men pitching the shoves up to them. There was quite an art in loading these waggons as the shoves could easily fall off if not stacked properly. The loaded waggon was then taken to the stack and the empty waggon returned for another load. There were usually four to six waggons operating at one time.

At four o'clock we stopped for tea, known as "fourses". At tea time we took the horses to the nearest pit for a drink. I always felt I might quite easily slip down the horse's neck into the pit myself. One horse I remember well – his name was Strawberry and he had belonged to my uncle and been used as a dray horse in London, with the result that he never walked but always tried to pull the waggon at a slow trot.'

THRESHING DAYS

'Towards the end of the year an exciting event took place – threshing the corn.

"It's coming, Dad" – we would rush out to meet the fiery monster as it trundled up the farm road. The engine driver would wave and we ran behind the very long load. It was no easy task to manoeuvre such a length through gateways and position it by the first stack. Standing in readiness was a tank of water and a huge heap of large shiny black coal that it would consume. The neat thatch that had protected the corn from the weather had been removed and action stations were taken. Men stood on the cornstack, feeding the sheaves into the drum which hummed and throbbed as it separated grain from chaff. The straw was taken by conveyor belt up an elevator (always painted a pretty pink) to form a straw stack that would be used for winter bedding. The golden grain poured into strong sacks, was weighed and stored in the barn until it was sold.

We loved the smell of the engine, the noise and the dust. The engine driver in his blue jacket and black leather cap was in charge of operations and his word was law. He spent the whole day with a rag in his hand, polishing and listening to the rhythm of his tackle. If we were lucky, he would lift us up into the engine and open the furnace door to see the roaring fire, but we were never allowed to touch anything or play near the engine.

As the cornstack became less and less rats and mice scampered out in all directions. Now was the time for dogs of all sorts and sizes to show their mettle. The experienced ones, with a nip behind the head, killed one rat after another and very few escaped. My brother and I kept well away, just in case any of the tales we had heard about rats were true.

After all the stacks had been threshed, the tackle made an impressive departure to a neighbouring farm.'

THE COMING OF THE COMBINE

'Word quickly spread round the village in the late 1940s that "Ole Harrold" (he was probably all of 40 years old!) had a new thing to cut the corn. This bright and shining monster with "Massey Ferguson" written on either side arrived at the barley field, ready for action. Oh dear! It was too big by far to get into the field. The gates were taken from their hinges, posts were uprooted, then with a scraping of edges it made its way finally into the field. What happened to the field gate and posts? – someone's kindling wood, I expect. What a sight it made with its driver aloft, churning out straw and muck, but where was the grain? Soon an old tractor and trailer pushed alongside, and down the long funnel gushed the golden grains, ready for the barn. Gone were the sheaves of corn which many a child had made into a fort or den, gone forever. Gone also days spent with cold tea, waiting, armed with sticks, to run the rabbits down. The aroma of the harvest rabbit roasting in the wall oven lingers, but myxomatosis put an end to that as well.'

IN SERVICE

While most young country boys went to work on the land, young girls went into service. From great halls to modest farmhouses, servants were in demand until well into the 1940s, and there were few other opportunities open to women in those days. It was just as hard a life in the house as it was out on the land, and experiences differed greatly – what a difference a 'good family' made to these children away from their homes for the first time.

A SERVANT GIRL'S STORY

'I was born in 1898 on the 17th December; my mother had six boys and then me, two sisters and another brother. We lived in a very nice cottage at the Wood Farm, St Faiths (which is now the aerodrome).

My mother used to do the horse-hair weaving, she had a loom

at home and she taught me to do it. When my baby brother was two and a half I had to stay at home so that my mother could finish weaving and take it to Norwich to sell at 17s 6d or £1 for 21 yards. That would buy four or five pairs of boots for us children. One day a man came, Mr Fox was his name, he wanted to know why I had not been to school. My mother told him she had to finish her weaving to buy us some boots. He said, rather than stay away I had to take my brother with me to school, so I took him in a pushchair with my two sisters.

I left school at 14, that was a year before the First World War. My father would not let me take up weaving, although my mother had already taught me to do this, so I went as a servant day girl at the Wood Farm for a few weeks, then I went as a kitchenmaid at a school at Old Catton. There were five in the family, 35 boys at the school and five servants. I had to get up at 6.30 am, clean out and light the fire in a big black cooking range to get the water hot for the baths, take the cook a cup of tea, put a big iron saucepan on for the oatmeal porridge, clean the kitchen floor over on my knees (no mops in those days), then help with the breakfast. When all were served the servants had their breakfast. Porridge, toast and dripping and a cup of tea. Then the washing up, oh dear, what a pile of plates and dishes and all the cooking pots, I thought I should never get through them.

After that it was time to start preparing the vegetables for the midday meal. When this had been served and everyone fed, the Master would cut us one slice of meat each, a few vegetables, and we also had a pudding. Then washing up again. It used to take me all afternoon at first. I then had to clean up the scullery and start again on the vegetables for the supper. We had a tea in the afternoon, bread and jam and a piece of cake if there was any stale cake left. For supper they had soup, a meat or fish dish and a pudding. We had what was left over and then all the washing up once again.

I was allowed an outing once a week, 3.30 to 7 pm. I would walk home which took me half an hour. Mum used to be busy but we always had a cup of tea and a chat, then I would help her with the evening meal for my father and brothers then walk back to work again. In the winter my father would go with me, as it was a very lonely road, although he had already had a very long hard day on the farm, from 6 am to 6 pm for twelve shillings a week. He looked after the bullocks, milked the cows, and helped rear all the turkeys for Christmas, which he used to pluck and dress and take to Norwich to sell in the market, so at this time of year he could be working until 10.30 at night. We used to have a great big turkey at Christmas and we had turkey dripping for weeks after, lovely yellow fat. My father was a short fat man and weighed about 15 stone then but more later in life.

I had a half day on Sundays every other week and after I had been there six months I bought a bike from a gardener's wife who was too nervous to ride it. I paid two shillings and sixpence a month for it and she let me have it for 50 shillings. My wages were 16 shillings a month, from the 1st to 31st, and out of that I had to buy house shoes every month, which were two shillings and elevenpence, black stockings and white aprons and outdoor clothes. I also had to pay my mother back for the clothes she bought me to start work in.

In the summer we would go into the garden to pick the fruit to bottle and make jam. There was a lovely garden there, all kinds of fruits, raspberries, peaches, apricots, all kinds of apples, and they had a large greenhouse with a grapevine. There was only one gardener and a boy and they kept the whole house supplied with vegetables and fruits. The cook would tell him each day what she wanted and they would bring them up to the kitchens. The gardener's wife had a laundry and she did all the household washing and ours, this would come back ironed and all the caps and aprons starched, how hard those women worked in those days.

The cook was very strict. One day I made a pot of tea in a big enamel teapot for the maids and put it on the table, she stirred it with a tablespoon and then put the hot spoon on my arm because I had my elbows on the table. She said, "No joints without the dishes." I had a bad burn on my arm for weeks. The Mistress told her off for doing this. I often felt like putting some Epsom salts in her tea when I took it up in the mornings.

I was there in 1914 when the First World War started, what a difference it made. The students had to go to Sandhurst when they left school as they were 18 to 20 years old: they were all sons of the wealthy and had lovely clothes. Unfortunately many of them were killed during the war and the Mistress used to look in the paper every morning to see the reports of the soldiers and sailors who had been killed. I had five brothers in the army; two were killed in France in 1917, one of them was only 19 and just a year and a half older than me. What an awful time that was for everyone.

The cook left and I think she went to work in a munitions factory. We had another one who was no good at all, she had a barrel of ale in and was often drunk. I had to work harder still then as the other maids all left when the school was closed. This left us with just two maids, and the Lady got someone to come and train me to cook and she was also a very good cook herself. Well, as the war went on we did not have much food, only our rations. I used to have to make scones with barley meal or mashed potatoes, maize meal bread and flaked rice milk puddings. We used to burn barley and put it in the coffee mill and grind it to make coffee, it did not taste too bad. They also bought goats so that they could have milk and cheese.

When they sold the house and all the cottages that went with it, and bought a house in Surrey, they asked Louisa and me to go with them as we were the only two maids left, but Louisa got married and her husband went back to France and was killed a month later, and I went into service at a large Hall. Louisa and I remained friends until she died in 1977, in fact she was more like an older sister to me.

When the Armistice was signed there was a party in the park for the village people. I made huge cakes and cooked large joints of meat for that in a great black coal-fired cooking stove; this was a very happy time. It was a lovely place and I stopped there for about a year, and while I was there I was confirmed by the Bishop of Thetford.

Then I met my husband and went on a temporary basis to a house where there were two children, a boy and a girl. There were just two other maids and I found myself cooking a seven-course meal every night. They were very nice people but the Lady was very strict with the little boy and he would run to me and hide under my apron when his mother was chasing him with a stick. I wonder if he remembers that now. But I was very happy there.

I was married in 1920 when I was 21 as my father would not let me marry until I came of age.'

WE HAD OUR BRIGHT MOMENTS

'I left school in 1921, when I was 14 years old, and when I was 15 I had my first job as a nursemaid for a very nice couple. The mother was very ill and had to have a lot of care and attention. I helped to look after the baby, learning to bath, feed by bottle and change nappies etc in a lovely nursery. My wages were two shillings and sixpence a week.

I enjoyed this very much but unfortunately for me, the mother recovered in the spring and they moved away. I then got a job in Walsingham in a fruit and vegetable shop. I was "maid of all trades", serving in the shop, seeing after three children and doing the housework. This was really hard work and long hours. I lived at home with my parents but had a sparse lunch with my employers, my wage again being two shillings and sixpence a week.

I decided to change my job and applied for one in Norwich. I thought this would be different and it was! There was one other maid, a girl from Ber Street and she did most of the dirty work. We were up at 6 am each morning and went to bed at 10.30 pm. We had to wear a uniform – a print dress, white apron, mob cap and hessian apron in the mornings, but I had to change to serve lunch and wore a black dress, small white apron, white cuffs and small white cap.

We shared a bedroom right at the top of the house. It is true, however, that we had a bed each. The mistress was very unkind and nothing we did pleased her. She would place a sixpence under the carpet to see if we had swept the dirt under. Of course, we had no vacuum cleaner, it was all done with a brush and dustpan. Still we had our bright moments. It was a treat to take a hare down to the butcher's to be skinned and jointed! I received three shillings a week at this time.

I was very unhappy working there and one day my brother in law arrived to take me home. This caused quite a sensation as he went to the front door of the house (servants used the rear) and said that he had called for me and my luggage and marched through the house and up to the attic to get my trunk. Katie decided to leave as well and she was delivered to Ber Street, the lady of the house no doubt having an attack of the vapours. I vowed then that if I ever married and had a daughter she would not go into service.'

FARMHOUSE AND POST OFFICE

'When I was 14 I left school and went into service in a farmhouse a few miles from home. Mother couldn't afford to buy me a uniform so came to an arrangement with my employer that *she* would provide it and pay me four shillings a week instead of the usual five shillings until it was paid for. The uniform consisted of two blue print dresses for morning wear, a black dress for afternoons, about half a dozen large white aprons, three or four check ones and a couple of hessian ones to be worn when scrubbing, half a dozen white caps and three pairs of sleeves (white, elbow length). The aprons and the sleeves were made by the mother of the girl I was to work with and whose bed I would share. She was a nice friendly girl and we got along well together. I don't think my employer ever paid her mother for making the aprons etc for which the charge was just over £1 and that included the price of the material.

My employer decided to call me by the name of the girl whose place I had taken. Her name was May, which also happens to be my middle name, and I never did like it, so quite often I would not hear when I was called. It wasn't long before I was being called by my proper name and it was surprising how soon my deafness disappeared.

On my first day I was introduced to the children of the family and instructed to call them "Miss this" and "Master that".

I had quite an area of scrubbing to do – it seemed like an acre or two to me, and one day the Mistress said to me, "You are such a good scrubber I'm going to raise you sixpence." "Hooray," I thought, "now I shall be getting four and sixpence a week." Not likely: when

159

pay day came I received 16 shillings and sixpence instead of the 16 shillings I had been getting. We were paid on the first day of each month if we were lucky, as very often it was a few days late. So, like that I was really getting three-ha'pence a week for all my beautiful scrubbing.

I used to pay my poor mother two shillings each month for doing all my dirty washing. Incidentally, my mother used to come to do the household washing every week, and one week had 19 sheets to wash besides the usual family wash. These were new sheets the Mistress had made and had to be washed and laid out in the sun on the big lawn to bleach. Mother received her usual half-crown for this lot and not a penny extra as I remember. All washing was done by hand – there was no washing machine.

Our postman put me on to my next job. A girl was needed to live in at the post office and shop in the next village to deliver letters twice a day and do the housework. The postmistress, a lady in her sixties, seemed nice enough. When I went for the interview I told her I had only been getting 16 shillings and sixpence a month even after nearly two years. She said she would give me nine shillings a week. I was delighted, and felt I was in clover at last, especially when she let me out through the shop and handed me a fistful of toffees on the way. "It's going to be all right here," I thought, but they were the first and last sweets she ever gave me from the shop or anywhere else!

After I'd done the housework and delivered the letters I chopped up boxes from the shop for kindling, weeded flowerbeds and vegetable patches in the garden. It was also my job to cut the "gwass" about twice a week but first I had to "scwape" all the stones off the "gwass" with my fingers so that they would not damage the cutter. I had to get down and go round the edges of the lawn knocking off any gravel which might have bounced off the path on to the grass as people walked by. On Saturdays it was my job also to rake the gravel paths. One day I became over-zealous and trimmed the grass around a flower-bed in the middle of the lawn to a rounder shape. The lady didn't think much of my efforts and sent me over the hedge where we threw the rubbish to hunt for the pieces and fit them back again!

Cakes went in and out of the dining room until the family were sick of the sight of them, then they were put into the old dark green casserole that was my "cake dish". I'm afraid I wasn't very often tempted by them and would throw them out and let her think I had eaten them.

On Saturday evenings she would get me to help her weigh up ounces of shag tobacco. I was shown how to cut paper from the *Radio Times* to the correct size to hold one ounce. Then she would

160

weigh the tobacco ounce by ounce and place it on my papers for me to do up as she had shown me. She could get 16 full ounces from the pound, weighing to the last tiny shred on her little scales.

I couldn't have a proper half-day off during the week as I had to deliver the afternoon post, but if I liked I could get someone from the village to do it for me, but I had to pay them a shilling so I couldn't often afford to do that. When the daughter and her family came on my Sunday off, I had to wash the lunch dishes and then take the two children for a walk before I could go home. I served as an errand girl when she decided to retire and have a house built at a nearby seaside village. I had to take messages to the estate agent at Sheringham and bring back replies. She didn't mind me taking a friend along for company on the long bicycle ride, and, wonder of wonders, I remember she once gave me a shilling!'

I CRIED MYSELF TO SLEEP

'In my young days the school leaving age was 14. My father was adamant that I should go into domestic service in spite of my mother's protests. There were domestic agencies where one went to see what posts were available, and in this way a position was found for me quite a distance from home.

There were several maids and gardeners employed, and I had to start at the bottom as a kitchenmaid, doing all the menial jobs. The cook was very fond of showing her authority and I was really a slave to her, as she was always giving me orders, and I expect you would have called me a drudge as I always seemed to be cleaning, scrubbing or washing up.

No modern facilities in those days. A shared bedroom with other members of staff, only a candle for light and no heat in the room, which was very sparsely furnished and situated in an attic at the top of the house. Up at 6 am each morning to clean the kitchen range and prepare the ingredients for breakfast before the cook came on the scene. I cried myself to sleep many times, as I missed my mother. I was allowed home once a month for two days. Travelling was by train and I had to forego my one half-day a week and save them up so I could have my visits home.

After staying in this post about two years I wanted to leave and improve my position, but I had to get permission from my parents first, also a reference had to be obtained from my present employer and if it wasn't satisfactory it would not be easy to get a post elsewhere. I again went to the agency, and had to give a month's notice from my present post, where I was treated most unkindly while serving my month. I finally left and started my new job near Norwich for the princely sum of £1 a month and my keep, which

161

was considered a good wage in those days. This was a much happier post, although I still had to accept many restrictions.'

YOU HAD TO MOVE ON

'When I first started work at 14 in Swaffham in the 1930s my wages were five shillings a week plus keep. If all went well at the end of three months the wages went up to £18 a year. The next rise after that was £24 a year but you had to move on to another house, that was how you got more money.

We were up at 6 am to light all the fires and carry coal upstairs to an invalid's room. We worked all day – in the morning we did the housework, in the afternoon we cleaned the silver and brass and prepared the evening dinner which was at 7.30 pm and consisted of three or four courses; we then washed up. At 10.30 pm we took the whisky and soda in on a silver tray, after which we went to bed. The food for ourselves wasn't very special, we certainly earned our money. One of the jobs we did at springcleaning time was to clean the carpets by soaking newspaper with water, shredding it up into small pieces and then throwing it over the carpet and leaving it for a short while. Then we went on our hands and knees and swept all the newspaper up and hopefully all the dirt. We had one half day off a week and every other Sunday, but we had to be in by 9.30 pm.'

A HARD LIFE FOR A YOUNG GIRL

'Domestic service in the 1930s was a hard life for a young girl. At the time there was no electricity laid on, so all the lighting consisted of oil lamps and candles. The working day would begin at 6 am when I rose from my attic bedroom. The first chore was to light the fires, then the carpets were swept with a brush and dustpan, which meant getting down on hands and knees. Hot water then had to be taken to all the bedrooms for the family. Following this, the breakfast table had to be laid. All of these jobs had to be completed by 8 am. Work through the rest of the day was endless. The day finished at 8 pm after supper. Time off consisted of one half day each week, and Sunday afternoons once a fortnight. All this for five shillings a week.'

'Among my memories of days gone by are those of leaving school and going to work at Barwick House as a housemaid in 1932. We had to be up at 6.30 am as all the downstairs cleaning had to be done before breakfast. I had one half day off a week and every other Sunday afternoon and evening, and had to be back in by 9.30 pm. My wages were £12 a year, so to buy a new coat or shoes meant saving about a month's wages. There were nine indoor staff there altogether. All in all they were happy days.'

'I was born in 1924 at Clenchwarton, then moved to Sporle in 1926 and to South Pickenham when I was twelve. My father was a farmworker and we lived in a tied cottage with water from a tap outside, tin baths for bathtime and an open fire with an oven at the side for cooking.

On leaving school I went into domestic service, which was long hours from six or seven in the morning till ten o'clock at night, half a day off every week and every other Sunday afternoon, having to be back in the house by nine o'clock. It was hard work scrubbing floors and polishing, and when there were shooting parties I have cleaned over 30 large copper water jugs with Brasso – it was hard work getting water spots off. Later I did the work of a parlourmaid, which was busier but easier.

I saw many hardships of girls in domestic service, especially when daughters of workers in tied cottages were more or less blackmailed to stay or else their parents would have been turned out of their homes.'

'I was born at Ludham in 1919, just after the end of the First World War. My father was team-man on Ludham Hall Farm and my grandfather was farm steward.

I would have liked to be a schoolteacher, but I passed the written part of the scholarship and failed the oral. Without a secondary education it was either shop work or domestic service, so when I left school I went into service at Ludham Hall. My wages were six shillings a week plus one shilling for my mother for washing my aprons etc. The most I earned was 15 shillings when I was 19. I had a half day off on a Wednesday and a Sunday off once a month and a few hours on other Sundays. I lived there for just over five years and had just one more job for six months before I was married at 20 to a threshing contractor. Women did not work after marriage in those days.'

'I left school in 1932 at the age of 14 and went to work for the butcher in Castle Acre. I received three shillings and sixpence a week for this. I had one half day off during the week and a half day every other Sunday. The butcher's mother was disabled and sat in an ancient bath chair in which I had to push her about. I was very small for my age and I could hardly see over the top.'

'I left school when I was 14. I was quite sad, but my parents could no longer keep me. The only jobs for girls were in domestic service, so I went to a farm at Fakenham. My mother got me a few clothes which were put in a tin trunk, and she walked me the two miles there with my little brother in the pram.

It was very hard work, being up at six o'clock in the morning to lay the fires, then out to feed the turkeys and chickens, then all day scrubbing, cleaning, and collecting and washing eggs to be packed to go away. The milk used to be brought up to the kitchen door twice a day from the cowsheds, some was sold at the door by dipping the measure into the churn and serving the people in their milk cans. The milk that was left was put through a separator to get the cream which would then be put into a butter churn, and I used to have to turn this a lot of times before the butter was ready.

I stayed there until I was 17, then I went into a gentleman's service, with a staff of seven. I was the under-parlourmaid. I served at table and looked after the gentleman's clothes. It was very different to the farm housework. By this time the war had started and I was married soon afterwards.'

WORK IN THE VILLAGE

Villages were practically self sufficient and many people found work locally. Some had more than one job, perhaps keeping the village inn as well as working in the smithy or running a smallholding. It was a time when farming was at the heart of all our lives, whether we ran the village shop or looked after the game on the estate.

THE VILLAGE INN

'My grandparents kept the Grapes Inn at Snettisham in the 1930s. I can remember the cleaning lady wearing a man's cap, her apron made from a hessian sack. She would sweep and scrub the bar floor, then sprinkle over a covering of sawdust every day. My grandmother had to bring the beer up from the cellar in jugs, and in cold weather the men warmed their drink with a red-hot poker from the fire.

My grandfather was always busy outside making horseshoes for he was the blacksmith and usually had several large horses in the yard waiting for new shoes. In the same area my father had a carpenter's shop; he was the wheelwright, making many different types of carts for local tradesmen, as all our deliveries in those days were made by horse and cart.'

'My Gran kept the Rose and Crown at Snettisham. I loved to turn the taps on of the large wooden barrels to fill the glasses with beer. One of my best memories is of the shooting season, when my Gran would cook 40 lbs of beef at a time for lunch for the beaters. The lunches were packed in wicker hampers, with large jars of beer and minerals. You can imagine the lovely dripping you would get from such large joints. This was the early 1930s when work was scarce and money was short, and people were very pleased to get a bowl of dripping. She also made lovely soup – I'm afraid the old dear liked a little tipple and some days if she was in a good mind she would give the soup away to neighbours, another day she would charge them fourpence. I had a wonderful childhood at the Rose and Crown. The field opposite, now full of bungalows, would hold fairs and a circus once a year. All the children would wait from early morning until the afternoon for the elephant to arrive.'

'The Three Horse Shoes at Titchwell was a free house and in the early part of the century consisted of a cellar, taproom and living space for the landlord and his family. The taproom had a wooden floor liberally covered with sand, and cast iron spittoons in convenient positions. The landlord would go down to the cellar to fill the beer mugs and glasses straight from the barrel. In the 1920s half the house was demolished and rebuilding began. When the new half was finished, the family moved across and opened for business while the rest of the pub was demolished and rebuilt. The landlord was also a smallholder, keeping pigs, bullocks and milking cows. At times he would drive to Hunstanton beach and load his tumbril with mussels, taking them to the "mussel lays" at Brancaster Staithe to mature. He also kept a pony and trap for hire.'

'The Bridge Inn at St Germans (demolished in the 1960s) was managed by my maternal grandparents and later by an aunt. This was a really old pub with a thatched roof, and used well water until the 1940s. The floors were uneven brick, and a huge wall oven, blackleaded cooking range, oil lamps and wooden closets furnished the interior. It was a popular meeting place for local men. The chief of the work was done by my aunt, lighting fires, filling lamps, and cooking for seven adults. One of them was a tramp called Charlie. He appeared one day, looking for work. Grandad set him on, Grandma found linen and Charlie bought a bed and a chair. He settled down and worked hard, ate with the family, but refused to sleep anywhere except in his shed. He kept this spotlessly clean, as he did himself and his clothes. He smoked a clay pipe and he helped with animals and crops. From time to time he would vanish, with no goodbyes, and we would think we would see him no more. He would return as if nothing had happened, bringing back something from his travels, and settle again. He was quite a character, well liked, popular with children too.

In the late 1940s and early 1950s many men were still in the forces. An old searchlight station was turned into a camp to house foreign university students who came to help with the fruit picking. There were many acres of soft fruit and later the orchards. The students spoke very little English. At night most of them met at The Bridge, sitting in groups and spilling outside on to the lane leading to the pub. They all had different tastes, some drank cider, some mixed brews. They sang and drank till closing time. I was kept busy trotting back and forth to the cellar and trying to sort out the money and the languages. Once a week all the local young folk were invited to a dance, held in a barn, sawdust on a concrete floor. We wore many pairs of sandals out during their stay.'

OSIER PEELING

'My aunt, now 95 years of age, remembers that as a young girl living at St Faiths she spent many days stripping the bark off willows for basket weaving – osier peeling, or as she said in her Norfolk dialect, "oosie pilin". The willows were kept in the beck to keep them moist and each girl wore a sack round her waist and pulled the willows through a device similar to a two-pronged fork to strip the bark. They were paid fourpence a bundle and it took them all day to do one bundle.'

APPRENTICE GAMEKEEPER

'In the early 1920s, as being a warrener and vermin killer on three farms in hand meant close contact with the estate keepers, I thought I'd join that fraternity. Easier said than done! Having good references and experience I found was no qualification to secure a keeper's post in those days. With few vacancies, employers were choosy: one had to be experienced or connected family-wise. Advertising throughout the eastern counties brought not one reply. I could have had a job with a farmer having his own shoot, but I wanted to get on a large sporting estate. Taking advice, I put an advert to try as head keeper's assistant and help on the rearing field in *The Gamekeeper*, which circulated countrywide. Receiving only one reply to go for an interview at Pond Hills, Hempstead, I got the job with immediate start.

Going early on Saturday, I was introduced to my lodgings, then shown round the head's partridge ground which I was to take over. After breakfast on Monday I met the other keepers by the aviaries

166

where rows of nesting boxes were lined up, and helped to take off the sitting hens. All were tethered, watered and fed, and after approximately 20 minutes put back on the eggs again. This was done daily till hatching was completed. Thousands of pheasants were reared annually, requiring a large field for rearing, which for my first season was a hay field, entailing much preparation in getting rides trimmed to set out rows of coops and to get the huts, two large coppers and all other gear there. As the young birds hatched, they were taken when dry and placed with given numbers to each hen in the coops.

My job was to do all cooking: literally hundreds of rabbits to skin, boil so flesh easily left the bones, and then mince; thousands of eggs to hard boil, then rub through a sieve; biscuit meals to scald and then all to be mixed in exact proportions with special meal. In those days pheasant rearing was a specialist job. With soft food one had to put down only as much as the birds would devour, no more, otherwise it would soon turn sour. Most keepers had their own remedies for any ailments, while today with dry feeding and modern medication it's so simple.

I was the fourth keeper on the estate. We each had to take our turn with night-watching while the birds were on the field, roughly eight

A great deal of work went on behind the scenes for a successful shooting party. This group from the 1890s at Gunton Hall includes Edward, Prince of Wales (centre).

167

weeks. Many a night I walked out and sat on a coop in the cool air to avoid falling asleep in the warm hut, and could hear the nightingale singing in the copse beyond. A large wood was opposite our field: as day began to break a cock blackbird would start to sing, soon to be followed by others and very soon the whole wood seemed alive with many species. It was my first experience of the real dawn chorus; it was great, but faded somewhat in June due to the many fledglings having to be fed.

I was fortunate indeed to get that job. My lodgings were at Church Farm. The people were marvellous, and it really was home from home. They had a son my age who saw after the horses, and we all got along fine.

Secondly, my head keeper certainly knew the whole job from A to Z, and being under him I had a lot to be grateful for. Until the birds were off our hands, so to speak, it was hard work and long hours, but he was fair to all and asked no one to do what he would not and did his full share.

With the young birds ready for the woods the gamecart driver brought his horse and trolley, which carried five stretchers at a time, each holding two coops complete with hen and chicks. So each load meant ten coops to the woods, then back for more. We worked from 9 pm till dawn for three solid nights and then did our usual day's work. I shall never forget going for my breakfast at the end of the third night – with my head nodding I was too tired to eat. My landlord, who had arthritis and was mostly at home when I went for meals, told me to lie on the couch and have a nap, promising to wake me in 15 minutes. True to his word, I was amazed how fresh I felt. I soon ate my food and was gone again. It took two nights the following week to clear the field.

As the young birds grew we lessened the cooking, bringing in split maize and wheat, which at first had to be steeped. After a time they began to wander and with a trained dog it was a constant job running them home. Our woods were very hilly with valleys, and the next stage was to prepare for shooting. The valleys had to be mown by hand (no machines) and we had to get a quantity of stakes to be numbered and placed for the guns. We ran out wire netting on the brow of the hills to stop the pheasants from running right down to their feet, and it was usually my job to go forward with my spaniel and flush the birds up a few at a time. At that time I daren't voice what I thought, but on looking back drives like that were not too special, though the drives out of one wood over valleys to another were more sporting, with the pheasants gathering both height and speed by the time they passed over the guns. After the day's shoot we had all the game to hang up and all the guns to clean, and then tea.

By starting at the foot of the ladder, I realized the advantages in later life more than if I'd gone in fully blown at the deep end.'

WHEEL SHOEING

'How many of you remember the yellow hand carts used by local roadmen in the days when every village had its own roadman? These men continually walked the roads keeping the verges tidy and the ditches and holes cleaned out and deep enough to take the surface water from the roads.

In the 1940s I used to spend most of my holidays and weekends staying with my aunt and grandfather at Martham. My grandfather was a builder and wheelwright, and several uncles and cousins worked for him. The firm also had its own blacksmith. One of the contracts they had was making roadmen's hand carts for Norfolk County Council.

The wooden carts and wheels were made by the carpenters and the iron rims for the wheels by the blacksmith. When the wheels were ready to be shoed, or shod, the iron rims were piled up and a bonfire built in and around them. Nearby was a huge iron disc, some five to six feet across, with a hole in the centre for the wheel hubs. When the rims were red hot, one wheel at a time was laid on the disc. A rim was removed from the bonfire with long tongs, dropped over the wheel and hammered into place. The ensuing flames were quickly quenched with buckets of water.

Wheel shoeing day was always regarded as quite an event and there were always plenty of onlookers.

When the carts were ready for delivery they had to be wheeled through the village to the railway station. Plenty of help was needed here as one person could only take one cart. This was no easy task for children who helped because if they didn't keep the handle high enough the legs hit the ground and the cart came to an abrupt stop.'

THE MILL

'My childhood was spent at Hardwick Mill near Long Stratton. My father was a millwright who made and repaired many windmill sails, including several local mills. Our post mill was burnt down in 1920, ten years before my parents moved to Hardwick in 1930 from Tasburgh water mill.

The new mill was built on top of the windmill's base, called the "roundhouse". It was run by a large oil engine, with a huge wheel that had a wide belt on it which set the rest of the machinery running and the millstones turning.

The local farmers used to bring their corn by horse and tumbril to be ground by the huge millstones, and would collect it a few days later ready to feed to their animals. I remember some of the particular sayings in conversation with my mother, who often barrowed the coomb sacks of meal to the mill door to be loaded on to the tumbrils. "Cartainly so ma'am, cartainly so!", or "Well, ma'am, the point is this, the point is this . . ." – wagging his finger, and "Well, tha'as like this here, ma'am!" and so on.

The mill became redundant in the early 1950s, and was dismantled in 1970 and the land sold for building, but the mill house is still lived in.'

THE CORNER SHOP

'A visit to a modern supermarket provides a startling contrast to the small corner shops of the 1940s and 1950s. My father had a shop in Gorleston with a sub post office attached.

All the fats, sugar, cheese and bacon had to be weighed. We even had to twist the blue sugar paper into cones before weighing up the half pounds of sugar. We sold everything, including paraffin; my father had made a rule that all the cans had to be left by 10 am. This reduced the necessity for handwashing to a minimum. However, as we sold greengrocery there were still the potatoes to be weighed up, and this meant that one's hands were virtually always in water.

Added to all the problems there were the rations to cope with. At one stage the bacon ration was a mere two ounces a week. Most people who lived alone saved up the ration until they could have a reasonable amount. However, two of our customers (elderly sisters who lived together) insisted on having their ration of bacon separately. One day, the elder sister rushed into the shop in a great state of anguish – she had posted her two ounces of bacon with the letters! I calmed her down and assured her that I would see the postman and return her bacon to her.

Most of our customers had sons in the forces and however difficult they found letter writing they sent them aerograms every week. The difficulty with these was that it was very hard not to read them. One of the funniest conclusions I remember seeing was "If God spears us", written as the writer, a true Norfolk woman, would have said it.'

'My father had damaged his arm during the Great War and he tried to make a living from a council smallholding but in the depression of the 1930s that wasn't easy, so when the shopkeeper and his wife at Barroway Drove both contracted tuberculosis, my mother and father opened a shop and took on the post office. Mother had had a good

170

education so managed the bookkeeping with ease. During the war my Saturday job (and on many evenings too) was to cut up the large blocks of butter, margarine and cheese into ration portions. We also sold bacon and what a job it was to keep the slicer clean. The bones had to be taken out of the bacon and we had them in pea soup. One thing we always had plenty of was soap powder. We just got a large supply in before it went "on coupon". Many customers came from other villages to buy their soap from us; not only did we have powder but blocks of Windsor brown and Fairy green that was often grated into the copper as the water began to boil.'

OTHER WAYS WE MADE A LIVING

There were, of course, dozens of other ways we made a living in the past, from fishing along Norfolk's coastline to working in a city shop. Here are just a few memories of times past.

SCOTS LASSIES AND FISHERMEN

'As a very young child in the late 1920s and early 1930s, my favourite walk was along the quay at Gorleston during the fishing season. The gutting sheds would have their shutters raised, and the brawny "Scots lassies" faced the bitter east wind, while they deftly gutted the "silver darlings" – the herrings. The girls were dressed in thick woollen jumpers, sleeves pushed up to the elbows, oilskin aprons, and their fingers tied in rags or bandages. They seemed not to notice the bitter cold, their faces glowed with health and their fingers flashed – pick up herring, nick, throw. The herrings would be picked up, gutted and thrown unerringly into the barrel behind, rarely missing, in just a second. I could have watched for hours, it was fascinating. When they were not working the girls could be seen walking about the town, still in their working clothes – woollens, oilskins and bandages – knitting furiously.

When I was a little older, a favourite pastime was meeting the boats coming into harbour. At Brush Bend the fishermen would throw us a few fish as they passed, we would carefully thread them on a handy piece of string, and proudly carry them home for tea! Also on Brush Quay, all the barrels were stacked, awaiting transportation, having been filled with herrings, sprinkled with coarse salt and the lids hammered into place. Climbing, running

Mending crab pots on Mundesley beach at the turn of the century. Fishermen worked all along Norfolk's long coastline.

and jumping over these barrels became one of our favourite games. It would be frowned on in these enlightened days and deemed too dangerous!

A few years later still saw me sitting on a bollard at the end of the pier, complete with notebook and pencil, striving to write down the registration numbers as the boats entered harbour in their hundreds, quite a feat for small fingers. When they were all safely moored, there was just about enough space in the middle for one boat to pass through.'

CHAMBERLINS OF NORWICH

'My mother began a millinery apprenticeship at Chamberlins during the First World War. The young trainees all lived in a large house in Willow Lane, under strict supervision, and many friendships were made, some of which lasted life-long.

Chamberlins was a very high-class ladies' fashion store, a family firm with Sir George Chamberlin as managing director. My mother eventually became millinery buyer and made hats for the Norfolk aristocracy to wear to Ascot and other great events. My parents moved to Dereham but I remember being taken on fortnightly visits to see my godmother, one of mother's Willow Lane friends called Peggy Inverarty, who had remained at Chamberlins as head of the lingerie department.

We entered the main door opposite the Guildhall, up wide shallow steps and under vast, glittering golden letters announcing "Chamberlins". Elegant window displays, changed weekly, flanked the steps and large glass front doors. Mother said that in the 1920s there was a gentleman in a top hat to carry ladies' parcels to their cars and to open the doors. There were always flowers in the hallway and in discreet spots throughout the store, and every department had its own head dressed in a smart black suit and white blouse or shirt. Aunty Peggy's blouse, I remember, always had white frills at the throat. We had to pass right to the back of the shop to see her, where the lingerie was discreetly hidden away. I loved the beautiful shining satin and silk nightdresses and slips.

The carpets everywhere were thick and soft, and I remember mirrors with gold scrolly edges, highly polished mahogany fitments and counters, although these had glass fronts to display special articles to the best advantage. Everything was priced in guineas, which was £1 and one shilling, for some reason considered more aristocratic. Most of the customers would have had accounts, paid quarterly.

Every counter had one or two chairs for customers to rest, and no one was ever hurried or left unattended. The fitting rooms were enormous by today's standards, with chairs of course, and an alteration hand was summoned if the fit of any garment was not perfect.

An elegant, luxurious emporium for an elegant, sophisticated clientele, it was bought eventually by Marshall & Snelgrove.

My grandmother did her shopping for clothes and household goods in Butchers of Swan Lane, as they were much cheaper. They put your money and the bill into little cylinders which buzzed along overhead wires to the central cash desk, and the change came quickly buzzing back.'

THE SHOE FACTORIES

'I was 14 years old the day after war was declared in 1939. It was announced just afterwards that schools would be closed for a time, so I thought I could start work. Off I went to get a job at Southalls shoe factory (Startrite), but when I went to the Employment Bureau in Norwich for my cards to start they wouldn't let me have them as I was too young. I had to wait till the following Christmas before I could leave school. We only went to school for a few hours a week anyway, I was attending Angel Road school at the time.

When I did leave I got a job at the Florida shoe factory on Salhouse Road, close to Mousehold Heath. My two sisters were working there at the time in the trimming room, one was a socker and the other a slasher. I joined them in this room, but to start with I put laces in shoes and tied ribbon bows, and got the boxes ready for the ladies called passers, who had to make sure there was nothing wrong with the shoes before boxing them. I also had to sweep up at the end of the day.

When the air raid sirens sounded we used to run out to Mousehold Heath and hide under the trees, as there weren't any air raid shelters to begin with. One day Barnards factory which was next to the Florida was bombed, I think it was the same day that Colman's was hit. It was nearly leaving off time and I was sweeping up, of course we all ran on to Mousehold, it was quite frightening. I never did find the broom I had been using. I left this factory when I was 16; it is now known as Van-Dal.

I then went to work at Southalls in the making room which was a men's department, but with so many men being called up for the forces, women and girls took over some of the jobs. My brother was working there as well. I nailed what were called springs into the waists (insteps) of shoes before the soles were attached. The men who put the soles on were on piecework, so we had to keep them going, which meant no wasting time.

After a while I was moved to another department which entailed booking shoe uppers from the machine room into the making room. I then put the uppers into boxes with the soles, inner soles, toe puffs etc which were then linked up with the lasts which were on racks, and they started their journey round the rest of the factory to be made up. This was called the marrying department. I left Southalls when I married in December 1953. Most of my family worked in shoe factories at some time; besides myself, three brothers, three sisters, sister in law, nephew, nieces and uncles of mine all worked at Southalls over the years.'

COMPTOMETERS AT COLMAN'S

'I took a three months' course in comptometer operating at Aldwych House in the Strand in London, then returned to my family in Norwich and joined Haldenstein, shoe manufacturers of Norwich, and later Boulton and Paul for a short time as a comptometer operator, until my family moved to London in 1936. We returned to Norfolk in 1942, to Mundham where my parents were fruit farmers.

I started work at Colman's in 1954 as a comptometer operator;

recommendation was required to secure a position at Colman's. Living in the country, I walked about half a mile to a neighbouring farm in order to get a lift in a car with a friend who worked in a bank in the city. There were four of us in the office, which was situated in the attic of Colman House in Carrow Road, a very old elegant building.

A comptometer was the forerunner of the modern electronic calculator, and could do all arithmetic functions, ie subtract, divide, multiply and add. It used decimals, so £sd had to be converted before use. We used these machines to check invoices of goods inwards against delivery notes, and pricing goods outwards. We had a large export market to South Africa, Australia and Europe and the paperwork was considerable for export orders. We carried out accounts procedures for all departments of the company.

The company gave an annual bonus, and we in the comptometer room were responsible for the calculations. This was done in the utmost secrecy, we were locked in the room while we worked out the amount for every employee on the percentage of their annual wage. Employees were given a number (no names) for confidentiality.

We were paid weekly, by cash. We queued up outside the Company Secretary's office and went in one at a time, shutting the door behind us, and were paid in cash, again in a secret and discreet way. We did not discuss with our fellow workmates what our wage was.

Colman's were good, caring employers, and I always enjoyed working among happy friendly people. There was an excellent luncheon club, four shillings was deducted monthly from our wages for a two-course hot meal. Every month there was a free issue to staff of one of the company's products, eg a tin of mustard or a bottle of squash. There was also a company shop where one could buy company products at discounted prices. Good sports facilities included a bowling green at Carrow Road which was used in the lunch break by the men.'

NURSING AT DITCHINGHAM

'I first came to Norfolk in 1926 at the age of 18. I had spent the previous two years working in an orthopaedic hospital for children and wanted to train as a nurse. I had hoped to be accepted at the Jenny Lind Hospital in Norwich, but was refused on health grounds. I was then given a recommendation to the Sisters at All Hallows, Ditchingham, to start as a trainee nurse.

I arrived at Ditchingham station and was met by the garden boy, one Charlie Bird, who took my bags and we walked to All Hallows. Ditchingham Hospital in those days was a general cottage hospital

175

run by Anglo-Catholic Sisters. It was an endowed hospital and existed on charitable donations. Sister Augustus was in overall charge. Sister Margaret was the nurse in charge and my tutor. On arrival I was given my own room and measured for a uniform by a dressmaker from Bungay. Two uniforms, two starched caps and about ten aprons were supplied. They had never had a trainee nurse before me, my wage was five shillings a week paid monthly.

The day started at 7 am, when a maid called me for chapel, and then it was into the wards to make beds and give the patients their breakfasts, then our breakfast at 8 am and back to the wards for washing patients, cleaning bedpans etc. There were no sterilisers and bedpans and urinals had to be scrubbed by hand with Lysol and Milton. My hands soon became red raw. The working day finished at 8 pm and we worked a six and a half day week. I was always so hungry, and had parcels of goodies sent from home. The food was poor and sparse, as it was mostly donated or scrounged by Sister Augustus. We were given two hours off on a Sunday when we were expected to go to the chapel at the convent.

The hospital had eight beds in the men's ward, eight beds in the women's ward, four beds in a side ward, and four beds on a balcony if we were very busy. We also took private patients. The income from this source was very important, and these private patients had the nurses' rooms and they had to sleep in the village. Patients paid what they were able, but no patient was ever turned away through poverty.

The most common complaint was pneumonia, for which the treatment was antiphlogiston heated on the open fire in the ward in an old saucepan, then pasted onto lint and applied to the upper body which was then encased in a cotton jacket. It was an effective treatment with the menthol vapours helping to loosen the congested lungs. Tonsillectomies were very common, and anyone with stomach ache had an appendicectomy regardless of their problem! Operations were carried out by a specialist coming from Norwich, assisted by the patients' own doctors, one as assistant surgeon and the other as anaesthetist. The only anaesthetic available was ether, which was dripped over a gauze held over the patient's face.

Typhoid and scarlet fever were also very common, and were treated in semi isolation. We treated a lot of farm accidents, for example horse and cow kicks, and I remember a shotgun accident when the patient was carried on a farm gate as a stretcher and brought in a waggonette. The mortality rate was quite high and we had our own mortuary. After a patient left, all bedding, pillows and the horsehair mattresses were put in a room which we had to seal with paper and formaldehyde smoke cones were lit to fumigate everything.

176

In my second year I did night duty. I was quite alone, but could call the Sisters if necessary. I was always rushed off my feet and in my twelve-hour shift only stopped to eat the cold meal that had been left for me. There was no electricity on at night and we only had very small paraffin lamps, three on a table in a ward and one or two in the corridors. We did a month at a time on night duty. I also did theatre work. We did have a steriliser in theatre, instruments and swabs were sterilised over a methylated spirit stove. My first operation was a gangrenous leg amputation. I am afraid I was ordered out of the theatre, having been told to hold the limb, before I passed out.

In spite of all the hard work and constant hunger (I was once caught returning from cycling to Bungay late at night with a parcel of fish and chips!) I really enjoyed life at Ditchingham and in what little spare time I had I took on the Ditchingham Girl Guides.'

THE IRONMONGER

'"A pound of nails, please Mister," was a familiar cry in an ironmonger's shop until the coming of the bubble-pack. Screws were stored in small cardboard boxes according to type and size, but nails were always loose in strong purpose-built open compartments ranged along the back of my grandfather's shop in Norwich. The nails were graded by length, and usually picked up in a metal scoop before being placed in the scale-pan. Then there was the joy to a child of placing the weights on the balance-pan.

Next to the nails was kept the drum of putty, the smell of which to this day evokes many memories. Putty had to be cut out before weighing and this was great fun.

The customer who wanted paraffin, turpentine or other inflammable liquids would have to be prepared to wait while an assistant would go downstairs, through the storage area in the basement and across a yard to the out-buildings where such materials were stored. The real danger of fire was constantly taken into consideration.

Goods were wrapped in brown paper and tied with string, and every sale was recorded by hand. Normally the till roll was totalled in the shop, but on market day it was always taken home for my grandmother to add up – her mental arithmetic was second to none.

At the end of the day, the wooden shop floor was always watered from a can to lay the dust before sweeping up, and I'm not surprised that the assistants wore grey overalls, as ironmongery was quite a heavy and dirty trade.'

BEHIND THE FACADE

A look at life behind the scenes as an apprentice hairdresser in the 1920s.

'It was the mid 1920s. Cloche hats, low waisted dresses, skirts just above the knee. Beaded garters, some even sporting little bells, and pink lisle (fine cotton) stockings. And the vogue was flattened bosoms. Not that the latter worried me. Mine had not started sprouting yet. I was the youngest apprentice at Mr Naylor's hairdressing establishment. I was small, skinny, pale faced, with red nose and straight hair.

On arrival at the salon over the umbrella shop at 9 am Mr Naylor would be unlocking the door to the lobby, where stairs led to the landing above. The first door along the corridor was the gents' room, the second the ladies'.

My first two years would be spent in the gents' room, mostly keeping the place clean. Brushing the long plush settees situated under the windows and sweeping the floors, and on Mr Naylor's instructions, mopping the lino floor with linseed oil. In the ladies' room, elegant Eileen was the main hairdresser. Brenda, the cheerful chubby one, in her third year, was her assistant.

After my first week at this emporium the girls christened me "Cherry the bold charlady", Eileen having asked me politely; "Did I suffer from indigestion?" "No," I retorted, "and I don't drink." I was a constant amusement to the two girls. I liked them, and their taking the mickey was like water off the proverbial duck's back.

Marble stands and washbasins were cleaned with a block of substance called Monkey soap. Shampoo and various substances were kept in brass containers which I cleaned with Globe polish. Nothing so up to date as Brasso. Mr Naylor called his shampoo "Egg Julep", but I suspected it was nothing more than Hudson's soap powder plus a little water. Large stocks of soap powder, with larger stocks of Tolley's Ale, reposed under the settees, craftily covered with sheets of brown paper.

My wage was five shillings a week, plus beer money. The latter was when the boss ran dry and the latest consignment had not arrived. I was then detailed off to replenish his stock. Oh, how I hated going into a pub!

Mr Naylor was very secretive about his own brand of hair restorer. Whilst the distilling was going on, I was locked out and told to dust the lower banisters or take the brass containers up the next flight of stairs to an old workroom and clean them again. He sold one bottle of this elixir a year. The label had the name Naylor's Pro Dit Hair Restorer, and depicted a bosomy lady wearing a boned wasp-waisted corset, holding a mirror in one hand and a brush in the other. A bottle of this precious concoction had to be delivered by me to a certain lady in Curls, the drapery store. What good it did her I shall never know, for Mr Naylor had a bald patch on the top of his head, which he concealed by putting his hand up the chimney and transferring the soot thereon to his pate.

Mr Naylor had no teeth – I'm sorry, that's not strictly correct. If you were lying back in the red upholstered chair with a white cloth round you and being lathered by yours truly, your eye wandering among the assortment of bottles before you, it's possible you might catch a glimpse of a drinking glass containing a pair of uppers and downers. Yes! but not your ordinary dentures. The uppers were connected to the downers by a pair of springs at either side. On occasions when I misbehaved, I was confronted by a very fierce Mr Naylor wearing the aforementioned impedimenta. His mouth would open like a jack-in-the-box, and the noise that issued forth would sound like yaagh! I was very intimidated and tried to find jobs that took me from his presence. On my return I would find the offending article sitting coyly in its bath of water disporting a happy grin.

Our half day was Thursday. Other days we worked till eight o'clock at night and nine on Saturdays. On that day the two long settees would be full, mostly of farmers, all ogling me as I plied the shaving brush. Mr Naylor would move to my chair with his razor. I would remove the cloth from the gentleman in his chair, brush him down and help him on with his coat. Next gentleman, please! On went the cloth and lathering commenced. Very often a brush slipped into the mouth of a cheeky one. Sometimes Mr Naylor's client needed a shave, haircut and shampoo. It was a wonder the poor chap I was working on had any skin left.

It was one of those Saturdays when Mr Naylor wanted me out of the way. I was a very innocent young person, so I didn't know the reason. I wouldn't have known what these peculiar articles were for, anyway. I was tidying glass cases one day. There was a conglomeration of all sorts of junk. Hairnets, hairpins, cigarettes, twopenny boxes of Phulnana and Shelmnesim face powder. As I was sorting these out I came across a rolled up rubber with a teat. "What shall I do with this balloon?" I asked the boss. He took it from me. "I'll give it to some little boy when he comes in," he said. I had asked the girls what was on the top shelf in Mr Naylor's room with "Silk finish double dipped and guaranteed for one year" on the label. They

179

roared with laughter, but didn't enlighten me. Thereafter anything they bought of special quality was "Yes, silk finish double dipped" etc. They thought it was a huge joke that I was so mystified.

In our establishment wigs and hairpieces were made to order. Sometimes customers brought in their own combings. These had to be carded on steel spikes, then on finer cards to get all the roots in one direction. Mr Naylor taught me to do knotting, using a very fine hook and taking a couple of hairs and knotting them into a very fine fabric, very similar to pegging a rug. I practised by making moustaches. Wigs were made on a wooden head block. Fine net was shaped onto the block and hair knotted into the net. On the rare occasions when wigs were ordered, I was sent to the jeweller's in the same street to ask for some old clock springs. These Mr Naylor would cut to size, and I was sent up to the workroom with a block of sandstone and told to round the edges of the steel. When this was done the piece of steel was sewn into a narrow tape until it was completely enclosed. Then these were sewn into the wig lining and would keep the wig in place when worn.

Perms had not arrived yet, so hair was marcel waved. Mr Naylor's method of teaching was very complicated. A tail of hair was hung on a hook. The tongs were heated on a gas ring. The lesson began with many contortions of the toothless face muscles, and lots of clickings of the tongs. Under-over-click, over-under-click. What was a very simple operation was made to look very complicated. The method of permanently curling hair for made-up pieces was Mr Naylor's secret, but I observed him winding hair round bone bobbins, securing them with tape, putting them in a saucepan of water on the fire and boiling them for a certain length of time. The result was a very natural curl.

The ladies' room had two large curtained windows, a long and broad red plush settee, a tortoise stove, two washbasins with two chairs, and a medieval-looking object high enough to go behind a chair. There was a gas ring at the bottom of this object, the top had a helmet-like construction. The unfortunate victim who needed her hair drying, lay back in her chair. The gas was lit with a taper, and the hinged visor was dropped. This monstrosity was made of brass, which I occasionally cleaned with hydrochloric acid. No protective gloves were worn in those days.

After two years I broke my apprenticeship in order to help in my parents' business. My father was always able to have a free haircut, as later did my husband. Perms came in, marcel waves went out. As for moustaches, they were only intended for theatrical people. Me? I grew up!'

WAR & PEACE

THE GREAT WAR 1914–1918

The war brought great sorrow to many families in Norfolk, and for the first time a fear of being bombed in their own homes. The sound of a Zeppelin overhead brought many a child from its bed in the middle of the night. Norfolk was also vulnerable from the sea, as Great Yarmouth found out one Easter Monday.

ON THEIR WAY

'My grandfather kept an old coaching inn near the cathedral in Norwich. This was used by the country folk who would stable their horses while they went to market. My father was expected to groom and feed them while their owners were away.

During the First World War 17 soldiers were billeted in the attic at the inn. They were young men on their way to France. Before leaving they would sometimes leave personal items in the care of my grandfather hoping to collect them on their return. Sad to say, many did not and they were still in grandfather's possession when he retired in 1955 after 50 years as a licensee.'

ZEPPELIN!

'I was born in 1914 and lived in a little house on Southdown Road, Great Yarmouth, with my mother and father. One of my earliest memories (it was on 28th November 1916) is of a Zeppelin hovering over our house for some time. My father took me into the garden to look at it, a horrible grey shape. Then it burst into flames and lit up the sky, and bits of flaming material were flying about. I was very frightened after that for a long time.'

'I was five when the war began, living at Northwold, and we were scared of Zeppelins. I can remember Mother getting us out of bed and bringing us downstairs for a while when there was one about.'

'In 1915 the Army built blockhouses in the sand dunes at Titchwell armed with machine guns and connected by telephone to Bircham Newton aerodrome. Dummies of German planes were put out on the pastures and used for gunnery practice by fighter planes from Bircham Newton. Accidents were common.

To escape Zeppelin raids families would get out of bed and go into the open fields at night, returning home when the danger was past. Farmers were ordered to have horses and waggons on standby to evacuate villagers in case of an invasion threat.'

BOMBARDED FROM THE SEA

'While living at Wymondham I saw a German Zeppelin in the night sky, heading for Norwich.

At Easter in 1916, my mother took the three of us to Great Yarmouth to stay with her sister. My aunt lived with her family at White House Farm, Runham Vauxhall. This was a small community not far from Vauxhall station on the Caister side of the A47 – the Acle New Road in those days. On the Easter Monday morning just before six o'clock, we were woken by the most awful banging and booming noise. Yarmouth was being bombarded from the sea! We looked out of the bedroom windows and could see people fleeing from the town along the Acle New Road, mothers pushing prams, their long white nightdresses flapping round their ankles below their coats. Needless to say, my mother did not stay on as intended but took us off home to Harleston as soon as things simmered down and we could get a train.'

CHAMBERLINS FIRE BRIGADE

'In 1915 my mother became a millinery apprentice at Chamberlins of Norwich. Sir George Chamberlin was a caring employer and the young trainees lived in a large house in Willow Lane, carefully supervised – no staying out after 9 pm!

Because of the wartime manpower shortage, the firm formed their own ladies' fire brigade, with "CFB" as the insignia on their uniforms. Thereafter they became known as Chamberlins Funny Bugs.

One day they gave a demonstration of their expertise for the press and public. My mother was photographed holding the hose. What was not mentioned in the press report was that instructions were given to turn the water on at half strength as the hose was very heavy. In the excitement this was forgotten and the whole force of the water suddenly came through. After what my mother described as a great struggle to hold on, she dropped the hose and the nearest members of the crowd were drenched.'

ANOTHER DAY

'My father was wounded in the war, in fact he was the only one to survive a shelling on his post on the Somme. When the morning

Chamberlins Ladies Fire Brigade at Norwich in 1915. The photocall went well until the water was turned on at full strength!

came he was the only one still warm, and in later years after a happy day he often said, "That's another day my mates haven't had." He was ever thankful for what he had; he did not even envy a neighbour who was rather well off in our eyes. "He hasn't got any children, I wouldn't be without mine." He considered himself far richer than the neighbour.'

THE SECOND WORLD WAR 1939–1945
THE BOMBING BEGINS

Once again we were at war and Norfolk was in the front line.
Bombs and incendiaries fell and we struggled with gas masks
and the knowledge that our lives would never be quite the same
again.

WHEN THE SIRENS SOUNDED

'I was born only a few months before the start of the Second World
War and grew up accepting the state of war as normal. Such things
as rationing and bombing were just part of life as I knew it. I lived
with my parents and elder sister in a new house in the northern
suburbs of Norwich. We had a good sized garden which Father had
to redesign at the beginning of the war and which provided us with
an abundance of fruit and vegetables, chickens and eggs. Next to
the chicken run was the air raid shelter, to a small child a place of
mystery and adventure. One had to descend several steep steps to
enter this brick-lined room. It was quite small and could only just
about accommodate the metal bunks and stools. There was a small
flap for a table and a ledge for a candle. Fifty years on I can still smell
the damp and the candle wax.

When the sirens sounded I soon learned that we had to hurry
down to this place of safety. I well remember running into my
parents' room one night at the start of an air raid only to find
my mother putting on her corsets! Surely, I thought, she should
not bother with that!

Father was not called up as he was running his own business but
he did serve with the Royal Observer Corps so was frequently on
duty during the nights of the raids. Our next door neighbour was
an air raid warden and his wife and teenaged son were both terribly
nervous and although they had their own shelter, they would often
come and sit out the raids with us. I do not know if Mother really
welcomed two extra bodies in our small space but I was always
pleased to see them. You see Mrs P. usually found the time to make
a pot of tea and brought it down to the shelter together with some
orange plastic cups and saucers. Such delight! The tea must have

tasted awful but those orange cups have shone down through the years in my memory.

Living where we did, we did not experience the heavy raids and dangers of some areas but on the one night when the bombs dropped on the end of our garden we did not have time to reach the shelter. Father pushed my mother, sister and me under the stairs and wearing his tin hat, lay down on the hall floor. During that raid we lost all our windows, many of the roof tiles and an internal wall cracked across. The house at the bottom of the garden was sliced in half. Two bombs failed to explode so we were evacuated. We went to stay with my mother's sister who lived in the country. Unfortunately several other of our relatives, in similar states, also descended upon her so the tiny two up, two down cottage with an earth closet and pump in the yard was stretched at the seams. My only memory of that visit is of having to use a pot instead of a WC and managing to drop my knitted toy duck into it (full, of course).'

ALL CLEAR?

'One day at the beginning of 1940, I set off shopping with my three children and a huge Marmet pram, black with white enamel handles. I had a baby boy of six months in the body of the pram, a girl of two (with whooping cough) sitting on the end, and a little boy of four holding on to the pram handle, so I also had four gas masks with me – a large one for the baby and three in cardboard boxes. The alarm went. First I had to get the two year old off the pram and manoeuvre the baby into the big gas mask, then the two children (now crying) into theirs, and last of all put mine on. You can imagine quite well that by now the all clear was sounding.'

I DREADED CLOUDY DAYS

'One evening in October 1940, as it was getting dusk, I was at my kitchen window when I heard and saw an aeroplane, flying low. I stepped outside just as it reached the bungalow and saw seven bombs released. I drew back on to the step and there was an almighty crash as debris and tiles off the roof went flying all around me. The bombs had dropped on the field, which was a poultry farm.

One large hut was demolished but no hens were killed. Luckily, the bombs did not fall on to the road or I would not be here now. It transpired that the Germans thought they were bombing a military camp as there were several poultry farms round this area at the time and it was near RAF Swanton Morley.

The aeroplane then turned around and dropped incendiaries in a wood which is opposite the new Gressenhall Museum. We had about 300 tiles off the roof and everything that could open, did, even the clock face, and one door lay across the bed.

During the war years I dreaded cloudy days as then the Germans sneaked in and machine gunned anything. One day I was in my garden when an aeroplane dived from the clouds and machine gunned near me. We had a lurcher dog at the time who was loose. He ran straight indoors and put his head in a pail of water which was standing on the kitchen floor!'

GONE FOR LUNCH

'We had a company of soldiers billeted in Burnham Market. They set up and manned a Bren gun in the Market Place, but when a German plane came low over the village and dropped a bomb near the station there was no one on duty – they had gone for lunch!

Three bombs were dropped near the village and the blast sucked out a plate glass window of a draper's shop, and some goods out of the window display. Then the window went back while the goods remained outside.'

A MOONLIT NIGHT

'Once the Germans dropped a lot of flares over Sparham. It was like a moonlit night. They mistook the field opposite for a camp; the corn had been cut and shocked up in groups of fours and sixes so I suppose it looked like a camp from the air. They dropped a lot of incendiary bombs on the field and when it was all over the Home Guard went to clear up. Dad brought home a tin container that the Germans had thrown out of the plane and we kept it in our front garden for many years.'

THE NORWICH BLITZ

'In April 1942 Norwich suffered one of its worst air raids, part of the so-called Baedeker Raids. Exeter, Bristol, Canterbury and Norwich, all historic places with no real role in the war, were bombed at the same time. Curls (where Debenhams now stands) was demolished and so was St Benedict's and the surrounding area. I was in the ATS stationed at Britannia barracks at the time and all the ATS personnel had to go into the large air raid shelter behind the barracks. It was very frightening hearing all the noise and not knowing what we would find. When we emerged later, Norwich was hidden by clouds of smoke.

The following afternoon my fiancé was very late for our Saturday

187

date. This was most unusual for him and I was very annoyed and told him so, but I was ashamed when he explained the reason why. While Norwich was being bombed, the Germans had also dropped bombs on Little Plumstead green, destroying four out of the ten houses there. A most unlikely target, certainly not historical! Two people were killed and others injured and badly shocked, and four families made homeless. My fiancé had been helping to rescue them and their belongings. In spite of the shortage of materials and labour, permission was given to build four new houses there to rehouse the farm workers, but only two of the families returned to the green.'

'When the blitz was on in Norwich in April 1942, I remember seeing people walking with prams and barrows out of the city at night to sleep in the country. Our school at Sprowston was a rest centre so we did not go to school that week, but those of us in the top classes went to help the folk who had been bombed out of the city and were sleeping in the school hall.'

GARRISON TOWNS

'We had moved to Avondale Road, Gorleston by the time the war started. In March 1939 there was a trial blackout which seemed very eerie, with no street lights anywhere for about three hours. Nobody realised then that six months later it would be for real for many years.

I went to Great Yarmouth High School, and we were not allowed to start the autumn term in 1939 until an air raid shelter had been built in the playground, so we did not start till October. We didn't mind at all.

From December 1940 I worked at Gorleston telephone exchange as a telephonist. It was a reserved occupation, and we had no uniform, badge, or means of identification. We were often insulted because we were civilians, especially by the ATS girls. We tried to join up – one girl even getting as far as a medical for the WRNS, but the Head Postmaster found out and forbade it. Trained telephonists were like gold dust then. As well as switchboard work, I did 48 hours a month ARP duty, and being trained by the Red Cross, used to go to the dressing station at Stradbroke School, Lowestoft Road. The exchange was in Baker Street. My mother was there as well. As well as duty hours, you had to report when there was a raid, day or night, so many a night found Mother and me running up there, tin hats, on, diving under a hedge or against a wall if we heard a bomb dropping. On the exchange we covered 8 am to 8 pm, working three shifts, and male telephonists worked overnight. Many times because of disruption by air raids we had to stay on duty till 11 pm or later till they could get there, working at least a 15 hour day. We had a good fish and chip shop next door which helped a lot!

In 1941 the Germans blitzed Yarmouth and Gorleston for five days running. The first night they aimed for the river as there were usually ML and MTB boats in. They were out and the Rows in Yarmouth got flattened by landmines and incendiaries. They moved a bit further south the next night and hit Southtown. The north end of Gorleston came next, and on the fourth night our turn came. Springfield Road was hit and we got the blast. All our windows were out and ceilings down. We had two WAAFs billeted with us, both were in bed, one had a complete window frame come down on her (unbroken) and the other was covered with broken glass. Neither was hurt. My bike was blown right across the kitchen table, and I fell over it in the dark. The first night there was no opposition to the raid at all, but the next night there were guns, balloons and fighters. My father was on duty all the week at Report Centre in Yarmouth.

We had an emergency shelter at the exchange, but didn't use it or we would not have done any work! We used to have anything up to 13 raids a day, so there was no point. We just took our chances. The windows were blown in four times, so we were bricked up with two tiny windows high in the wall.

Yarmouth and Gorleston were very much garrison towns. Most of the civilians fled when the blitz started, and soldiers were in the empty houses. At work we were under Army Command for a time, with officers from Brigade HQ inspecting us from time to time. I had to sign the Official Secrets Act so there is probably a great deal I cannot divulge!

We were bombed, strafed, had V1 and V2 bombs. When it all finished we could not understand the silence, also the lights took a bit of getting used to when they came on again. Before D-Day there were troops everywhere, then they were gone. One of the best kept secrets was the radar station on the cliffs where our WAAFs were. Nobody knew about it, and on the exchange we worked with them a lot.'

IN THE DITCH WITH THE POSTMAN

'I attended school in Thorpe and cycled the three miles there and back each day from Sprowston. Our school had the "crash warning" system for air raids. This meant that although the air raid sirens had sounded, we did not have to go to the dug-out trenches until the crash warning went, indicating that there was enemy action overhead. This saved endless hours of sitting in the trench, waiting for the all clear.

One afternoon when the crash all-clear had sounded, I was

allowed to cycle home. I had just got into Blue Boar Lane when through the trees came the sound of someone throwing pebbles at me. There was also the sound of a low-flying aircraft. Further along the road was our friendly postman who jumped off his bike and yelled to me to get in the ditch. This I did very quickly as I now realised that the pebbles were machine-gun bullets. The postman and I stayed in the ditch until all was quiet and then I cycled home at top speed.

I wondered what people would say if I told them I spent ten minutes in a ditch with the postman – each of us too frightened to say a word! – but both praying the enemy aircraft had gone over and there were no more on the way.'

SHUT THE DOOR!

'Maybe once or twice a year there would be a social evening held in the village school to raise money for some special concern. It was while attending one such occasion that we had our one and only V2 rocket over the Downham Market area. Some folks ran outside to have a look while others yelled to "shut the door" because of the blackout – forgetting that the flying bombs were unmanned.

I saw a plane crash one evening that set fire to a straw stack, and we also had a Flying Fortress bomber explode over the village one morning. Later that day I was leading the horse while father was horse-hoeing some corn, and picked up a man's finger.'

THE CHURCH WAS DESTROYED

'All Saint's church at Bawdeswell was destroyed on 6th November 1944 when an Allied plane crashed into it. The plane was a Mosquito from 608 Squadron based in Downham Market, and was on its way back from a bombing raid over Germany.

I lived in the Gables, next door to the church. It used to be the old workhouse so it was quite a big place. It was dark when it happened. My wife was in the bedroom trying to get our two year old son off to sleep. I walked into the other bedroom; I had an apple in my pocket, I took it out and just as I was about to bite into it the lights went out and there was a lot of banging. It was a cold November and the plane was flying low because it had iced up. It went into some overhead cables and then on to the church. The two engines came off and went across the road. One hit Chancer House and the other hit Miss Secker's house. The church went up in flames.

I decided I'd better get outside to see if there was anything I could do. I trained for the Fire Service pre-war and was in charge of the local fire contraption that we towed with a 1927 Morris Cowley.

There wasn't much that we could do, but someone got a ladder and got into Miss Secker's house to rescue her, fortunately she was unharmed. Three fire engines soon arrived, one from Reepham, one from Dereham and one from Norwich. We directed the firemen to the pond that was in the field. It was a big fire at first, but fortunately it was raining and everywhere was wet, so that helped.

The two young Americans on board, Pilot Officer James McLean and Sgt Mervyn Tansley were killed. Pieces of the wrecked plane still remain. Mr John Ames has used part of the fuselage and petrol pump to make a plaque in honour of the pilots. A new church was built in its place in 1955.'

LIFE GOES ON

Despite the bombing life had to go on. The harvest still had to be got in and families fed and clothed. In time it began to feel as if we had always lived this way.

THE WAR CHANGED OUR VILLAGE

'The war brought many changes to Ludham. "Flat Norfolk" meant an ideal site for an airfield and the marshland area was suitable training ground for the Army. We were soon surrounded by Nissen huts built by the Pioneer Corps, Italian prisoners of war (who found our large snails a delicacy), Royal Engineers and Irish labourers. The RAF moved in and aircraft activity became normal. They were providing escort for heavy bombers and for coastal defence.

A visit to the airfield by George VI and Queen Elizabeth did much for the morale of pilots and staff. The different regiments came and went from the Army camp, which was built surrounding the village and within it to disguise the fact that it was a military base. The Bren gun carriers broke up the surface of the roads as they clattered through the village to their practice areas on the marshes.

Americans came for a short duration to wire the telephone system for the airfield. How quickly those boys worked, and what strange garb they wore. How friendly and noisy they were. So relaxed and different from our forces. I still correspond with the sister of one, who returned to his home town of Chicago. We had Canadians too, generous to the schoolchildren with sweets and chocolate. We had no fear of being molested with all these men in the village. They

Mundesley children in fancy dress as part of War Weapons Week – we all did our bit to collect for the war effort.

were all decent fellows. Of course harmless romances flourished, and some of the non-drinking soldiers came to tea instead of propping up the bar at the King's Arms.

The Free French were always trying to buy soap to send home. There were Spaniards in the Pioneer Corps who were excellent dancers and sang in harmony, songs of their homeland. There was even a Burmese in the RAF, and of course many pilots were Polish and Czech. It was strange to notice the odd gold tooth, something the English did not go in for in dentures.

I corresponded with one widow whose pilot husband was killed in a flying accident on his return to Prague. Her letter mentions several of the Czech pilots who were stationed at Ludham and how tragic it was that three of them had been shot down by our own guns when returning to the base. The pilots continually wore their flying gear and had very few hours' leisure. We had a few bombs, mostly when the pilots were making a hurried exit and wished to travel light. A stable was demolished and horses were killed. We children would watch with interest all air activity, and saw land mines descending on parachutes, caught in the cross-beams of the searchlights. Tracer bullets looked spectacular at night. The grocer's wife was killed by a machine gun bullet while in her house, the shop was opposite the King's Arms. Her husband died a month later from shock. We had several daylight raids, but considering the activity and obvious Nissen huts, we were fortunate not to have had many more with serious consequences.

In the early hours of the morning of D-Day and still in darkness, the lorries containing troops evacuated the village. The continuous rumble of vehicles went on for some time. I had been given parcels to pack, watches, rings, money, photos etc, to send to the wives and families of soldiers. This I did and put a note in some of the parcels, as these boys were our customers and had become our friends. So many did not return from that day of the war.'

'In the summer of 1942 two men from the Ministry arrived unexpectedly at Stalland Farm, Deopham. It was a Sunday afternoon. They came with a compulsory purchasing order to acquire 40 acres, thus halving the size of the farm. The land was needed to be part of what became known as Deopham Green Airfield.

Within weeks the main contractors, Laings, arrived. Many of the labourers were Irish. Overnight, it seemed, this quiet corner of Norfolk became a hive of industry. One farmhouse was knocked down and the farmer and his family were given temporary accommodation in a wooden prefabricated house in a nearby meadow. Two cottages were also knocked down, hedges were uprooted, trees were felled, ponds were filled in and roads disappeared. Soon there were to be acres of concrete instead of fields. Two big hangars were built and a control tower. On the edges of the airfield Nissen huts provided homes for the men of the 452nd Bomb Group, part of the American Air Force.

The first Americans arrived in November 1943. By the new year the first flights were leaving Deopham for daylight raids over Europe. From then on our days were punctuated by the drone of planes leaving in the morning and it was noticeable that not so many returned in the evening. During the light evenings of 1944 we would walk across the fields to the wire netting on the edge of the airfield. A few yards on the other side were the dispersal points where the B-17s (Flying Fortresses) were stationed. All the planes had names and emblems painted on the side and raids were recorded by a bomb sign. We got to know the planes and became quite upset when there was an empty space where one of "our" planes had stood.

The war ended in May 1945 and there were great celebrations on the 'drome. We sat on a haystack in our farmyard and watched. Horns hooted, Very lights were shot into the air, guns exploded and the airmen seemed to go mad with joy. In the distance we could see a fire which proved to be a straw stack alight.

In their zeal to celebrate a couple of airmen fired the stack, and we learned later that they had to pay compensation to the farmer. Their high spirits could be understood, for not only was the war in Europe over, but they would be going home.

Some of the GIs used to visit us at the farmhouse and enjoyed our hospitality. They loved my mother in law's shortcakes.

In the autumn of 1945 we were able to rent from the Air Ministry roughly the same acreage as we lost. Much of it was under concrete. What was ploughable had in many ways been damaged. Over the following years, with good farming practices, the land has improved. We gradually took down the Nissen huts, dismantled one of the hangars and had acres of the concrete taken up. We were able to buy the land in the early 1960s.

One of the good things to come out of this upheaval was the friendships which were forged. Many of the Americans have made return visits, bringing their wives with them.'

'The war brought quite a different way of life to the Norfolk countryside, as all fit young men and women except those in specialised jobs were called into the forces. Older men joined the Home Guard, women helped with land work and most people had some training in first aid, gas drill and the use of stirrup pumps to put out fires from incendiary bombs. People joined the Red Cross, ARP and WVS and women met weekly to knit comforts for the troops. There were aerodromes every five miles or so around Little

194

Ellingham with searchlights and gun sites dotted in between. By 1943 villages were surrounded by American servicemen and men on bicycles were to be seen everywhere. They found their way to village pubs for company and friendship. Their huge Flying Fortresses and Liberators were thick in the skies. In many ways this influx of troops brought prosperity to villages. Women helped in base canteens and took in the Yanks' washing and they in turn supplied families with many extras to supplement rationing. They helped with entertainment, especially for the children. Many uses were found for damaged parachutes, and nylons were seen for the first time!'

WE GREW USED TO THE WAR

'I was born in Feltwell, a quiet village in the south-west corner of Norfolk. Our neighbours had previously lived in a cottage on land recently bought by the Air Ministry. The government had requisitioned a large tract of agricultural land bordering our village and the neighbouring one of Hockwold. During the 1914 to 1918 war there had been a small airfield with wooden huts on some of this land but this time they had a much larger and more elaborate plan in mind and the removal of a few country folk was of little consequence.

When the aerodrome was built prior to the outbreak of war the tempo of the village changed dramatically. The billets were filled with personnel, the married quarters with families, heavy RAF lorries thundered through the main street and the constant sound of aircraft was to be heard in the sky above. However, with these changes came many benefits to compensate for any small inconveniences. Electricity and piped water had been brought to the village and most important of all was the employment the presence of the aerodrome provided; until then agriculture had been the main source of work for men, domestic service for women.

Children from the RAF families attended our village school, hence more teachers were provided, an improvement for us all. Some of the children had accents to which we were unaccustomed but we soon grew used to them and as far as I can remember there were no real barriers. However, their presence did not last for much longer than a year or so for on 3rd September 1939 all wives and families had gone and the married quarters filled with young recruits – the war had begun.

From the beginning we had the blackout, which caused great inconvenience as every door and window had to be covered during the hours of darkness so that no chink of light could be seen from outside. Blackout Time was published each day in the daily papers and a heavy fine could be imposed if these rules were not adhered to. Some managed successfully with heavy curtains, others used wooden shutters or made blinds from a special fabric known as blackout material. This new law meant no bonfire or fireworks on Guy Fawkes night which being an eight year old at the time disappointed me and my contemporaries considerably.

The wartime atmosphere seeped into our daily lives. At school gas mask practice and air raid drill become part of our lessons and sometimes we had the real thing, a genuine air raid with enemy aircraft flying overhead and real bombs being dropped. The target was of course our local aerodrome but sometimes the village itself was on the receiving end. We lived quite close to the accommodation part of the RAF station and we would often hear their air raid warnings given out over the tannoy system long before our village siren gave out its warning, so theirs was the warning we paid most heed to. I remember one Sunday afternoon quite early in the war when without warning three enemy fighters came from out of the blue, machine gunning the aerodrome as they went and we could see tracer bullets flying past the window. They were gone in a matter of seconds but it was rather alarming and we all ducked underneath the table.

There were one or two army camps on the outskirts of the village to help guard the RAF station so altogether there was quite a large influx of service personnel in the area. In view of this the proprietor of the cinemas at nearby Thetford and Brandon saw a good business opportunity and opened one in our village, from then on the old Coronation Hall became the Rex Cinema. It opened six nights a week and changed its programme twice a week, and what was of most interest to us children was that it also had a matinee on a Saturday afternoon to which we were allowed in for the sum of threepence. How we enjoyed it and children from neighbouring villages would bike three or four miles to see the show. Lacking the usual childhood treats such as sweets, oranges, bananas, seaside outings and numerous other things this small pleasure helped to compensate. The cinema had a near miss one night when some bombs were dropped, one fell behind the building and a nearby farmhouse received a direct hit from another one. Luckily no one was hurt but there was a considerable amount of damage done to the village that night and several families lost their homes.

We grew used to the war and it became part of our lives. At night we often went to sleep to the sound of Wellington bombers preparing to depart on their bombing operations and in the early hours of the morning heard the sound of those fortunate enough to return. There were times when the enemy would follow our returning aircraft home and bomb the aerodrome. There was one occasion when a German fighter followed ours in. He did not attack, instead he landed on the airfield, but before our defences had recognised him as the enemy he had taken off again and was away. This may now seem unbelievable but was witnessed by more than one person, and a few years back that same pilot returned to the village to see it at a more leisurely pace!

Our mothers had a difficult time coping with food rationing but on the whole we in the country fared better than those who lived in the towns. We had no long queues at the shops to contend with, most of us grew our own vegetables, we kept a few hens, those working in agriculture had extra cheese ration, and sometimes a rabbit would be caught, even so feeding the family was difficult.

Most people had one or more of their family away in the fighting forces and inevitably there were casualties. My own family did not go unscathed. In January 1942 my sister like many of her age group went to "do her bit" as it was then known. She chose the army where she was trained as a height finder on ack-ack guns, the crews made up of girls except for the one man who fired the gun. It was a dangerous job and she was unfortunately hit by shrapnel one night while on duty and was killed. She was 18 years old and her name is on our war memorial along with the names of half a dozen young men from our village.'

SURROUNDED BY AERODROMES

'I well remember the start of the war. My father had been in the First World War and had expected the second one, so on that fateful Sunday at Watton we gathered round the bakelite radio to hear Chamberlain say, "We are now at war with Germany." "Right," said Dad, "into the garden." He handed me a fork, Mum a spade and he had a pick-axe. He decided on the site of our dug-out and we worked hard all day, made seats, covered the hole with railway sleepers and camouflaged the whole site with soil so it looked just like a mound for marrows. Next day we went to look at our handiwork and the hole was full of water – we never used it.

Back to the drawing board – "Right," said Dad, "we'll clear out the cellar." This we did and installed camp beds plus our tools so that we could dig ourselves out if the house was hit. In between times we had to criss-cross our windows with sticky tape, look up in the attic to find any black material so we could make curtains to blackout our lights at night and Dad's butcher's shop vans had to be fitted with headlight shades. It was agreed that if the air raid warning went we were not to wait but go straight down to the cellar – our little dog was always first. We spent many nights down in that cellar, and we installed a primus stove and frying pan so that we could fry anything we could find for our supper. Mum always went down to the fish and chip shop to buy the chips. All this preparation was quite necessary because Watton was surrounded by aerodromes: Marham, Swanton Morley, Sculthorpe, Wretham, Bodney, Lakenheath etc. There was also a railway line for enemy planes to follow: trains showed red sparks, they were not diesel; not forgetting the battle area, filled with soldiers.

Rationing had started and everyone was issued with an identity card and ration book. We were rationed for meat, bacon, fats, cheese, eggs, sugar, tea and there was a points system for tinned goods and other rare goods and sweets. We had to register with the Watton shops and once registered could only get goods there for one year, the shops would guarantee our ration for one week at a time. Even if things were not rationed they were very scarce, we grew as many vegetables as we could possibly look after – potatoes and carrots gave very good crops and carrots appeared in every dish under the sun. We grew apples, pears, plums, strawberries, raspberries. These were bottled for winter. We didn't see bananas, grapes, lemons or pineapples for the whole war – lots of children didn't know what they were when they first came back.

We worked jolly hard. A typical day was for me to help Dad with the sausages, have breakfast, cycle five miles to work at the farm office – 12 noon cycle five miles home and go to bank, have lunch, cycle five miles to farm and later return home – help Dad either scrub up the shop or make pork cheese, lard or dripping, cut up meat for sausages for next day, have tea. Then we would go down to the Church Army hut near the cinema and serve mugs of tea to army boys on manoeuvres or from the camp – we met some weird chaps but mostly they were a very friendly bunch and very grateful for a cuppa. We worked there from 7 to 10 pm each day on a rota basis: on the way home we might call in at the dance hall for a bit of a dance and then off to bed. On weekends we went on a mobile canteen into the woods when the soldiers were on manoeuvres; what a weary bunch they were.

Offal was not included in the ration, sausages if you were lucky. One customer asked my father for some bones to make some soup, if possible ones that had not been sandpapered – he never left any meat on them!

We also had clothes coupons. Stockings were two coupons per pair, hence we knitted stockings, smart lacy ones (off the coupons yarn, if you were lucky), or we bought a bottle of liquid make-up and got a friend to draw a back seam with an eyebrow pencil and hoped they had a steady hand. We made do by cutting dresses down and decorating them with different coloured scarves, belts, buttons etc. We made earrings from buttons with shanks and fuse wire. Later we were able to buy wooden shoes with hinges in the soles, rather like platform shoes – not very comfortable.

Although we worked hard, money wasn't very plentiful and we saved for weeks for a day out. I well remember my friend and I went with our Mums for a day out in Norwich. We headed for Bonds. I found a lovely pair of green velvet trousers but they were a bit too big round the waist so I left them to be altered. My Mum bought a bone china tea service. The assistant tried to persuade her to have it delivered next day. Oh no, she insisted on taking it home. Bonds had a lovely restaurant on the ground floor, old oak beams and beautiful food for war time. We ate there and boarded the bus thoroughly satisfied with our day out – little did we know that it was the last really good visit to our lovely city. That night we were down in the cellar and we could hear the bombs and planes all night. The heart of the city was gutted – Bonds to Curls, all the Watton end of Norwich was a heap of smouldering rubble. My trousers had gone up in smoke, but Mum had her tea service safe in her china cabinet and I still have it intact. Mum felt she had beaten Hitler at his own game.'

ROTAS AND RATIONS

'Our childhood was one of lovely days on the farm until the war began just before I was a teenager. Never will I forget the first bombing of Norwich as my sister and I and our friends had cycled to a dance at Bawburgh village hall and all was well until the siren wailed and the sky soon became bright with Very lights. The soldiers who were with us and stationed at Model Farm, Easton, bundled all of us girls and our bikes into their lorry and took us home, to the relief of our frantic parents.

Our house was designated to be the "headquarters" of the farm workers' cottages at Honingham and a rota was formed so each night the man on duty would ring a connecting bell to all the farm cottages if the siren sounded. My sister and I took turns to take the duty man tea and Mother's shortcakes. Families would join us all at the "big house" which was well reinforced and we would all assemble in the cellar. Thankfully, many of the warnings proved to be false alarms and after the all clear had sounded we would walk back home by the river, all misty at dawn, and never seem to find sleep again.

By the time I was 14 I was working in a grocer's shop at Colton and rations were very meagre. I had the job of cutting up the extra rations allowed to farm workers every month consisting of no more than two ounces of margarine, cheese, butter and tea. It was very hard work as everything had to be weighed up in stiff blue paper bags including sugar, tea, dried fruit, soda etc, and cheeses had to be skinned of their hessian cloths. These were not always easy to remove and I remember being so tired while working late one night, that I fell asleep while skinning one with only a candle for a light.'

ACORNS AND EGGS

'During the war we collected acorns to feed to the pigs. Rosehips were collected for syrup for babies. Our mothers picked blackberries for the canning factory and to make jams. Before my father went to work he would take the goat on the common and stake it near the best blackberries to stop others picking them!'

'We felt the impact of the war as King's Lynn was bombed at various times. I remember the night The Eagle public house was destroyed. I was about twelve years old at the time and was having my weekly bath in the tin bath in front of the fire, when the impact of the bombs was heard and felt. I jumped out of the bath and fled under the kitchen table without a thought, and of course without any clothes on.

The food was a problem in wartime and looking back I think my mother, like many others, worked miracles in keeping us all fed on two ounces of butter, two ounces of margarine, four ounces of sugar, and a very little meat for each member of the family and supplemented by whatever she could get on points. We did have the abundance of vegetables my father grew in the garden. We also had a few chickens and two ducks which kept us supplied with eggs, although my mother had to use the dreadful dried egg powder for cooking. But we all remained healthy throughout this time and grew well. I remember my mother carefully preserving the eggs when the hens were laying well, in a big stone jar full of waterglass solution, so that when the hens stopped laying we were still able to have "proper" eggs. She also preserved runner beans in brine in stone jars, so that in the winter we still had vegetables to augment our rather bland wartime diet.'

BILLETING THE SOLDIERS

'Yanks would come from Billingsford to the King's Head at Scole to see "the scroungers", as they called the villagers. Claude Bowles invited them to his birthday party one day just to show them. He gave them chicken, vegetables, apple pie and cream and whisky. Later they came for their own party, and brought tinned fruit and ice cream. (A lorry came with it and the village had tinned fruit for weeks.) All local pubs and farm outbuildings were used for billeting the soldiers, and we got twopence a head for breakfast, fourpence for lunch and threepence for tea. Giving them cottage pie, vegetables and bread and butter pudding was the only way to cope, also rice pudding and suet pudding. Milk and flour was available with permits from the Ministry.'

AMERICAN GENEROSITY

'During the war I worked with a group of Dr Barnardo's boys who had been evacuated to a big house in Norfolk – 50 boys and six staff. We were surrounded by airfields, one of which was taken over by the Americans. As soon as they knew there was a children's home in the area, we had visitors on the doorstep. Some came spasmodically, but three spent practically all their off duty time with us.

They would stay with the boys, help put them to bed and then sit and chat to the staff. One of them had a very good tenor voice and as our headmaster was a keen pianist, we enjoyed some lovely musical evenings.

The first Christmas six of them came to dinner and presented us with three turkeys. They insisted on washing up and even washed the teacloths. The next Christmas they brought two trucks and took us all to the base where we were joined by other children for a huge party in one of the hangars. They were very generous and we never wanted for cookies or sweets. After the war ended some of them kept in touch. We found that those who visited regularly were missing their homes and families and were grateful to have someone they could visit and talk to – home from home.'

DOING OUR BIT

We all helped with the war effort in some way, whether it was by joining the Home Guard or the Women's Land Army, making jam or raising money.

WE ALL HELPED

'Men were called up for active service, therefore all able-bodied women, married or single, were called upon to help the war effort. Thus we saw women bus conductors in towns and villages where there were bus services. Women drove food delivery vans and milk vans. They worked on the land, especially when peas and fruit needed to be picked. Women also formed WVS and Red Cross groups; and had sewing and knitting afternoons to make garments for troops and for the hospitals. I can remember my mother's sewing machine being collected on a wheelbarrow to be taken to sewing meetings. WIs made jam and canned fruit. In North Creake when rationing was at its height, there was a scheme where farm workers were allowed two meat pies a week, also extra tea, cheese and sugar. The local baker made and baked the pies and they were brought to our house where we distributed them to the eligible workers.

"War weapons weeks" were held periodically when we raised money for ammunition by holding whist drives, socials and dances. I remember going round the village where I worked playing a barrel organ and collecting money en route. The larger houses were commandeered for troops, some were used as hospitals. Men not eligible for service joined the Home Guard or ARP, doing a day's work then on patrol at night in case of enemy landings on the nearby coast. Land Army hostels were also in the area. Italian prisoners of war worked on the farms. Make do and mend was the housewife's motto as clothing was rationed. Collectors went round selling saving stamps for the war effort.'

WARTIME IN THETFORD

'War made such a difference to Thetford, camps were everywhere – we were surrounded by them. Army and Air Force, and so many troops in the town at night – we young ladies were spoilt for choice and we all had many boyfriends. At night the Market Square was packed with lorries all wanting the ladies to go to their camp dances and of course there were usually dances in the town itself. We really thought we were the "creme de la creme".

In time I was sent to work at the canneries and I remained there throughout the war. It was a very primitive place and bitterly cold, and many times in the summer we were still working at 10 pm canning baked beans, peas etc for the troops – when all we wanted to do was to go dancing!

My friend and I thought we would join the WAAFs and filled in the forms but the manager wouldn't release us because they had taken all the young men and we were left with just two very old men. We did everything, even to unloading boxes of cans from the railways, and once when the water flooded into the factory from the river and came to the tops of our boots we went to work at the railway to "label up", so the troops could still get the cans.

Wartime in Thetford had its funny side as well. Most men and women had to do some kind of part-time work as well as their ordinary jobs and we women at the canneries were told to report

202

to do just that. My friend and I became part-time air raid wardens; we loved the smart navy blue uniforms and white shirts, navy ties etc. One night on patrol near the common where the workhouse was situated we spotted a light quite near where I lived. We moved in quickly because the siren sounded to discover it *was* my house; I really told Mother off, but she said it must have been a crack in the door.

My father was in the Home Guard and took his duties very seriously. One night my sister and I were going to a dance, but he wouldn't let us cross the Town Bridge, he said it was blown up (make believe). We were furious. We said, "It's us, Dad", but his reply was, "I don't care, you have to go round by the small three bridges", so it was a long way to get to the dance that night!

My sister was in the Fire Service – full time – and she also had some funny tales to tell in spite of the grimness of the war. One summer night they were dashing off to put out a plane that had caught fire on its return flight from Germany. It was in Brandon, the next little town to us, and on the way they "lost" one of the men; he fell off the back of the fire engine and landed on the grass verge. They realised he was missing when they went to work on the plane, but picked him up on the way back – still sitting in the same spot.

War was grim and it was only later when it was all over I fully realised the seriousness of it all, the terrible loss of lives; but for me and many other girls that lived in Thetford we had a lovely time, listened to some beautiful bands and heard Glenn Miller at Honington as well as many other stars.'

POSTED TO YARMOUTH

'When I went to the First Officer WRNS' office and was told I was being drafted to Yarmouth I immediately thought of the Isle of Wight, and I was really disappointed when I was told Great Yarmouth, Norfolk. I had just completed one year at *Royal Arthur*, Skegness, a shore establishment, and had become a Leading Wren Officers' Steward and wore my anchor on my sleeve with pride. I hadn't needed the training there as prior to 1941 I had been a parlourmaid for three years!

First Officer Jamieson told me there had been an air raid a day or so before, and the WRNS headquarters in Queen's Road had been hit. Arriving at Great Yarmouth I was sent to HMS *Watchful*, and our quarters and the officers' were the old Victoria Hotel (now the Carlton) and adjoining small hotels.

After a few months I was drafted to HMS *Miranda* at the river mouth. The officers' quarters and the WRNS' living accommodation there were converted from the fishing sheds. Our complement was a Lieutenant Commander and two Lieutenants who had offices nearby, and five WRNS – a Petty Officer, Leading Wren Cook, a Rating Cook and two Leading Wren Officers' Stewards. How hard we had to work to get the place ready, trying to get a polish on the Royal Navy lino, and with polish in short supply the Petty Officer would cycle into town for it. She also visited the market twice a week to purchase flowers, fruit and vegetables.

The Captain's barge was moored alongside, and when on the odd occasion a naval dance was held at the Floral Hall we were rowed over and back again by the Captain's Steward. On other occasions we had to cycle right up to the Haven Bridge and back on the other side, a distance of about six miles.

The ships going out were MTBs (motor torpedo boats) and minesweepers, French and Dutch boats as well as our own. At the river mouth there was an ack-ack battery with barrage balloons and one night during an air raid one of the balloons was set alight and drifted down, landing in the river. We had to run to dugout shelters in the sand dunes.

I had a year in *Miranda* and returned to *Watchful* when more officers were drafted in. Part of the time I worked at the naval barracks (it had been the mental hospital between the wars) and there Vera Lynn entertained us as part of a concert party.'

GRANDAD IN THE HOME GUARD

'My grandfather farmed at Winter's Farm, Gateley, North Elmham. He enlisted in the Home Guard straight away but at the beginning, all the men were given in lieu of uniforms was an armband and one rifle for every four men with only six rounds of ammunition. They drilled with pitchforks instead, and it was several months before they were fully kitted out. After about a year a regular army captain came to check the standard of their knowledge by challenging them to a mock fight lasting one day. In order not to be outdone by the local men's cunning, the captain brought three tanks with him.

My grandfather was very disgruntled for he had a lot of work to do on the farm and could ill afford to waste a day "messing about", especially as he knew an easy way to stop the Germans' advance: put an upturned soup plate in the lanes, it looks like a land mine!

Grandad had been hiding in a ditch for over an hour when he heard an odd rumble in the distance. He was unaware the opposition had tanks with them. The noise came nearer and nearer so he put out his cigarette, cocked his rifle and peeped out. An enormous mass appeared and right over his head pointed a six inch wide muzzle. The monster came to a halt abruptly and there was silence. A man popped out from the turret like a jack-in-a-box and said, "Bang!

You're dead!" Grandad was furious and grumbled, "Well, in that case I'm going back to my milking." The regular soldier was shocked: "You can't do that! You must wear a red badge to show you're dead. Or if you prefer only to be injured, you're our prisoner and we must count you at the end of the battle . . ." But Grandad just sheered off back to the farm. It didn't stop him becoming a corporal later on.'

JOINING THE LAND ARMY

'Up to the age of 17 I lived in London, and came to Norfolk in 1940 and lived on a farm at Deopham. I enjoyed helping about the farm which grew corn, sugar beet and hay but the main enterprise was in poultry. Day-old chicks were hatched and sent around the county.

In 1942 I had to register for war work and applied to go into the Land Army. I was accepted and a job was found on a farm near Wymondham, so I was able to keep in my lodgings and travelled the five miles to work by bike.

My main work was with the cows. I was the cowman's assistant and we milked the 24 cows by hand. On my first day I was given a three-legged stool and a pail and put to work on a very old, passive Friesian named Granny. I was assured that the milk would come eventually. After half an hour I had about a pint! Poor Granny! But after a few days I got the knack and soon became a fast and competent milker.

The milk was cooled and put into ten or twelve-gallon churns. Having put the cows on the meadow my next job was to take the churns on a pony-cart into Wymondham and through the town to the milk depot. I was never given any instruction about driving. Fortunately the traffic was very light compared with today. I was never very happy working with horses and had a sense of unease with them. Back in the yard I had to clean out the cow-houses and wash them down, then put in clean straw. Food was put in the bins ready for the afternoon milking, this consisted of a mixture of shredded mangold (made by putting the mangold in a hopper and then turning a large wheel with a wooden handle), chaff (straw cut into small pieces in a chaff box worked by a stationary engine), sugarbeet pulp (soaked in a barrel of water) and crushed linseed cake. In the racks above the hoppers hay was placed. All the work was very labour intensive.

Afternoon milking began at 3.30 pm. The cows calved in the autumn, so with many of them dry during the summer I was sent to help out with other jobs on the farm. Horse-hoeing went on for weeks. I led the horse while the team-man guided the hoes between the rows of sugar beet or mangolds. In hot weather the poor horse was troubled with flies and so we fixed some leaves on

Mary Flatt working as a land girl at Wymondham in 1944. It was hard and dirty work but many land girls loved their new life.

the harness between its eyes. As I held on to the bridle the horse's saliva dribbled down my arm – most unpleasant! In the evenings I used to join the rest of the workforce to hand-hoe the root crops, a chance to earn extra money. We were paid about £4 an acre, good money in those days.

The corn was cut with a binder and we stooked the sheaves. As the field was reduced to a small patch of standing corn all the workers and their families armed themselves with sticks to hit the rabbits as they ran out of the corn. The men then killed them. The rabbits would be shared out at the end of the day, this gave promise of a lovely rabbit pie.

I used to enjoy the stacking of the sheaves, which were brought into the stack-yard on waggons. My job was to assist the stacker who concentrated on placing the sheaves on the edges while I followed behind to bind them in the middle. The stacker was very experienced and an excellent craftsman, claiming that his stacks never needed a prop. "Keep your middle full, girl," he would shout to me. He took great pride in his work and would never be hurried. When all the corn was gathered in he would escort the last waggon into the yard holding a sheaf high on his pitchfork, saying, "This is the one I've been looking for!" He would thatch the finished stacks with wheat straw.

Harvesting the sugar beet was a long, tiring job, but I had nothing to do with it because I was back in the cow-house. The sugar beet was eased out of the ground by a horse-drawn machine, and the workers pulled them out to lay them in rows. Then they came along with a bill-hook and cut the tops off, throwing the roots in small heaps. These were forked into tumbrils and brought off the field and put in a heap near to where they could be loaded on to a lorry, using forks. I used to take a tumbril into the fields and gather up the tops which were fed to the cows, but in limited amounts as too many would taint the milk. It was hard work on the farm but the men were very tolerant and helpful and there was a good spirit of comradeship.'

'In 1944 I joined the Land Army. Leaving Norwich by train I alighted at East Rudham station, to be met with a closed-in carriage and two horses to take me to the hostel two miles away. This was part of the local taxi service.

I worked with horses, harrowing, rolling and hay turning. At harvest time I loaded the waggons with sheaves. At sugar beet harvest we picked the beet up with bare hands and threw them into the cart. At the end of each week, after 48 hours' hard work, I received my wages, £2, with £1 of this going to the hostel for my keep. The work was hard, the food poor, but we had lots of fun evenings and weekends.'

DELIVERING THE GROCERIES

'I left school at the age of 16 in 1941. I then went to work at Hannant and Sons, High Class Grocers, in Swaffham, where I lived. I worked in the office as book-keeper.

At this time the shops in the town had pooled delivery services to the outlying villages to save petrol, which was in short supply. Groceries would be packed in boxes and loaded on to the vans from the Co-op, International Stores, Hannants, and Mallets, and taken out to the villages. One day for instance, the Co-op van would go with their driver, and someone from one of the other shops, to deliver to the villages around Swaffham and take orders to be delivered the next week. About two years after I started work, our van driver was off work for some time and I was asked to go on the vans with drivers from the other shops to deliver groceries to our customers. We would start about eight o'clock, loading the van with groceries from the two shops; sometimes I would go with the Co-op, sometimes with International Stores, sometimes with Mr Mallet and our other van driver, Mr Mann.

When I went with the Co-op we used to collect "Industrial" pies made at the Co-op bakery in Swaffham, as extra rations for farm workers. We always had a lovely hot pie before we left; this was very welcome on a cold winter's day (no heated vans in those days). A Mr George Wilson was the driver on these days, and our first call was on his mother and there we would have a hot drink and an apple turnover. When we delivered the groceries we had to mark the ration books, cut out any points and soap coupons and sweet coupons, collect the money and take orders for the next week. Food was very short by this time and off-ration foods were eagerly sought after, and at every house we were asked if there was anything off the ration. We went to all types of houses – big country halls, pubs, cottages, and even an old converted railway carriage where an old lady lived; she had a fire which smoked, so you could hardly see and your eyes smarted. She looked a bit smoke-dried but she was a very well-educated and interesting lady.

Some of the houses were not very clean and we hoped we would not be asked to have a cup of tea. However, most of the places were very homely and everyone was very kind, offering us a hot drink and a warm-up by the fire in the winter and cool drinks in the summer. When they knew that I had no father and no garden, I was given vegetables to take home. We tried to save off-ration goods for people living out of town, as they only came in at weekends on bicycles, and were not able to shop every day as the people could in town. We had some very nasty weather to contend with, the winters were very hard with snow and icy roads. Sometimes we could not get the van down snow-covered tracks across fields to farm cottages. This meant we had to carry the groceries over the field path. There were not many things in the boxes but you knew you were carrying them by the time you reached the door. I met some wonderful people, and many years later, after I had married, they would still know me and greet me in the market on Saturday.'

JAM AND MEAT PIES

'From 1940 to 1941 a preserving centre was established at Aldborough Hall, and made 2,900 lb of jam, jelly and chutney, and bottled 381 lb of fruit. The Aldborough and Thurgarton Women's Institute was the first, in May 1942, to start the "Meat Pie Scheme" in response to the government's aim of getting extra rations to the farmworkers. The pies were made at the green bakery and sold every week in the church room.'

'During the war we could buy specially made meat pies. They were delivered to the lady who lived at Bradenham school house. My brothers and I attended the school and would pick up the pies after school. I don't think they ever got home in one piece. They were usually nibbled round the edges.'

A CHILD'S WAR

As children we soon came to accept this strange new world, helping where we could and finding fun in necessity.

WE DIDN'T REALLY UNDERSTAND

'"The day war broke out" I remember very well. We had just arrived in Happisburgh for a week's holiday in a small wooden bungalow. The garden ran to the edge of the cliffs and whilst we were exploring, out of the sky came a German plane. It was flying at cliff height and we could see the pilot quite clearly. We all waved but he did not return the gesture. Next day the outbreak of war was announced. Nothing much happened, our holiday continued. Daily we climbed down the cliffs, which were quite steep, to the beach by means of some very rickety wooden steps, which would certainly have been condemned on sight by the new breed of "Safety Officers". We played on the sand and bathed in the sea. The sea, as I remember, was always so cold. My aunt, a hardy soul, would towel us down briskly to get us warm. The towel, full of sand, felt like sandpaper. Soon we had a rosy glow, giving an illusion of warmth. In reality, a few layers of skin had been scoured off. This was probably the last time we went to the seaside for the next five years or so, as the beaches were mined and closed to the general public, with the exception of a very few small areas.

Back at school in Coltishall after the summer holidays, we were prepared for the war. Air raids, being an immediate possibility, were practised for. If the weather was fine, we all went outside to take cover in "The Dell". This was a small wooded area alongside the school playground. If it was wet, we had to sit underneath our desks until the all clear sounded. Luckily the system was never put to the test; the village was not bombed. The only damage suffered was minor and considering the close proximity to the aerodrome this was quite surprising.

Joint exercises in the event of an air raid were organised. The Red Cross, St John Ambulance, Home Guard and Air Raid Wardens all participated. The Scouts and Girl Guides were the mock casualties and the messengers. We were given labels listing our injuries and had to sit about at strategic points in the village awaiting rescue. The high point was getting a ride in an ambulance. Mostly you had to walk back to the Red Cross centre, sometimes with "broken legs" because of a shortage of transport. Then the "good ladies" would practise their bandaging skills, with slings and splints and quite a number of eye pads which would never stay on for long. I don't know if they ever ran a bodycount, but they were always a few short. Waiting for attention was sometimes tedious and we would sneak off home.

Sunday mornings would be the time for the Home Guard to practise. This was also a source of entertainment for children. A very mixed assortment of men would be drilling on the football field. Marching did not come easily to most of them, but they made valiant efforts to obey the commands of an ex-army sergeant with a very loud voice. The "target", which was hung on the goal post, was attacked with vigour and enthusiasm, but none too accurately. The noisy young critics watching would often get sent home with a clip on the ear for being cheeky.

Black gas masks were issued to everyone, except very young children, whose gas masks had colourful Mickey Mouse-type faces. These were to be carried at all times. At school, more practising. How quickly could we all get them on? Then to test them we would have to pick up a piece of paper on the bottom of the mask by taking in a deep breath. We soon found that gas masks were a rich source of rude noises. To get used to them we were made to do a whole lesson wearing them. That was the idea anyway. Usually practice was swiftly curtailed, order restored and lessons continued.

Coal was in very short supply. The classrooms, which were large and very draughty, were heated by one small fire. One particular teacher was short and very broad. During the winter term he would conduct all the lessons leaning against the fireguard, thus blocking off any warmth which might have permeated into the room. Sometimes the rooms were so cold the inkwells had ice crystals in them.

During the early days of the war, evacuee children from Bethnal Green descended on the village. This disrupted our schooling somewhat. We had to share the school with them. Alternate weeks we went to school in the mornings and then in the afternoons. The week we were not using the school we mostly went on nature walks or had games. Wet days we took shelter in the chapel. I have no doubt our schooling suffered a great deal. Gradually the evacuees returned home, leaving only a few who were integrated with the village children and normal hours returned.

We were encouraged to help with the war effort. We collected baskets of rose hips to be made into syrup; also acorns for pig food. More nature walks, but at least we were doing something useful then. Nothing was wasted, anything edible was preserved in something: fruit was bottled, vegetables salted, eggs "laid down" in waterglass. We scoured the hedgerows for blackberries. During the jam-making season preserving sugar was off ration. Hazelnuts grew in the hedgerows, and also a small red plum we called a "malabella" plum. It was sweet and delicious when ripe. Food and clothing were rationed for a very long time after the war. We were certainly not a "throw away society" then. One other thing I remember doing as war work was helping my granny thread ball and socket beads onto a length of thick wire, about three to four feet long. They were made of a white, waxy material very like plastic. For this she was paid a small amount for each strip. I have never been able to find out what these were used for, nor indeed have I ever met anyone else who can remember doing this.

Looking back, I don't think as children we were really aware of what war meant. The death and destruction wasn't really brought home to us. There was something rather exciting about watching "dogfights" overhead. I don't think we really thought about anyone being killed and maimed. Boys collected bits of shrapnel and if a plane crashed anywhere near, word soon went round the grapevine, and hordes of boys on bicycles would rush to find trophies before the authorities arrived and chased them away. With television bringing all the horror into our homes, children these days could never remain so carefree, living through such difficult years.'

HEAR THE BELLS?

'I lived in a village near Norwich. My mother seemed to think that if the Germans dropped gas the church bells would ring. One night she woke me up and told me to dress quickly. She said that she could hear bells and went off to investigate with her gas mask on. I was left to manage as best I could as a four year old with a liberty bodice to negotiate in the dark. My mother meanwhile had met up with a neighbour returning to his farm after delivering a cow. He was most surprised to see her (especially with the gas mask on, no doubt). They both stood still in the cold night air and listened, then all was revealed. My pet goat was caught up with his chain wrapped around his stake!'

211

GETTING TO SCHOOL

'During the war years between the ages of eleven and 16 I travelled from Terrington St Clement to school in King's Lynn.

Leaving home to catch the 8 am bus and arriving home at 4 pm meant that during the winter months journeys were made in the blackout. To this day we have few street lights in the village but then, of course, torches could not be freely used and there was no friendly gleam from windows and outside lamps to guide us on our way.

The double decker buses took children, workers and shoppers to and from Lynn – children sitting on the top deck often three and four to a seat and many people standing downstairs. However, we and the bus all survived thanks to good drivers, less speed and less traffic.

The windows were covered in a heavy netting, securely stuck down, with a small diamond shape left open in the centre from which to espy the outside world.

Later a "special" bus was allocated to schoolchildren. This was much more exciting having an open staircase to climb at the back to get to the upper deck. What fun the boys had in the winter throwing snowballs right into the open space and how the conductresses disliked having to brave the elements.

I don't think we really feared the times when the sirens sounded during the school day. In fact to file out into the corridors to a place of comparative safety was quite welcome during a maths or history lesson!

Much more of a dread were school dinners! No choice of dishes – but looking back it must have been a most difficult task for the catering staff with the small ration allowance.

Apart from our satchels which were usually heavy with homework books we always had our gas masks to carry – fortunately never needed.'

BULLETS AND BOMBS

'As we lived bordering the airfield at Ludham, we were allowed to go to all the concerts and entertainments with a special pass. We got to know several of the airmen and were once told confidentially that the Queen would be visiting the airfield. We all decided to stand at the end of the road and when a policeman came along to move us on we told him we were all out for a walk! He did let us stay and we had a lovely view of the Queen.

We were all issued with gas masks, which we took every day to school. My sister had a special sit-in mask for babies which she thought was great fun. All the windows at school were criss-crossed with tape against blast. I slept with my sister in a Morrison air raid shelter, and we used the top as a table. One night we had all the windows blown out as two bombs were dropped at the front of the bungalows and one at the back. Moonlight shone in and we thought the bungalow was on fire. The ARP were soon on the scene to help and we had the next day off school.

We would see all the planes start out and count them and would be there again when they returned, hoping they all came back. One day when I was hanging linen on the line for my mother I was machine gunned by a very low plane. I quickly fell into the hedge and as soon as I could, rushed indoors. Another time we had a bullet through the bedroom window. At times it was very frightening and we were always careful not to show any lights, being on the airfield boundary.'

HELPING AT HARVEST

'During the war, about 1941, we children – my two brothers and myself – had a pony and trap and used it to go about locally. In the summer (double summertime) we used to go in to Dereham to the first house at the cinema and leave the pony and cart at the George Hotel with Tom Pye, the ostler.

Most of the young men were called up so we were short of people at harvest and my brothers and I had to work as "hold gee" drivers. We had three horses – Beauty, Blossom and Kitty – who pulled the waggons which were loaded with the shocks of corn and we had to drive to the stacks. Oats and wheat weren't so bad, but the barley was dirty and the haulms from the ears of corn used to stick to us and itch. At the end of the day we rode the horses back to the stables, but they always went to the pit first and we had to hold tight or we would go over their heads into the water. My father often wouldn't wait for an empty waggon to move the thatching ladder and would ride a bicycle with it on his shoulder.'

LIFE WITH GRANDMOTHER

'It was during the late 1930s and early 1940s I went to stay with my widowed grandmother. She lived in a cottage seven miles south of Norwich and at that time had no running water or electricity. It was a great delight to me to accompany her several times a day to collect water from a nearby hand pump and also to sit listening to stories – she was a great storyteller – by the light of a paraffin lamp.

During the early part of the war she thought it unsafe to sleep upstairs and had her bed brought down into her "front" room. On this bed were put all the feather beds from the remaining bedrooms.

213

As a child I felt I was climbing way up to the ceiling when I slept in Granny's bed, but how warm and cosy it was.

We spent many summer days going for long walks together, picking flowers and gathering wild strawberries. Often we sat together by a small stream watching fish in the dark blue water and the bright dragonflies darting about. Every week my grandmother collected her pension from the local post office and I was given threepence plus her sweet ration – a great extra treat in those days. At home an older boy cousin and I exchanged apples, pears and plums from our orchard for candy from the Americans as they cycled past on their way to and from Norwich.

Various people descended on the village from London. My mother was busy helping to billet these folk within the village community. They tended to return quite quickly to their London homes. However, many also came from Norwich every night, returning in the morning. These too were housed in the homes of the villagers.

In spite of all the comings and goings in the village we contrived to spend our holidays paddling in a nearby stream, catching tiddlers, playing five-stones and flying kites. In the winter when it snowed we all made our way to a nearby slope where we had great fun either on our sledges or tin trays. Perhaps it was because I was a child then but life seemed so much gentler and great fun just within the village community. We all seemed to be part of one very large family.'

LITTLE PITCHERS

'Always, the smell of blackcurrants takes me back to the Norfolk of my childhood; sitting, a four year old blissfully unaware that a war was raging, under the blackcurrant bushes in the back garden listening to the bees buzzing and the voices of my mother and various neighbours in the background. They are gathered round the well which served a row of ten houses and was approached along a grassy path running along the ends of the back gardens. I can hear laughter and the occasional warning, "Little pitchers have big ears!" I was waiting for Raymond, the big boy from next door, to come along so I could catch him taking our strawberries and threaten to set the dog, who was always referred to as Gerry, on him. His name confused me. My father said there were "Gerries" everywhere but we only had the one dog.

The well was a very important feature of life. Every morning early there would be a procession of men and boys with pails – they were always "pails", not buckets – fetching the water for the household for the day. The older men still used yokes to carry the pails. Even in the darkest winter weather the water had to be fetched and no light could be used for fear of the unseen "Gerries" zooming in on

214

the well. None of the gardens had vegetables too close to the path as no one wanted to take a fall into a cabbage patch while carrying two pails of ice-cold water. Sometimes we ran out of water before Father came home and then Mother would venture out with a pail on to the ice-covered well paving. I used to hang on to her skirt in case she should tumble down the well. No one ever fell in but often someone would be held over the edge to fish out a pail that had come off the hook.

Well water was only used for drinking, cooking, washing faces, babies and teeth. Water for bathing, washing linen, washing hair, watering plants and animals came out of the water butts placed strategically around every available building. My brother got himself into severe trouble one year when he put a large amount of frogspawn into Grandfather's water butt, as the old man insisted that he owed his health and strength to always drinking rainwater!

The well featured in one wartime drama. One evening we were about to have tea when the aforementiond Raymond rushed in to say that there were German spies poisoning the well. My father was in the Home Guard and up till then had done very little apart from standing about by the cemetery on dark nights. He put on his greatcoat and ran down the garden path with his rifle. Mother called after him to take his gas mask but he was soon back safely with two men in uniform. They sat at the table and shared our tea, and one was crying and the other put his elbows on the table which I thought was very bad manners but nobody else took any notice. Raymond was told to clear off and I was put to bed, and in the morning all was back to normal. Years later I was told that the men, who were only teenagers, were Dutch soldiers who were on a training exercise, having been parachuted in and told to find their way back to base, living off the land and avoiding detection. They had hoped to get water to drink from our well, but their army training had not prepared them for boys like Raymond who went out raiding other people's strawberry beds. And he made friends with our dog Gerry, too.'

THE GAS VAN

'I was five years old when the war started. I went to Hillside Avenue School, Thorpe St Andrew. I remember being fitted for a gas mask which I had to take everywhere I went.

The "Gas Van" visited our school. It was large, like a single decker bus, but it didn't have windows. We put on our gas masks and about twelve children went in through a door at the back of the van; it was shut and another door opened and we were inside. We sat on seats down each side of the van and sang songs, or recited poems. We

End of the war celebrations included donning fancy dress at Shipdham in 1945!

were told not to touch our gas masks. Some kind of gas was released to enable our masks to be tested. After about ten to 15 minutes we left the van and ran around the playground, still with our masks on, to get the gas out of our clothes. Then it was back to the classroom and the next twelve children went to the van.

Goodness knows what kind of gas it was, but I don't remember anyone suffering any ill effects! I have never heard of any other school doing this.'

'ON YOUR BIRTHDAY'

'"When will the war be over, Daddy?" I was constantly asking. Father, no doubt tired of my constant badgering, replied, "On your birthday" and it was! On the very day. I was six. Of course he knew more of current affairs than I did so perhaps it was not such a lucky guess. I remember spending the evening curled up in a chair whilst the grown ups were partying. There was a cake that someone had decorated with white icing and covered with little flags of all the allied nations. At least I think it was a cake – it looked like one but I do not recall it being cut and eaten.

Later a bonfire was built on the bomb site at the rear of our house and someone sat a "guy" of Hitler on it. My parents could not understand why I was too frightened to go to the bonfire party, I could scarcely watch it through the bedroom window.

VJ Day was a much happier time. My mother, sister and I were staying at Bacton on Sea in a holiday bungalow. Father was at home in Norwich, working. One morning he came running down the lane to the bungalow shouting, "The war's over! the war's over!" Everyone was so excited. There were some soldiers stationed nearby. They were so overjoyed that they took the sergeant and put him in the water butt.'

THE EVACUEES

Even before war had been officially declared plans were in hand to move children out of the cities to safety in the countryside and many of these little evacuees came to Norfolk. Some never settled, and opened their country hosts' eyes to a very different way of life, but others loved their new homes.

OUR EXTENDED FAMILY

'Everyone knew that there was going to be a war, which meant that all children living in danger areas were to be sent to the country. Therefore, in each country town or village a billeting officer was appointed; ours at Burnham Market happened to be the postmaster. He visited each house in the village and ascertained how many children, and of what sex, could be accommodated. We did not know when they would arrive.

On Friday, 1st September 1939, news spread around the village that evacuees would be arriving during the afternoon. Most of the people who were to become their "foster parents" went to the Hall to collect their children. They had come the last part of their journey by coaches. Most of the children had come from Shoreditch secondary school but brought younger brothers or sisters with them. Thinking back to the Hall, it was rather like a slave market with people saying, "I'll have this one," or "I'll have those two." I can remember one lady, from a farm, saying, "I'll have my four boys," and driving them off in her car. We had a nine year old girl, Doreen, and her 13 year old brother, Leslie. We took them home, each with a gas mask, a small case of clothes and a postcard to send home to parents giving their new address. At the Hall they were given a brown paper carrier bag containing a tin of corned beef and a tin of evaporated milk to help provide an evening meal for the unexpected children.

Our children settled in after, to them, an exciting day, and went to bed too tired to be homesick. Next morning Leslie was anxious to find where his twin boy cousins were living as he was supposed to keep an eye on them. He soon found them housed nearby.

Doreen was a very lively child and very chatty. She was always tap dancing; our kitchen lino didn't take kindly to it! She used to sing all the latest songs. She wrote long letters home about what was happening in the village and about school. One teacher she did not like; we were always hearing about "Old Nagger". Her one desire was to scrub our front doorstep. "Can't I scrub 10, Downing Street?" she used to say. We had a fanlight, otherwise there was no resemblance in our eyes.

Leslie used to go out with his friends and read a lot. He had little to say except, "What's for afters?"

On appointed Sundays, special rail transport was laid on for parents to visit their children. This unsettled some of them. As there was no immediate activity in London many children returned home. After about a year ours went home too. Later on the mother, who also had a three year old boy, was evacuated with her children when her husband went in the Navy.

They had not been gone long before the billeting officer came to ask if my mother would accept a 14 year old girl, Florence. She was a very quiet, well spoken girl and had a younger sister, Nelly, and a little brother Dickie housed in the same road with, as we thought, a respected woman. She used to put things in their cases and say they had stolen them and then punish them. They were too frightened to say anything until they were going home. Florence only stayed a few months with us as it was time for her to leave school.

Soon after, a Young Soldiers' Regiment came to the village and was billeted in private houses. My mother was allocated three lads; one Irish, one English and one Welsh. She was told that if they were any trouble there were two of their officers billeted next door. They were lively lads, but behaved themselves. They used to meet their pals and discuss what they had all had to eat and whose "Mother" cooked the best apple pies. Their stay was for only a few weeks.

Hardly a breathing space before the billeting officer came again. Would my mother have Alan, a small seven year old boy? His mother had visited her three boys and didn't like the way her youngest was being brought up. Alan duly arrived, a very small boy in a brown blazer and school cap. I can remember my aged grandmother putting her arm round him when he arrived and saying, "You'll be all right, we'll look after you." He immediately settled in as one of the family. He was a cheerful little boy, never any bother and never got cross. He used to go to his friends to play Monopoly, and was a keen Cub.

Every Saturday morning a parcel arrived from "Our Mum". She sent comics, sweets, little extras and pocket money so that he could go to the local cinema – first house on a Saturday evening. He seemed to be with us forever. He went home for a short while; their house was bombed so back he came. At the end of the war he went home to continue his schooling. Then he returned for his holidays. For his National Service he joined the Navy and then used to spend his leaves with us. We missed him when he eventually married and had other interests, but he always sends a Christmas card.

During the war we had two different regiments billeted in empty houses in the village. The WVS ran an evening canteen for them. There we came in contact with the men and often had one or two home for Sunday tea. One Christmas we had two for lunch.

I think that my mother did very well to balance the rations, to feed and look after her "new children" besides playing her part in the Civil Defence Casualty Service, the WVS plus the WI.'

A group of evacuees on Aldborough Green in 1939. Many children found new friends and a happy life in Norfolk villages.

219

THE FIRST NIGHT ON STRAW

'I first came to Norfolk at the age of ten on 3rd September 1939. I was evacuated from Gravesend, Kent. We travelled on the *Royal Sovereign*, a paddle steamer.

By the time we reached Southend pier war was declared, and destroyers accompanied us. Needless to say it was a very traumatic journey. A large number of the children and teachers were sick. I was one of the lucky ones. When we reached Great Yarmouth we spent the first night sleeping on straw in the racing stables. The greatest thrill was to see our headmistress in her nightdress. She was human after all! With this excitement we forgot to feel homesick.

Next day we were taken by coach to Aldborough. By then I think we were all rather grubby and tired, but were warmly greeted by the WI with tea and currant buns (just like the ones my mother made).

We were taken by car to live with the Norman family – Mr Norman was a chauffeur for the Rev Lilley at the Hall. On the way my rather imaginative five year old sister was convinced she was going to a witch's house. Actually we were fortunate, we had a wonderful home.

Coming from the modern suburbs of London, Aldborough was so different. Water was still pumped and there were privies in the garden. The life and the hierarchy at the Hall fascinated me. We picked primroses and violets from the hedgerows, gleaned in the cornfields and paddled in the streams. School was in the church room sitting at trestle tables. The green was our playground. We loved it all. Although we were evacuated to Staffordshire after the fall of Dunkirk, we still kept in contact with the family in Aldborough. Norfolk has indeed been my second home.'

VOLUNTARY EVACUEE

'My grandmother owned a pig and poultry farm in a hamlet called Brookville. The village was always known as the "Fruit Colony" as it had been designed as a community for ex-servicemen after the First World War. It was sponsored by government funds to be self sufficient. There was a jam factory, a printing works, a pub, post office and even a small community centre. Sadly by 1939 only the shop and pub survived. On the first day of the war, 3rd September 1939, my grandmother and uncle drove in to London to fetch me, aged seven, and I was to spend the rest of the war with them.

During 1940 several children from the East End of London were evacuated to our village. They were housed in local homes but as there were so many of them the primary school was unable to place them in classes. This meant they were marched along the street to the large Methodist schoolroom, including me! It was a most miserable day, as I could not understand their Cockney accents, and I could not wait to get home that afternoon. My grandmother was a tiny lady, just four feet ten inches, but really strong willed and aggressive, so off she went to see the local school governor three miles away to tell him that on no account would I go to the Methodist school. "He was unable to alter things" was his response, so I was kept at home for two weeks and finally returned to the primary school. Until I left, "VE" was always written beside my name in the school register – Voluntary Evacuee!'

YARMOUTH EVACUEES

'As sixth formers at Great Yarmouth High School, we arrived on the first day of the autumn term 1939 to find that the juniors were to be sent home, while we remained to help with some of the newly arrived evacuees – mentally handicapped youngsters from a Dagenham school. With no experience in this field we found them very difficult to deal with. Their aspirations were so different from ours, and our hitherto sheltered existence had not equipped us for the job. I have a vivid mental picture of chasing couples whose sole interest appeared to be in kissing each other. One of their staff told me to stop this at all costs, but no sooner had I separated one "courting couple" than I had to tackle the next!

Our next task was knitting woolly ends to fit on gas masks – designed to filter smoke, I believe. As all the non-knitting juniors had to be catered for, the task seemed endless.

June 1940 came the day of our own evacuation, our only instructions being to assemble at Vauxhall station at 10 am, wearing our school uniform and carrying our gas masks.

We sixth formers patrolled the train and alternately controlled and comforted the younger children. It seemed to us to be the start of a great adventure. There was much speculation as to our destination until rumour had it that it was to be Retford in Nottinghamshire.

On arrival, we assembled on the station platform to be allocated to billets. Retford had already had evacuees from a city, and expected similar problems from us. Members of the Billeting Committee surveyed us anxiously as they took down essential particulars. Many of the younger children by now tired out and dispirited, dissolved into tears. The prospective billet parents remained in the waiting room until suitable evacuees had been selected for them.

We as seniors, did our best to console the diminishing band of forlorn children. A friend and I who were left until almost the last, began to feel that our adventure was rapidly turning into a disaster. We were, however, among the lucky ones, finding billet parents who genuinely welcomed us as members of the family.'

221

FROM THE EAST END

'My mother's first evacuees were a brother and sister, Gwen and Ken, from the East End of London; their father was a bus driver. A few minutes after they arrived, someone brought another brother and sister, younger, and they were Italian. Their language was filthy and they were beautiful but dirty. Mother said she could only have the two she'd got and they promised to find another place for the Italians. These last two refused to wash, they said they had washed the week before, and they wouldn't sit on chairs, they said they always sat on the floor. The children had each been given a tin of corned beef and you can imagine my mother's horror when the Italian boy opened his with his teeth and fished the meat out with his fingers. The vicar came and said he would take these two and Mother told him about the language as he had two small girls. However, he said that could be cured and took them away. A month afterwards, Mother met him and asked how they were getting on, and he said he had to let them go as his own little girls were swearing.

Gwen and Ken stayed a good while but their parents wanted them back. Mother was taken ill and I came home to nurse her. Some more children arrived, and two brothers nobody would take, they had been shifted around, and against the doctor's advice I said give them to me.

I didn't like the idea of school dinners so had them come home, and good meals caused the youngest to come full of sores, at least that was what the doctor said it was. I had to dress and treat them, all over his little body, twice a day. I got him well, and when it was time for them to go home they threatened to run away, they cried and screamed. Apparently they were knocked about by their father and starved by their mother.'

ONE OF THE LUCKY VICTIMS

'Early in 1944 my mother and I were evacuated to Norfolk along with several other families. I don't remember much about the journey except waking up on the bus as we rounded a bend and seeing a white fence with a letter box in it, and then discovering my teddy bear had lost a leg! (I believe the fence in question was the gateway to Hoveton Hall.)

We were taken to Stalham school and into the hall through what seemed to me to be very tall green doors and from there were distributed to our various hosts. Mum and I were sent to Holly Farm, Ingham, along with another lady and her two children. Her name was Mrs Esther Rose and the two children were Terry, who was about three and a half, and Wendy who was about 18 months or possibly younger. It's hard to remember exactly as I was only about four years old myself.

Mr and Mrs Russell and their son Oliver owned the farm and went out of their way to make us welcome. We lived in one half of the farmhouse and they lived in the other, each half being completely self contained.

My Mum and Auntie Essie (as I called Mrs Rose) must have found things a bit daunting to say the least, as we had all come from the suburbs where we lived in houses with all mod cons and at the farm there was nothing. We had oil lamps and cooking stoves, a toilet at the bottom of the garden path and all the water had to be pumped into buckets in the pump house and brought into the house in the buckets. I remember my Mum dropping a bucket with a shriek one day as a lizard ran out from underneath it. Fortunately she was in the pump house, as it was a full one.

We had great fun on bath night in the tin tub in front of the fire. At least we children thought it was fun!

What happy days we had outside amongst the animals. There were pigs, calves, chickens and cows to be fed. We spent hours hunting for eggs in all the most unlikely places and were so excited when we found one. The broody hens and their baby chicks were also a great delight.

I think my greatest love was the lovely old cart horses which we would ride for hours on end. I spent more time on the back of old Gypsy than anywhere else, plodding endlessly up and down the furrows as we ploughed and sowed fields, with Jeffrey the ploughman singing *The old lamplighter* time after time.

Another activity I was introduced to was "rabbiting". Each evening one of the farmworkers would take me out with him and his ferrets, and we would come home laden. I must admit now I couldn't eat rabbit pie if I was paid – we seemed to live on it.

We would spend hours at a time lying in the clover fields looking for four-leafed clover, but I don't remember ever finding one. At other times we would roam the fields looking for the strips of silver paper that were dropped to confuse the radar. This was put to great use for Christmas tree decorations. Our tree was extra special as it was cut from one of the holly trees around the farm and great deliberations took place deciding which branch was to be cut. Oliver would then chop it off and place it firmly in a bucket and bring it indoors for us to decorate. Not an easy task with all the prickly leaves!

I started going to the local village school for a while and of course got teased unmercifully about my funny accent. However, I survived and thoroughly enjoyed being there, except for having to drink ice cold milk (I was now used to having it straight from

223

the cow), and having to run outside and across the playground to the outside loos.

One day my Mum got up in the morning and announced that we were going back home, for no apparent reason she felt she had to go, so everything was hurriedly packed and off we went. We didn't go straight home to our own house in South Woodford but to my mother's parents in Hainault. We had hardly been in the house an hour when the phone rang and it was my father, phoning to let my Nana know that he was home and off to Norfolk. Imagine the surprise he had when Nana told him, "There is no need, they are here." Of course I didn't understand what all the tears and smiles were about, and when he arrived I remember kicking this strange man who was hugging and kissing *my* Mum. All was revealed eventually and I was quite happy to be hugged and kissed myself, although I remember his uniform was very prickly.

Once we got back to our own home things began to settle down but I started picking up every illness that was going and was really quite ill. In the end the doctors said there was nothing for it but to take me back to live in the country and it was decided to sell up our home and move back to Norfolk. We were very lucky and able to come back to Holly Farm. Dad got a job in a local market garden and we lived at the farm until Mum and Dad bought their own place at Hickling a few years later.

I really feel I was one of the *lucky* victims of the war, it brought terrible sorrow and unhappiness to many people, but to me it brought the opportunity to grow up in the country amongst some of the kindest and friendliest people I have ever been fortunate enough to meet.'

HIGHDAYS & HOLIDAYS

SPECIAL TIMES

Most villages could provide their own entertainment in days gone by, from parish teas and magic lantern shows to amateur dramatics. We had little time for leisure but made sure we enjoyed what we had, whether it was listening to the new wireless or joining in celebrations for Royal jubilees and coronations. Our horizons were so much narrower then, before the days of television and long distance travel.

TREADING THE BOARDS

'In the 1920s at Swaffham we did not have a lot of entertainment, but groups of about 15 or 16 people from the village got together and put on one or two shows a year for charity. It was great fun and very surprising to discover the talent everyone had.'

'The first we children knew was a poster appearing on the back of the shop door, advertising the latest production of Honingham

Honingham Drama Group performing If Four Walls Tell *in 1956.*

226

Drama Group. For the next few weeks excitement grew. What was the play? Who would be in it?

On that long awaited evening in the 1950s the village hall was transformed. We entered by a side door, one end of the hall was curtained off and a stage had appeared. Children were allowed to sit on benches in front of the rows of chairs, and much pushing and jostling went on; the braver boys tried to peep under the curtain. Some threw sweet papers over the top. This usually had the desired effect of bringing someone out from backstage, if only to tell us off for our impatience.

At last, the curtains parted. Of course, we knew everybody in the cast, but tonight was different. The make-up altered them and we could forget who they had been. We were carried into the world of make-believe, become reality through the village drama group.'

AN ENTERTAINMENT

'As small children living in Norwich in the 1920s (with no television or radio) we greeted with delight any entertainment outside the board games of ludo and snakes and ladders that filled our leisure hours. The streets of Norwich were safe for even a young child to walk in, and so at seven I was allowed to accompany my friend and neighbour of eight to the local church hall for lantern lectures usually showing grateful coloured children smiling at the camera. On this particular evening we heard of a different programme – something to do with a Blue Riband. It sounded interesting so we hurried and entered a church hall packed with rows of children. Unfortunately we arrived in the middle of the proceedings and missed the introductory talk (no doubt about the Blue Riband) but in time to hear the lady in charge asking for items of entertainment.

We heard two recitations which we thought rather dull, but were amazed to see the artistes rewarded with a shining new penny. Requests for more volunteers met with silence. I could stand it no longer – think how many liquorice allsorts one could buy for even a halfpenny. A normally shy child, to my companion's amazement I sped up the hall on to the platform and produced, with histrionic talents no one had suspected, a spirited rendering of "And Shall Trelawny die? Here's twenty thousand Cornishmen shall know the reason why"! A thunder of applause greeted my descent from the platform but far more important, a tiny, shiny threepenny "joey" was pressed into my hand. The evening then closed with an exhortation for us all to swear to avoid the demon drink and to sign the pledge. It seemed only right to repay their generosity by signing, but the queue was so long, and our return home long past curfew time, so regretfully we hurried from the hall. So I can now drink my occasional glass of sherry with a clear conscience.'

PARISH TEAS AND MAGIC LANTERNS

'The annual parish tea was a social gathering at Little Ellingham between the wars. Farmers' wives would each provide a sitdown meat tea with trifles, pies and cakes for twelve people. This meant getting crockery, cutlery and sometimes the tables as well as the food to the parish room. Tickets were one shilling so it was usually only the menfolk who came for the meal. His ticket would be purchased from the person whose food he preferred. Mother and the family would come along later for the social evening that followed and for a few pence they would be entertained. There would be crackers and streamers for the children, who scrambled for nuts and oranges, and they would enjoy the leftovers from the meal.

The King's Messengers, a Society for the Propagation of the Gospel, would meet one evening of the week and make toys and various small items from fretwork, supervised by Rev R. M. Boys, who also had a magic lantern. During Lent this would be used at meetings in the parish room, showing slides of far-off places. Sometimes eyes would be watering and noses held to fend against the smell of carbide which fuelled the lantern.'

CINEMA AND REPERTORY

'Occasionally in the 1950s a travelling cinema show would come to the village halls. We certainly had our fair share of Laurel and Hardy, Old Mother Riley and George Formby films at Bradenham, amongst a variety of others. Without fail, every time the projector would break down and amidst the groans and whistling from the audience the lights would come on as we waited for the repairs to take place. This was an accepted part of the show and we all returned the next time for more of the same.

We also had repertory companies who visited the villages and performed plays. They sometimes needed a child in their plays and there was always a willing volunteer who would take to the stage and receive a small wage in return for helping the company out and becoming a star for the evening.'

THE WIRELESS

'When wireless first came out not many people could afford one, so some young men made their own. I remember in 1930 one boy at Sparham had his out in a field. I was sitting on a stile nearby when I heard it announced that Amy Johnson had just landed from her

Aldborough ladies' football team played a home match against the ladies of Aylsham in 1958 in aid of the village green fund. Everyone in the village turned out to watch.

adventurous flight to Australia. I remember everyone clapping and cheering.'

'Apart from an occasional village concert, entertainment was a very home-made affair and my first pleasure was when we had a radio, or wireless as we called them then, which worked by a dry and a wet battery. Each week the accumulator man came to exchange the wet batteries. The best programme to me was *Monday Night at Seven* (which I think later became *Monday Night at Eight*). There was always a little quiz and a story in drama, which the narrator would end by saying, "What would you do, chum?" Later on he would come back and say what had happened in the story. The last item was always a beautiful piece by a choir, which must have been the first "good" music I had ever heard.'

WHEN THE BBC CAME TO NORWICH

'I well remember the week the BBC came to Norwich – 27th April to 4th May 1946. As a pupil at the Blyth School I went to the temporary BBC studio at the Norwich Castle Museum and listened to auditions for *Children's Hour*. Three of my fellow pupils were chosen to broadcast and another young singer from the cathedral choir. Others successful at the auditions were a quintet from the City of Norwich School and the Reepham Junior Band. After the auditions we all crowded round Stuart Hibberd, the senior BBC announcer, and he signed our autograph books.

For me and my fellow pupils, television had not even entered our thoughts. We would have thought it magic if someone had said that in only a few years' time the results could have been televised!'

OFF TO THE EMPIRE EXHIBITION

'In April 1924 the Empire was celebrated at the British Empire Exhibition at Wembley. I was a child of nine years and there was great excitement in our home: Mother was taking my sister and me and a few other friends to Wembley. Norwich Co-op had chartered a train and were picking up at North Walsham.

The great day arrived and early in the morning we boarded the train. On arriving at Liverpool Street station we were met by a fleet of coaches which took us on a tour of London and on to Wembley. Lunch was laid on at a restaurant which had been built for the occasion – they seated 30,000 visitors at a time. You could have lunch in South Africa, take tea in India and dine in New Zealand, Canada or Australia.

There were flower gardens intersected by waterways and broad avenues. The world's first never-stop railway conveyed thousands of visitors over 15 miles of road. The amusement park was the then largest ever built and the thrills and sideshows were never ending. A Mr J. Cochrane, a theatrical producer, brought from Canada, United States, Australia and Argentina cowboys and cowgirls plus hundreds of horses and cattle. There was wild horse racing, broncho riding contests, calf roping and steer racing, all for money prizes. The ladies were catered for with dress exhibitions, arts and crafts, sports and hobbies. I remember a parade of The Wembley Beauties who appeared at The Palace of Beauty representing women of history and fiction.

All parts of the Empire seemed to be represented. It really was to show to the world the great resources of the Empire and British Industry. We listened to the King's recorded speech, and this in itself was exciting as very few people possessed a wireless. There were wonderful exhibits, I remember a replica of the Niagara Falls, an effigy of the then Prince of Wales in butter, a coal mine with real pit ponies, but it was Queen Mary's dolls house which seemed to attract the biggest crowds. As the day came to a close we made our way to the stadium where there was a pageant, a portrayal of Captain Cook capturing Botany Bay. I remember the vessels with full sails and full of seamen slowly moving across the arena, soldiers, guns, hundreds of performers acting this event.

The last thing I remember as I fell asleep on the train was hearing singing:

Let's go to the Exhibition, Exhibition 1924
That's the place to be, Oh! it's better than the sea
So all take a holiday and go to Wemberley!'

JUBILEE AND CORONATION

'I told everyone I was going to "The Pageant", although I had no idea what a pageant was. I was wildly excited, the King and Queen were going to be there too. The occasion was to commemorate the Silver Jubilee of George V and Queen Mary in 1935 and the pageant was being held at Blickling Hall.

Even more important, we were having new clothes for the occasion. Mother had a new hat. It was a large straw hat which she decorated with floating ribbons. Granny had a new dress. I had only ever seen her in one dress. In the mornings she always wore a long black skirt, summer or winter, over which she wore a large white cook's apron. Every afternoon she washed and changed into her only dress. It was a dark maroon with a cream pattern. The new dress, which was being paid for "on the book" with a shilling a week, was very smart indeed. It was black with a coloured embroidered panel on the front bodice and two loose panels down the front of the skirt.

My mother made my dress with new material. Usually she cut down old clothes for me, but this was new. It was a small blue and white gingham with puff sleeves, a Peter Pan collar and little blue buttons down the front. My life would have been complete had I been able to have a pair of black patent leather ankle-strap shoes. But no, brown sensible sandals it had to be. My brother must also have had new clothes but I don't seem to have been very interested in his sartorial splendour.

Off we went on the train from Coltishall to Aylsham and then by bus to Blickling Hall. We sat on tiered seats along the drive leading to the hall. The pageant was a series of historical tableaux as far as I can remember. Then came the King and Queen in an open carriage. I was

231

very disappointed. I had expected them to be wearing their crowns and ermine and jewels. The memory of the new clothes lasted a long time though. I grew out of the dress but I still have the little blue buttons. And Granny, well, every afternoon until she died in 1948 she changed into her "new" dress.'

'The Coronation Day of 2nd June 1953 turned out dreadful, with wind and rain all day. North Wootton had arranged a great programme of events by village volunteers but the day was spent mostly watching television in the village hall. Very few people had their own sets in those days, or had even seen television before. Tea was served in the barn at the rear of the Priory as, of course, the food had all been catered for. The sports and games were held on the following weekend.'

HOLIDAY TIME

A holiday at the seaside was the high spot in many summers, or perhaps a quiet cruise on the Broads, memories held dear by generations of Norfolk children and those who came from further afield.

AN EDWARDIAN SEASIDE HOLIDAY

'We all have treasured memories, and mine go back to the time when Edward VII was on the throne. A family holiday by the sea was indeed an event.

First came all the preparation, with Father going to the station to pay just one silver shilling to have our large well-roped tin trunk transported "luggage in advance" in just one day. As suitcases were not then in general use, we had a rigid, woven straw dress-basket, which travelled with us on the train. It consisted of two overlapping separate sections which thus acted as an expanding carrier, well strapped for transport.

The children all had their own spades, wooden ones for the younger children, but with blades of metal for the older ones. The pails, decorated red, blue and white, were to become treasure houses as the holiday proceeded, returning home laden with coloured seaweeds, shining patterned pebbles and shells of all descriptions. The beach was everyone's main thought, but on arrival, all were first bought special "sand shoes".

The sand itself gave lots of fun, with sand pies, castles with turrets, moats and tunnels. Games with shuttlecocks and battledore, bats and balls and quoits were played, and whirligigs and kites soared to the skies. Before the popular donkey rides, toddlers were thrilled with rides in little carts pulled by nanny goats.

Of course, all seaside towns hosted a Punch and Judy show, and special Minstrels also had their show. No litter spoilt the golden sand. A man with pointed stick spiked and bagged up any stray untidy pieces, and in those days, children all obeyed parents saying that "bits" were not allowed.

Before the days when stacks of lounging deckchairs were piled up for hire, the ladies, in their white, high-neck, long-sleeved blouses and long skirts, complete with hats secured by large hat pins front and back, sat erect on little wooden chairs.

Paddling time was strictly rationed to avoid possible chills on holiday. The boys, in knickerbocker suits, were quickly ready for this pursuit, but girls, with long black stockings and dresses to their knees, had petticoats and frocks to crush hurriedly into their bloomers. The toddler had special stretching pants pulled over her dress, and looking rather like a balloon was taken, hand in hand, by Father, with his trousers rolled up to the knees, to dip the toes into the rippling waves, and then to search the rocky pools for shells and starfish, known from books.

Gradually the fashion had arrived for both male and female to bathe in the sea. Father had a stockinette, stripey swimsuit, buttoned from close up to the neck down the front and with short elbow-length sleeves – rather wasp-like in appearance with grey and black stripes. Mother wore a really rather elegant blue and white creation, made of alpaca, with cuffs and collar, skirt, pants too, with frills below the knee. A bright red suit for the dark-haired girl, a blue one for the auburn girl, navy blue for both the boys and pretty blue for the toddler completed the family attire. But how to get from beach to sea? It would have been quite indecent for such a parade across the sand! However, bathing machines were close at hand, with wheels and shafts, and seats inside, where we could change into our special gear. Then the box on wheels was hauled by a horse into the foam, where strong steps were fixed from the door into the waves. We held tightly to a very strong rope, to help us feel brave, as we all went down to get quite wet! This was an experience never to be forgotten. Swimmers went out into the sea, but ladies bobbed up and down, and children soon found the fun of sitting in the surf. My special joy as the toddler, was to sit very still on Father's shoulders, while he swam out into the sea and I rode high in glee. Oh, what joy we had beside the sunlit sparkling sea!'

SUMMER AT GORLESTON IN THE 1920s

'We came from London to Gorleston for three weeks every summer. This was the high spot of the year, and started with the big trunk being brought down from the attic ready to be packed. It was collected by Carter Paterson at least two weeks in advance (in a horse-drawn van), and was usually awaiting our arrival.

Living in a London suburb, my brother and I would be woken up in what seemed to be the middle of the night for the taxi ride to Liverpool Street station. This was an adventure in itself, for there were few cars around in those days. The station was a noisy bedlam of steam and smoke and engines hissing, and it was a great relief to find our compartment and to rush around seeing which pictures of seaside resorts were framed above the seats. Some years, our train went to Yarmouth and from there we caught an open-top tram to Gorleston; this took us past yards piled high with timber and gave us our first glimpse of the busy river traffic – from fishing boats to paddlesteamers and cargo boats.

It was usual to stay in "rooms with attendance"; that meant a bedroom and a living room – Mother did the shopping and the landlady prepared the meals. For some years we stayed in Springfield Road; later when my brother and I were older we needed two bedrooms and moved to Albermarle Road, which was further from the beach. We always had a midday dinner, and the trek to and from the beach twice a day seemed endless to small legs, but in reality it wasn't much more than half a mile. I have been back to prove it!

There were wooden huts on the beach at the breakwater end, but these gave way further along to rows of tents. Our tent was way past the three red stone shelters (which are still there), and was owned by a man called Austin. We had a little hut where we left buckets and spades overnight; a blunt wooden spade for me and a much-envied sharper metal one for my brother. Mr Austin took the canvas off the tents every night, leaving rows of wooden skeleton frameworks all along the beach. We always had the same tent every year and we met the same families and played with the same children. There were endless games of cricket and rounders, and on windy days, combined efforts to dig huge holes in which to sit – windbreaks hadn't been thought of then. On the first day of the holiday there would be frantic digging in the tent to see if the previous occupants had dropped any money. Once, my father was sitting in a deckchair idly riffling through the sand and found half a crown, and then a whole handful of coins which had obviously fallen from someone's trouser pocket.

During heavy August thunderstorms, the children all crowded into

Having your photograph taken in a motor on the beach was one of the attractions at Great Yarmouth in 1927, just a ferry trip away from Gorleston holidaymakers.

one tent singing and playing noisy games, whilst the adults chatted in the one next door. There were always several wrecks just off-shore, and sometimes a fisherman would row us out to one. I remember him prising mussels off the barnacled spars, opening them with a knife and swallowing them raw.

One memorable year Grampa came for a week, he stayed at a boarding house overlooking the sea, which we thought very grand. Every morning he walked down to join us on the beach wearing suit and waistcoat, hat, black boots and carrying an umbrella. There was no concession to holiday clothes. He didn't like the beach much and said the sand got into everything. Every morning I was given a penny of my pocket money to spend, but while Grampa was there, I got another penny to spend in the afternoon. This was riches indeed when one penny would buy two ounces of boiled sweets, and an ice cream cornet was a halfpenny.

Walking along the promenade, we were often photographed by "Jackson's Faces", and there would be a rush the next morning to pick ourselves out from dozens of other photos displayed on a wall opposite the jetty. Once a week, I could choose a comic from those laid out on the edge of the "prom" – *Rainbow, Bubbles, Playbox* etc. The choice was difficult because they all gave away different free gifts such as cardboard models, bundles of flags for sandcastles, balloons, and so on. One year, one of the comics ran a competition for a picture in the sand. I spent the morning collecting a bucketful of white pebbles and shells for this, and was delighted to win a huge inflatable beach ball.

On the corner of Beach Road was a palmist; the teenage daughter of some friends went to see her, but would never reveal what she had been told. A great treat during the holiday was a visit to Hill's Cafe in Beach Road to eat a real ice cream out of a glass dish (as opposed to the usual cornet). I must have held the record for making this last a long time, but nobody hurried me – I think parents were much more patient then.

Further along in what was known as Pops Meadow was a large wooden building where Pops Concert Party used to perform. This was very special as it meant staying up late. The programme had a lucky number, and there was great excitement if one of our group won a prize, or if one of us caught any of the coloured cottonwool balls which were thrown at the audience. We often heard the band playing as we walked past the bandstand enclosure (now the Floral Hall), and at least once would go and sit inside for the afternoon, sometimes taking part in a fancy dress parade. Nearby was a rifle range where my older brother practised shooting at a cardboard target. This was run by a retired clown from Bertram Mills Circus. I think he was the famous Whimsical Walker, but have not been able to verify this. He occasionally appeared in his clown's costume.

Every summer, my mother and I embarked on a paddle steamer bound for Yarmouth, whilst my father and brother walked along the riverside and met us there. My memories of Yarmouth are rather fragmented. I remember an exhibition of pictures on the beach in a boat called "Peggotty's Hut"; there was a man who sculpted wonderful pictures in the sand – mostly horses or scenes from the Great War. Of course he had to do them again every morning. There were comical figures with a hole through which you looked to have your photo taken; and a charabanc on the beach for the same purpose. There was the "weighing-machine man" with a highly polished brass stand from which an armchair was suspended, with shiny weights alongside. He estimated your weight before you sat on it and was surprisingly accurate. A visit to the prison was rather frightening, dark and dank.

We always had to call at the bloater shop to send a box of bloaters to friends. Back in Gorleston, we often heard a fisherman walking down the street shouting "Yarmouth Bloa'ers". There was a rowing-boat ferry which crossed the river not far from the harbour mouth. In those days there was open ground on the Yarmouth side with many railings on which the fishermen hung their nets to dry. One year we went over on the ferry and spent the evening watching a small plane taking people up for short joyrides. It may have been Sir Alan Cobham of Flying Circus fame who came in 1929 to encourage interest in flying. That evening, the returning ferry was full of people and sat very low in the water. I refused to go in it as I thought it was going to sink, and I wouldn't stop screaming until my poor father decided to walk up the river quite a long way to the next ferry with me on his shoulders! I think the fare was a halfpenny.

Many evenings were spent wandering on the old Dutch pier, peering at the sea through gaps in the wooden boards, climbing on the capstans, watching the constant stream of boats entering and leaving the harbour, and scrambling through the "cosies" – which were niches on the south side of the pier formed by the numerous timbers. These were a favourite haunt of fishermen. My brother sometimes caught small dabs using a hand line.

A favourite walk in the evening after our high tea was along the road at the back of the town bordered on one side by hedges and fields of corn scattered with great patches of scarlet poppies. We could walk until we reached the end of the houses, with open fields beyond, then turn down a lane towards the sea, past the Links Hotel and back along the top of the cliffs.

There was a timeless sense of permanence and security about those holidays, and although nothing ever seemed to change, I don't remember ever feeling bored.'

HUNSTANTON AND WELLS

'We always went to Hunstanton for our holidays in the late 1920s. We arrived at the railway station, beautifully cared for with rambler roses climbing up posts – "American Pillar", so my father said. Delights included playing on the nicely rounded rocks to the east of the pier, below the cliffs, with our "jumping poles" (about five foot long, like broom handles), and finding interesting sea-life in the pools left by the tide. On the "prom" there were slot machines like hens, on low pedestals, which "laid an egg" when a penny was inserted, a penny being then quite an outlay of pocket money. The eggs were of thin metal, and contained small sweets or chocolates.'

'My first memories of Norfolk are unhappy ones! Living in Peterborough until 1946, as children we had many day trips to Hunstanton. Unfortunately I was a very poor traveller and always managed to be sick when we reached the level crossing gates at King's Lynn. I once overheard my father suggesting to my mother it had become psychological as I always had to get out at the same spot. Friends of my parents had a small car with a "dickey" seat which meant I sat in the open air and therefore had no travel sickness. My father could never understand why I preferred their "bone-shaker" to the comparative luxury of his Vauxhall 21.

In the sea below Hunstanton cliffs with 'jumping poles' in the late 1920s.

We normally stayed at Hunstanton for Easter. I don't know whether Easter time was warmer in the 1930s or whether we were tougher, but sometimes we would go swimming under the pier with the hotel owner. As she was riddled with arthritis I can't think, with hindsight, that it did her much good but she seemed to thrive on it. When we returned to the hotel the cook would have produced a plateful of home-made lemon curd tarts to eat with our cups of tea. They were the most delicious tarts ever, and my sister Lorna and I would eat until they had all gone.

The first Easter following the outbreak of war my parents, two sisters and I were walking across Hunstanton Green when she saw an army officer, lady, gentleman and two girls coming towards us. As they drew nearer my father exclaimed, "It's the King and Queen!" We passed within about three yards of each other, no bowing, no curtsying, just all staring at each other. Most of all Lorna and I, as we were wearing almost identical camel coats to the princesses. From then onwards they were referred to as our "princess coats".

We spent our long summer holidays in Wells-on-Sea. I loved it then and I love it now. We would have dinner, bed and breakfast in the hotel and then spend the days in my great aunt Emily's beach hut. We would collect fresh rolls, ham, cheese, butter, fruit and salad together with milk, tea, coffee and ginger beer, park the car in the pine woods behind the sandhills and then walk through the lovely-smelling woods to the hut. The sun always seemed to shine, the beach was full of golden sand and we would dig and create all day. Castles, cars and shell designs were our specialities. Occasionally our great aunt Emily would bathe with us. As she was an extremely large lady there were always jokes about only going in when the tide was out! I was fascinated by her hand-knitted costume which, when wet, would droop right down to her knees. She appeared to be completely unconscious of the fact that she was something of a spectacle.

The next beach hut was owned by a lady and her sister from London. One of them taught at the Royal School of Needlework, and on one holiday taught my mother to do the most exquisite smocking. My children were to benefit from this many years later. I loved to listen as she told of the famous items she had helped to embroider. She related how every pupil and tutor had put in at least one stitch in the coronation dress of Queen Elizabeth.

Two beach huts away was a jolly bachelor who, on his half days, cooked himself steak, onions and chips. What a delicious smell wafted across the beach!

My mother's cousin, a music teacher, took her pupils on an annual day trip over to the island. When the tide was out I would go with them, being rowed over the channel, complete with our packed lunches. Here we would play games and enjoy our picnics until the tide told us it was time to return to the mainland. There was an old abandoned boat on the island, occupied, so Gwen said, by a hermit. As I had never seen such a person I hoped he would appear, but I never saw him. I was told he had been crossed in love, but it was years before I knew what that actually was!

During our summers in Wells there was always an Annual Regatta. Another cousin of my mother's used to sail in the races, and there was great excitement as we cheered him into harbour. There was a fair on the harbour, and we would feel as though we were flying over the water as we went round and round on the horses, as well as up and down.

We wore pleated shorts, aertex shirts, and occasionally a heavy sweater although it never seemed cold in those days.

One day my father took me to the East Quay to see where the

crabs were boiled. Oh, the squealing of the poor crabs – the lids of the heavy pots kept rising as they tried desperately to get out. I couldn't watch. I was assured they were incapable of feeling pain. If so, why did they make so much noise?

In August 1939, after our annual spell in Wells, I stayed with a second cousin in Walsingham. One night I heard lots of noises and voices. When I asked about it in the morning, I was told it was "only the pilgrims". It transpired "they" were emptying the "privies" – as a townie this was something quite unknown to me and very intriguing.

The great-aunt and uncle in Walsingham were farmers and butchers. A cousin some five years older than I helped around generally. I loved watching her churn the butter and cream and then would go with her in the pony trap to deliver it in the neighbouring villages. I envied her not having to go to school and study, I thought it an idyllic life in my tender years. One evening she told me that as soon as it became dusk we were going to walk to a nearby field to watch the searchlights "play". In later years, I strongly suspected she was more interested in the soldiers than the searchlights!

One of my favourite occupations was to cross the channel with my father, look for the little pinholes and delve for cockles. The "stukey" blues were to be found here. When we returned to the beach hut they would be put into a bucket of water to clean. Next day they would be boiled and my father – the only taker – would eat them with vinegar and Hovis bread and butter.

Our sailing cousin would sometimes take us around the creeks, showing me how the samphire grew and how to eat it. "Poor man's asparagus" is its other name, he informed me. It certainly does taste like asparagus.

When approaching Norfolk we always played a guessing game. When we did, my father would announce, "We are in Norfolk!" What excitement this conjured up: long days on the sand, the smell of the pines and the sea, collecting shells and coloured pebbles, making castles, eating sandy sandwiches, running in the air of the sea all day. And did the sun really shine all the day, every day? It seemed so. I was always sad to leave Norfolk but was told I was lucky because many children didn't have holidays to go home from. The flint walls and houses were seen in reverse and we would say, "Goodbye, Norfolk". My mother always brought us back with "It will be nice to be home again, won't it?"

ON THE BROADS

'For a week in the summer of 1946, we came to the Broads – my fairly new husband, his best man and my sister. The slow train

240

Enjoying a day on a wherry boat moored outside The Acle Bridge hotel.

from Birmingham had deposited us at Stalham station with a walk down to the yachting pier carrying all our gear, which in those days of rationing included a certain amount of food we had saved up for the holiday.

The rather decrepit looking converted lifeboat was handed over to us with a few instructions about not trying to stop or reverse it as if it was a car, and a warning that due to fuel rationing we must keep to the northern rivers. No guesses as to which two spent the first hour unpacking and making a meal, and which two managed to navigate us into Sutton Broad.

Only essential reed clearing had been done for several years, and channels were narrow. A lookout was useful as a fouled propeller meant a strip off and dive by our ex-navy crew member. So we took care. Hickling was a particular delight as the shallow, then clear, water revealed a varied plant life and shoals of small darting fishes. There was no difficulty in finding mooring places and we had many quiet and beautiful walks along banks and into villages. At Coltishall Common, we could order delivery of morning milk and a newspaper for a mooring fee of two shillings and sixpence paid at the hotel, and at Wroxham we tied up at the town quay and shopped at a village store called Roys.

We were rather horrified at what we saw floating in the river water on one occasion when we took a dip too near houses, and we stood on the bank afterwards flinging buckets of precious drinking water over each other. Our boat had the luxury of a pump-flush toilet and a very tiny hand basin like a metal shell which let down from the wall and was emptied by a hose, so I suppose we did our bit for pollution. It was easier to wash in a basin outside and use the water for swabbing the decks – our ex-navy man said this should be done each day.

We lived by daylight as we had only calor gas for a small cooking stove and a lamp in each cabin. There were two narrow seats meeting in the prow where my sister and I slept feet to feet, and the lads had a wooden two-tier bunk in the main cabin on the wall opposite the "kitchen". Social life and "driving" the boat took place in the open rear cockpit where there were seats all round and a canvas roof cover which could be pulled over like the hood of a huge open car. There were hanging side flaps which let in the rain, but I don't remember there was very much, and in our idyllic state there was only sunshine, clear air and birdsong – including the quacking of ducks. We did have to repel wasps and moths, but gnats were rather too numerous so we had to retreat.

There was very little river traffic in those times, and we learned to give yachts plenty of room and avoid getting caught up in fishing lines. We moored at Great Yarmouth, which was as far as we thought our fuel would take us, and went to the cinema. Coming back in great spirits, eating fish and chips out of paper, we were amazed to see our boat suspended above the water by its mooring ropes. We had not thought about the fall of the tide in the river and I doubt whether so soon after the war there were any public warning notices.

How lucky we were to have a holiday on the Broads just at that time when the tension of war had been released, but before the holiday potential of the waterways was fully exploited. With our children we came several times, the boats becoming more comfortable but the mooring less attractive to us. Our wonderful solitudes were no more. Still the memories of that first holiday never dimmed.'

A BUSY HOLIDAY VILLAGE

'Hopton was a very busy holiday village from pre-war years until the 1960s when the demand for new housing swallowed up two of the five holiday "camps" (as they were then known) in the village centre.

The three remaining camps still operated and provided work for a large number of local people and also from the surrounding areas.

The chalets were of wooden construction with very basic services, consisting of a hand basin and cold tap. Toilets were in blocks scattered around the chalets and it was not until the 1950s that

242

built-in bathrooms appeared.

Most holidaymakers arrived by train and coach, mostly from London and the Midlands. Hopton station was very busy on Saturdays as was the A12 when they all arrived. Travellers were met by the village children with their luggage barrows, ready to carry cases and bags to various camps. On occasions holiday camp entertainment staff would be on hand with a band to accompany the visitors on their walk to the camps.

Sunday was usually the day for a football match between rival camps, cheered on by visitors suitably dressed, with balloons for the children. During the week country walks were organised together with games on the beach etc.

August being a very busy month with all camps booked up, villagers would take in bed and breakfast visitors. Yes, Hopton was a very busy village in those days. During the war all the camps were taken over by the army and air force, and many local girls married servicemen from the camps.'

ST VALENTINE'S DAY

St Valentine's Day was eagerly anticipated by Norfolk children, a special day which brought gifts, pranks and its own traditions.

A RED LETTER DAY

'St Valentine's Day was very special for Norfolk children. Dusk falls about 5.30 pm on that day and that is when the excitement and fun began. A loud knock or the shrill sound of the bell would send the children scampering to either the back or the front door. On opening the door they would find a parcel on the step. Taken into the house, the parcel would be given to the one whose name was on it. However, not much time was spent over it as another summons would sound and there was more scampering and laughter as another present was found. The dashing backwards and forwards would continue until all in the house had received a present. The excitement was often prolonged when the presents disappeared into the dimness outside (a string having been attached to pull them back into hiding). This worked as everyone obeyed the rule not to go beyond the step. It was known as Snatch Valentine. The presents

243

were not of great expense – a notebook, pencil box, bar of chocolate etc – but it was a red letter day to the children of pre-war Norfolk.'

HOT PENNIES

'On Valentine's Day, during the dinner hour, the children from Little Ellingham sang songs round the village from house to house. They would chant "Good morrow, Valentine" and be given apples and cakes and sometimes pennies in reward for their songs. If the weather was snowy, these pennies would sometimes be heated on a dustpan and flung into the snow to be scrambled for. Money would be divided amongst the singers and quickly spent on sweets at the village shop. This custom ceased when school dinners were introduced.

After dark, small parcels would be placed on steps with a very loud banging on the door. Neighbours also gave each other "Valentines" but these were usually in the form of a piece of coal or wood or a few apples.'

VALENTINING

'Ingoldisthorpe where I was born is a village between King's Lynn and Hunstanton. We had a custom there when I was a girl of Valentining on 14th February.

On Valentine Day morning it was early breakfast, with as much of the village as possible to be covered before we went to school. We all assembled at a prearranged place and started off. We went to every house and sang at the door until someone came out and gave us some money. At most places we were expected and were soon on our way. About six of the older children ran to the outlying houses, Long Row, over the line and over the laundry, and left the main group to go round the rest of the houses.

Of course we were always late for school, and Miss Yaxley, our head teacher, used to keep the register open until we all arrived. She always let us out early at midday as we had the big houses to visit.

First of all we ran to the rectory, only across the road. The Rev Wynne made us stand in a half circle while he counted us and gave us a penny each. Then we ran along to the Hall where Colonel Davey made us sing and be counted all over again. Another penny each here, and then on to the Manor, where we went into the courtyard and the gardener threw apples and sixpences for us to pick up – not very good really as the big children pushed the small ones out of the way, so we small ones didn't get anything.

After all that we all ran down to the village shop, owned by my aunt and uncle, where the money was taken in and counted and

244

then divided between us all. What was left over was used to buy sweets, and we usually ended up with two or three sweets each. Then home to a hurried meal and back to school before the register was closed.'

VALENTINE SONGS

'When I was a child in the 1930s I lived at Aldborough Green. On Valentine's Day the girls next door and I went round the village, knocking on doors. This is what we sang about Jack Valentine:

> Good Mother Valentine
> God bless the baker
> Who'll be the giver?
> We'll be the taker
> Please Mum, please Mum
> Would you be so kind
> To give us something for Valentine?
> If you haven't got a penny, a ha'penny will do
> If you haven't a ha'penny we'll bless you.

The pennies we collected were spent on sweets at the village shop.'

'Valentine's Day at Little Barningham was celebrated not only by the finding of presents on the doorstep, but also by going in groups to the larger houses and farms and singing:

> Old Mother Valentine
> Draw up your window blind
> If you wish to hear us sing
> Open the door and let us in
> Please ma'am, please ma'am,
> Would you be so kind
> Give us a penny for a Valentine
> You be the giver
> We'll be the taker
> Please ma'am, please ma'am
> Would you be so kind.'

CELEBRATIONS THROUGH THE YEAR

There were many other occasions of celebration and traditional fun through the year, some quieter and more reflective such as at Easter and others full of joy and magic. Empire Day, once part of every schoolchild's calendar, has now gone for ever.

EASTER TIME

'I was born and brought up in Norwich and when a teenager from 1945 to 1952 Good Friday for me followed a fairly regular pattern.

First thing in the morning I would jump on my bike and cycle down to the local bakery on Brunswick Road and queue up for freshly made hot cross buns, straight out of the oven on Good Friday morning.

In the afternoon I would make my way to St Andrew's Hall and listen to the Norwich Philharmonic Orchestra and Chorus perform Handel's *Messiah*. They did this work every year and sometimes I, as a Guider, was asked to sell programmes.

I rushed home to tea and then I went to St Peter Mancroft church, close to Norwich Market Place, and waited outside with several hundred other people for the start of the Annual Procession of Witness.

Preceded by the episcopal cross and headed by the Bishop of Norwich, then Dr Herbert, white-robed clergy and choirs of all the Norwich Anglican churches, together with the congregations, took part in this annual procession from St Peter Mancroft to Norwich Cathedral. We were accompanied by two bands, the British Legion at the front and the Salvation Army at the back, and we sang *Onward Christian Soldiers* and *Stand up, stand up for Jesus* and other well known hymns as we wended our way through the large crowds of citizens that assembled along the route to watch us. As dusk fell we reached the west door of Norwich Cathedral, and as we entered the mighty organ played its welcome and the bishop was standing in the pulpit as we filed in to find a seat in the nave or side aisles.

One year I went with my father up the many steps to the triforium and sat looking down on the vast congregation, but I did not look over too many times as I don't like heights.

The bishop conducted a short service and gave an address on the meaning of Good Friday. The final hymn at the service was always *When I survey the wondrous cross*. Then we left the cathedral and walked home through the streets of Norwich with many clergy and choristers carrying their white surplices.

The next morning, I accompanied my mother with armfuls of spring flowers to the local parish church where I helped her to decorate for Easter Day. This was a quiet task after the singing and band playing of the previous evening.'

EMPIRE DAY

'Empire Day, 24th May, was a great treat when I was a child at Watton. We had a holiday from school in the afternoon. Everyone assembled at the war memorial, which was then at the bottom of Church Walk, and then paraded through the streets waving Union Jacks. On a meadow off Norwich Road there were sports with money prizes. I once won seven shillings and sixpence, a fortune in those days. Afterwards there was a tea to round off the day. I don't remember a rainy Empire Day. Usually the tar was oozing from the road in the heat.'

'On Empire Day in the 1920s we always went from Ickburgh by decorated horse and waggon to Watton to the sports, held in a meadow belonging to Hall and Palmer the auctioneers.'

THE FAIR

'My mother had happy memories of the fair which came to Thurton each year. This was held opposite the George and Dragon and the children looked forward to it coming each year. She remembered particularly the "Rock Lady", as she was called, who sold sticks of rock to the children.'

'One of the happiest memories of my childhood was the sports day and the fair at Whitsun holidays. A part of Hempton was roped off on Whit Monday and everybody joined in the sports that were held there – sack races, bike races, egg and spoon races, all the races you could think of for young and old. Then of course we had eats and drinks and then we trooped off to the fair and had as many rides as our few pennies could get us.

I also looked forward to the annual Hempton sheep fair. The village green was the place for all the activities. The grass was cut short, the hurdles were put ready and the men came and built them into pens and long passages for the sheep to go into on the big day.

247

Watton carnival in 1953 naturally had a royal theme!

After school we would all go and make camps inside these pens and play all sorts of games. The fair would come then, with its dodgems and coconut shies. After the end of the sheep sale the fairground would come alive with music and people. Afterwards we would all troop home tired with excitement and ready for bed.'

THE GREAT DAY

'Watton Show was held some time in the later part of September, giving farming folk time to finish harvest. If they hadn't finished by the appointed date owing to a wet season, the attendance at the show was very poor. For that was what it was all about; farming. Most of the people in the district were connected with farming; if they were not farmers or farm labourers, they were blacksmiths, wheelwrights, saddlers, millers, or foundry workers employed in the making of farm implements. Now these trades are almost nonexistent. The tradesmen relied on a good harvest to get paid promptly for their goods and services, while the shopkeepers also benefited from good crops gathered in.

How we counted the weeks and then the days to the show. My father and brothers were busy getting the stock ready. Pigs were scrubbed to a spotless pink; horses groomed till their coats shone like silk; roots were staked out in the fields long before the day. There were mangolds – Golden Globe and Red Intermediate; sugar beet, long and straight with no offending fangs; also swedes and

248

turnips, solid as the truth. Waggons and tumbrils were washed free of mud and painted red and blue. Such a lot of work went on in the evenings, but how enjoyable it all was.

Mother was making me a new coat for the occasion. She was making it from a remnant bought during Durrant's sale. I was in a great state of anxiety as to it getting made in time, for it would have been terrible to have to wear my shabby school coat. But yes, all was well, the buttons were sewn on that very morning.

What a wonderful feeling, the Great Day had arrived at last! The members of the family were all up very early. The roots were already lying in rows on the bottom of the waggon. We hoped that when they were cut in two by the judges on the show ground, they would be solid and not have a hole in their centre.

The pigs were loaded into a tumbril with lots of squeaking and squalling, a rope pignet was pulled tight over them. Those protesting pigs had no desire to go to the show.

No one worried about breakfast that morning, but my brothers took a packed lunch with them before driving their horses and waggons down the fields towards the Watton road.

Mother, Father and I followed later in the pony and trap. There was more traffic on the road than I would have thought possible, everyone was going in the same direction. We arrived in town, stabled the pony at the sale yard, and walked towards the show ground.

The pavements were packed with people. All the farmhands had been given the day off and were out with their wives and families. Cheap jacks and stalls selling all manner of things were stationed along the street and for the folk who could not afford the shilling to go on to the show ground it was most entertaining to watch the traders display their wares and also watch the many exhibits going to the show in their gaily painted waggons.

The great cart horses looked very proud with their manes and tails braided, their brasses shining and their heads held high, just as if they were all first prize winners. The muscles under their polished coats rippled like the waves of the sea. The huge bulls, led by the rings in their noses, got their share of admiration, also the cows as they minced along, their great silky udders swinging from right to left at every step.

Mother had the entrance money ready. Half a crown, for it was half price for me. I felt very pleased with life as I walked with my parents under the great banner stretched across the gateway. It read "God Speed The Plough".

We hurried to where the roots were laid out on the ground, marked out by tightly drawn ropes. Yes, some of the roots were neatly cut in two, but praise be, ours were solid rocks. Prize cards of red and blue were on sugar beet and mangolds, also several "highly commended" cards.

We then moved to the pigs' pens. There was a red rosette tacked to the wooden hurdles that made a temporary sty for our sow and litter of pigs. If they didn't look too pleased, my brother Harold standing in charge looked as pleased as Punch.

We could now look round the rest of the show with happy hearts. This was the day the public met with friends and relations they hadn't seen for a year. There was a great wagging of tongues. I was sure to get a sixpence or two from my many uncles, as the festival atmosphere made them more benevolent than usual.

The vegetable tent was always worth seeing, to think of all the anxious toil that went into the growing of those wonderful onions, carrots, beans, cauliflowers etc. And the mixed baskets; all that produce brought to perfection at the same time.

There is something special about an agricultural show, the smell of the animals, the crowds and the noise of the band. Some exceptional quality that cannot be defined.

The animals started to leave in the later part of the afternoon for some had come from a distance. They made a colourful display with their rosettes and prize cards proudly hung round their necks. A small crowd still remained at the entrance of the show ground, as if unwilling to miss a thing.

In the evening we went to the fair that was held every show day on a meadow in the town. Roundabouts, swings, the cake walk, they were all there and so were the crowds, all wanting to try one or other of those delights. The noise was almost deafening.

We were all very tired when we climbed into the little trap behind a willing Pansy, the pony, so glad to be going home at last. The carriage lamps were lit by two candles which shew little light, but I was too exhausted to enjoy the ride home in the dark. I nodded off to the tune of the pony's hoofs on the hard road. A happy day was over to be discussed again and again in the weeks to follow. (NB – shew, pronounced "shoo" is still in use here as the past tense of show.)'

CHRISTMAS MAGIC

'From the log book of the Aldborough and Thurgarton Women's Institute, an account of the children's party held on 31 December 1919: "Children and old people of the two villages received invitations to a party held in the Church Room from two o'clock until five.

The afternoon of the last day of the year was pleasantly spent by our members, their children and as many old people who could venture out into the very cold weather.

The room, which is such a suitable one for such occasions (containing two dressing rooms and a platform) had been decorated by members earlier in the day with evergreen and flags, and looked especially bright when filled with all the bright faced little ones, ranging from two to 16 years, as they joined with their mothers and sisters in the old round games they all enjoy. The old people were comfortably seated, with rugs at their feet, around a stove on the platform where they could watch the youngsters at their fun. Oranges and sweets were handed round and at four o'clock tea was served, most of the children bringing their "peace mugs", which had been given to them during the year by Mrs Gay of Aldborough Hall.

Members serving tea were kept busy for nearly one hour, after which there was a gramophone selection by the Rev Lilley, musical items by Miss Spink, the Misses Underwood and Miss Harris, and a recitation by Mrs Groom which caused much laughter.

The most attractive item of the party must be mentioned last, as it happened last, and this was the arrival at the front door of a scarlet clad "Father Christmas", who distributed to each child as they marched past, an orange and a packet of sweets. When every child had received its gift, they joined hands round their welcome visitor and sang "For He's a Jolly Good Fellow", followed by cheer after cheer.

This surprise item had been prepared by Mrs Lilley and Mrs Edmund Gay, the latter kindly acting the part, in which she had so well disguised herself as to be quite unrecognisable, which needless to say caused all the more wonder and excitement to the little ones.

Upon dispersal, regrets were heard that five o'clock had arrived all too soon, every member feeling that she had had a share not only in providing, but in sharing the afternoon's enjoyment for young and old." '

'At Christmas we would have a chicken or roast beef and Yorkshire pudding. Christmas pudding was of course a must, and mince pies: these would have been prepared some weeks before, stoning the raisins, cutting up the crystallized orange and lemon peel, and when the puddings were mixed everyone had to stir. At the last the threepenny bits were put in and of course on Christmas Day everyone looked for a coin.

Christmas was a lovely time, Christmas Eve hanging the paper chains which we had made from coloured paper cut into strips and stuck together, the tree decorated, cakes iced and jellies made, we also made toffee with treacle and then we had to go early to bed. Mother would make sure I was asleep before the stocking full of things was hung on the bedpost or my iron bedstead with brass rails, then Christmas morning I would awake early to find Father Christmas had been, with orange or apple in the toe, sweets, chocolate, hanky, beads, scent, games book, doll, golliwog and perhaps a drum! Not like the expensive gifts of today, but we were happy with them, then when we had dressed and had breakfast the postman would come with parcels and cards, perhaps a friend would pop in with a parcel and have a drink. Then it was time to go to Snettisham church, having left the dinner cooking in the oven and the vegetables on the hobs.

After dinner we opened our presents and had a sing-song and Dad would roast chestnuts on an iron pan over the open fire. I loved to sit round the fire; mind you, I'm afraid I sometimes sat too close and burnt my legs, but it was lovely and cosy. Sometimes friends would spend the evening and we played hide the thimble and postman's knock and had a drink. We could buy flagons of wine then and ginger wine, and there were nuts, dates, figs and orange and lemon slices in plenty for the festival season.'

'As one of a family of ten children, Christmas at our home at Hemsby was a very exciting time. The yard cockerel was fattened up, sweet coupons saved and Father would spend hours in the shed after dark making toys.

On Christmas morning we would be awake early as ten of us would be piled into beds in two rooms. It was impossible to move out of bed without waking each other, but we were not allowed to open our stockings till seven o'clock, then we all piled on our parents' bed and with great excitement each in turn opened their stocking, which did not have much in, a colouring book, crayons, and a tangerine. Perhaps a tube of sweets, but as we had nothing much through the year this was quite something. I can remember Mother making us a doll from rags one year and four of us had to share it, which we always did.

Then we would all go down and see the Christmas tree which Mum and Dad must have been up half the night decorating with silver paper and paper chains. On the tree was always a small present for each child – usually sugar mice – but they would not be opened till after the carols on Christmas night.

I can remember our day was so happy, we played games with Mum and Dad all day and with having ten children there was nearly always a new baby for Christmas. We were hungry most days of the year but never on Christmas Day.'

Index

254

List of Contributing W.I.s

Contributions were received from the following Norfolk Women's Institutes:

Aldborough & Thurgarton, Alpington & Yelverton, Ashill, Aylsham Afternoon, Aylsham Bureside, Banham, The Beck, The Birchams, Blofield Heath, Bradenham, Bradwell, Brooke, Broome, Brundall & Braydeston, Burnham Market, Buxton & District, Caston, Chedgrave & District, Coltishall & Horstead, Corpusty & Saxthorpe, Cringleford Afternoon, Cromer, Deopham, Dersingham, Diss, East Harling, East Thorpe, Erpingham with Calthorpe, Fakenham Afternoon, Falcon (Sprowston), Feltwell, Gayton, Gorleston, Great Ormesby, Great & Little Plumstead, Gressenhall & District, Hellesdon, Hempton, Hemsby, Hethersett, Holme Hale, Honingham, Hopton-on-Sea, Keswick & Intwood, Little Ellingham, Loddon & District Evening, The Lophams, Ludham, Mettingham, Mundesley, Neatishead, Barton Turf & District, New Hunstanton, North & South Creake & District, Northrepps, North Walsham & District, North Walsham Market Cross, Northwold, North Wootton Evening, Norwich – Evelyn Suffield, Old Catton Evening, Overstrand Evening, Pentney & West Bilney, Pulham Market, Reepham & District Afternoon, Rockland St. Mary & District, The Runtons & District, Saham, St. Faiths, St. Germans, Sandringham, Scole, Sea Palling, Waxham & District, Sheringham Evening, Shipdham, Snettisham, Southrepps & District, South Walsham & District, Sprowston, Stalham, Stanhoe & Barwick, Sutton, Swaffham Afternoon, Swaffham Evening, Terrington St. Clement, Thorpe End, Thurlton & District, Tilney St. Lawrence, former members of Trowse, Upper Thorpe, Walpole Marsh, Walsingham & District, Watlington, Watton Evening, Whissonsett & Horningtoft, Wimbotsham, Witton & Ridlington, Woodside, Worstead, Wroxham, Yaxham.